Volume Zero

X Protocol Reference Manual

---

for Version 11 of the X Window System

by Robert W. Scheifler

edited and with an Introduction by Adrian Nye

O'Reilly & Associates, Inc.

Revision and Printing History

July 1989:   First Printing

Small Print

The X Window System Series

The books in the X Window System series from O'Reilly and
Associates are becoming the standard manuals for X. They are based
in part on the original MIT X Window System documentation, but go
far beyond it in comprehensiveness and ease of use. Over 20 computer
vendors recommend or license volumes in the series. In short, these
are the definitive guides to the X Window System.

Volume 0, X Protocol Reference Manaul

A complete programmer's reference to the X Network Protocol, the
language in which computers communicate all the information
between the X server and X clients. 418 pages, $30.00

Volume 1, Xlib Programming Manual

A complete guide to programming with the X library (Xlib), the lowest
level of programming interface to X. 659 pages, $34.95—or sold as a
set with the *Xlib Reference Manual* for $60.00.

Volume 2, Xlib Reference Manual

A complete programmer's reference for Xlib. 723 pages, $34.95—or
sold as a set with the *Xlib Programming Manual* for $60.00.

Volume 3, X Window System User's Guide

Describes window system concepts and the most common client applications available for X, Release 3. For experienced users, later
chapters explain customizing the X environment and include an
alternate *.uwmrc* file. 576 pages, $26.95

X Toolkit volumes soon to be available

Two volumes on X Toolkit programming are being developed. Volumes 4 and 5, *X Toolkit Intrinsics Programming Manual* and *X Toolkit
Intrinsics Reference Manual*, will be available in the Fall of 1989.

For orders or a free catalog of all our books, please contact us.

O'Reilly & Associates, Inc.

Creators and publishers of Nutshell Handbooks
632 Petaluma Avenue • Sebastopol CA 95472
email: uunet!ora!nuts • 1-800-338-6887 • in CA 1-800-533-6887

Table of Contents

Preface

About This Manual

This reference manual describes the X Network Protocol which underlines all software for Version 11 of the X Window System. The X protocol is the language in which computers communicate all the information between the X server and X clients, whether the server and clients are operating on different systems in the network or on the same system.

The C-language X library, known as Xlib, is the lowest level of C programming interface to the X protocol. The Lisp library CLX is the lowest level library for Lisp. These libraries translate procedure calls into the X Protocol described in this volume. Additional higher level software such as the X Toolkit, CLUE, XView, Andrew, and InterViews are written using these low-level libraries to make X application programming easier.

In general, application programmers do not need to know the details of the protocol. However, it can be helpful to have access to the protocol specification when things do not work the way you expect.

Summary of Contents

This manual is divided into three major parts. Part One provides a conceptual introduction to the X protocol. It describes the role of the server and client and demonstrates the network transactions that take place during a minimal client session. Part Two contains an extensive set of reference pages for each protocol request and event. Part Three consists of several appendices describing particular parts of the X protocol and also several reference aids.

The reference pages contain a reformatted version of the Release 3 version of Robert Scheifler's original X protocol specification. The original document was formatted as running text. The reference section in this document treats each protocol request or event on a separate alphabetical reference page. Introductory material from the original document is presented on two separate reference pages—one entitled *Intro*, which describes the format and syntax of the reference pages, and one entitled *Connection Setup*. The encoding of requests and replies, presented as an appendix in the original document, have been placed on the reference pages with each request. Every word and sentence in the original document is present in this manual with as little editing as possible to reduce the chance of errors. Therefore, the only difference between the reference section in this book and the original document is the organization of the material (which is intended to provide greater ease of access).

The appendices in Part Three contain several miscellaneous topics from the original document and several reference tables:

Appendix A, *Connection Close*, describes the server's operations to clean up after a client connection terminates.

Appendix B, *Keysyms*, describes the keyboard key symbols.

Appendix C, *Errors*, describes the problems that cause the server to generate each type of error.

Appendix D, *Predefined Atoms*, lists the predefined atoms.

Appendix E, *Keyboards and Pointers*, describes the X Window System model of keyboard handling.

Appendix F, *Flow Control and Concurrency*, specifies the constraints on server implementations for multi-threaded computer architectures.

Appendix G, *Request Group Summary*, lists the protocol requests by function with a brief description of each.

Appendix H, *Alphabetical Listing of Requests*, lists the requests alphabetically with a brief description of each.

Appendix I, *Xlib Functions to Protocol Requests*, lists each Xlib function and the protocol request it generates. This table is useful because there is sometimes more than one Xlib function that calls a particular protocol request.

Appendix J, *Protocol Requests to Xlib Functions*, lists each protocol request and the Xlib function that calls it.

Appendix K, *Events Briefly Described*, summarizes the conditions that trigger each event type.

Glossary describes many of the terms used in the reference section. This glossary is unedited from the original protocol document.

How to Use This Manual

This manual is intended for server implementors and client-library programmers and for application programmers who want to increase their knowledge of the underlying principles of the X Window System. The tutorial section contains how the protocol works and some of the issues involved in implementing it. The reference section contains the true definition of the protocol.

For application programmers seeking a deeper understanding of how Xlib works, probably the most effective way to use the manual is to read the tutorial introduction and then turn to

Appendix I, *Xlib Functions to Protocol Requests*. This appendix lists the protocol requests corresponding to a given Xlib call (though not every Xlib call generates a protocol request). From there, simply turn to the alphabetical reference page for the appropriate request. The "Introduction" reference page contains additional information (such as definitions of data types) necessary for a complete understanding of many of the reference pages.

The more serious student of the protocol should probably read the "Introduction" and "Connection Setup" reference pages thoroughly, before working systematically through the reference pages and appendices. Appendix H, *Alphabetical Listing of Requests*, provides a useful overview in the form of brief descriptions of each request.

Assumptions

The tutorial section is written for the experienced programmer familiar with the principles of raster graphics but who knows little about X. The reference section assumes a strong familiarity with X, but much of this information can be learned by reading the tutorial.

Font Conventions Used in This Manual

Italics is used for:

- UNIX pathnames, filenames, program names, user command names, and options for user commands.

- Text added to reference pages by the editor that was not part of the original protocol document written at MIT.

Helvetica Italics is used for:

- Titles of examples, figures, and tables.

`Typewriter Font` is used for:

- C language function calls such as Xlib functions and UNIX system calls.

Boldface is used for:

- Chapter and section headings.

- X protocol terms and defined constants.

Related Documents

This manual is Volume Zero of the X Window System series by O'Reilly & Associates, Inc. Other documents from O'Reilly & Associates, Inc.:

Volume One — *Xlib Programming Manual*
Volume Two — *Xlib Reference Manual*

Volume Three — *X Window System User's Guide*

Forthcoming from O'Reilly & Associates, Inc.:

Volume Four — *X Toolkit Intrinsics Programming Manual*
Volume Five — *X Toolkit Intrinsics Reference Manual*
Volume Six — *XView Programming Manual*

Request for Comments

Please write to tell us about any flaws you find in this manual or how you think it could be improved, to help us provide you with the best documentation possible.

Our U.S. mail address, e-mail address, and telephone number are as follows:

Ordering

O'Reilly & Associates, Inc.
632 Petaluma Avenue
Sebastopol, CA 95472
(800) 338-6887

Internet: nuts@ora.com
UUCP: uunet!ora!nuts

Editorial (Adrian Nye)

O'Reilly & Associates, Inc.
90 Sherman Street
Cambridge, MA 02140
(617) 354-5800

Internet: adrian@ora.com
UUCP: uunet!ora!adrian

Licensing Information

This manual has been designed for licensing and customization by manufacturers or distributors of systems supporting X11. For information on licensing, contact Tim O'Reilly at O'Reilly & Associates, Inc., at (800) 338-6887 (in CA 800-533-6887) or send e-mail to tim@ora.com.

Acknowledgements

The information contained in this manual is based in large part on the *X Window System Protocol, Version 11*, by Robert Scheifler (with many contributors). The X Window System software and the protocol document were written under the auspices of the Laboratory for Computer Science at MIT and are now controlled by the X Consortium.

The tutorial introduction has benefited from the review and suggestions of several people, including Jim Fulton of the X Consortium, Dave Striker of Convex Computer Corp., Pat Wood of Pipeline Associates, and Tim O'Reilly. Any errors that remain are my own.

— Adrian Nye

Part One:

Introduction to the X Protocol

Part One consists of a lengthy introduction to the concepts embodied in the X protocol, the tradeoffs involved in its design, and the techniques used in the implementation of servers and client libraries. It also describes the network interaction that takes place during a minimal client session.

The Server and Client
The X Protocol
A Sample Session
Implementing the X Protocol
Future Directions

Introduction to the X Protocol

The X Window System (or simply X) provides a hierarchy of resizable windows and supports high performance device-independent graphics (see Figure 1-1). Unlike most other window systems for UNIX that have a built-in user interface, X is a substrate on which almost any style of user interface can be built. But what is most unusual about X is that it is based on an asynchronous network protocol rather than on procedure or system calls. This protocol basis has a number of advantages:

- Both local and network connections can be operated in the same way using the protocol, making the network transparent both from the user's point of view and from the application programmer's point of view.

- The X protocol can be implemented using a wide variety of languages and operating systems.

- The X protocol can be used over any reliable byte stream (through local interprocess communication or over a network), several of which are standard and available on most architectures.

- For most applications, the X protocol has little performance penalty. Performance is limited more by the time required to draw graphics than by the overhead in the protocol.

It makes sense that networks and window systems should be used together. Since the window makes no distinction between local and network connections, the applications automatically provide a user interface to the network. The window system lets users get the benefit of access to remote computing abstractions using the same commands they use for running programs locally.

The protocol basis and concomitant portability of the X Window System is especially important today, when it is common to have several makes of machines in a single network. Until X, there was no common window system, and the common graphics languages that did exist did little to hide the differences between operating systems and graphics hardware. On the other hand, code that implements X is freely available and has shown itself to be extremely portable. Implementations exist for machines ranging from personal computers to supercomputers. The system is so hardware and operating system independent that properly written application software will compile and run on any system.

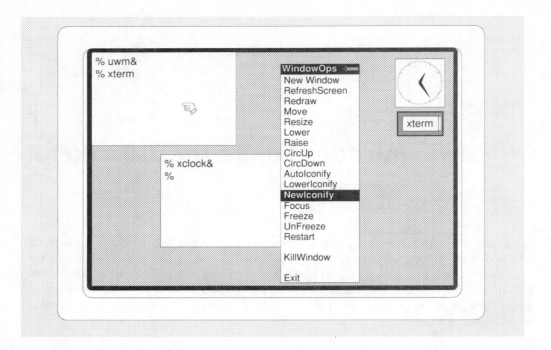

Figure 1-1. A typical X Window System display

1.1 The Server and Client*

The use of the terms *server* and *client* in X may at first seem different from their use in other computing contexts. To X, the *server* is the software that manages one display, keyboard, and mouse. One user is controlling the keyboard and mouse and looking at the display controlled by a server. The *client* is a program displaying on the screen and taking input from that keyboard and mouse. A client sends drawing requests and information requests to the server, and the server sends back to the client user input, replies to information requests, and error reports. The client may be running on the same machine as the server or on a different machine over the network.

You are probably familiar with the concept of a "file server," which is a remote machine with a disk drive from which several machines can read and write files. But in X, the server is the local system, whose abstractions the (perhaps remote) client programs are accessing. Figure 1-2 shows a server and client and their relationship to the network.

The X Window System is not limited to a single client interacting with a single server. There may be several clients interacting with a single server, which is the case when several applications are displaying on a single screen. Also, a single client can communicate with several servers, which would happen when an announcement program is displaying the same thing on several people's screens.

---

*If you have already programmed X applications or used the X Window System extensively, feel free to skip the sections early in this chapter that cover familiar topics.

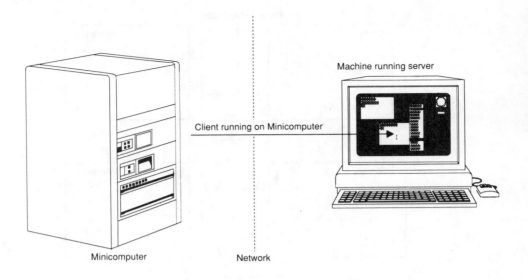

Figure 1-2. The server and client

A client may be running on the same machine as the server if that machine supports multi-tasking, or the client may run on a different machine connected over the network. On multi-tasking UNIX workstations, it is normal to have some clients running locally and others operating over the network. Naturally, other users will probably have clients running on their own system and perhaps on yours as well, but most will be displayed only on their own screens. With servers running on single-tasking systems such as IBM or compatible PC and AT class computers, all clients must run on other systems over the network. The same is true of specialized X terminals that have the server software built into ROM, and have an integral Ethernet™ network interface. Figure 1-3 shows a network with two servers, in which clients can run on any node and display on either server.

The *window manager* is a client that has authority over the layout of windows on the screen. Certain X protocol features are used only by the window manager to enforce this authority. Otherwise, the window manager is just like any other client.

X clients are programmed using various client programming libraries in C and Lisp. The C libraries are the most widely used. They include a low level procedural interface to the X protocol called Xlib and a higher level toolkit written in object-oriented style called the Xt Intrinsics. The Intrinsics are used to build user interface components called widgets. Several widget sets that implement certain user interface conventions are available from various vendors. The one supplied by MIT is called the Athena widgets. Figure 1-4 shows how the various programming interfaces for C are combined to write clients that utilize the X protocol to communicate with the server.

Xlib and the Xt Intrinsics were developed at MIT. Several other toolkit layers that use Xlib to interface to the protocol have been developed outside of MIT, some written in C and some in C++. These include Andrew, InterViews, and XView.

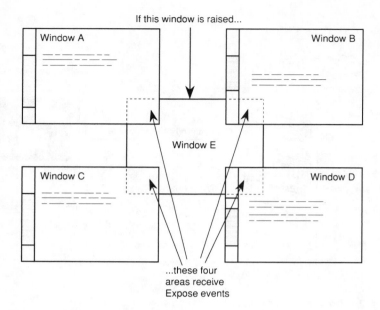

Figure 1-3. A distributed X environment

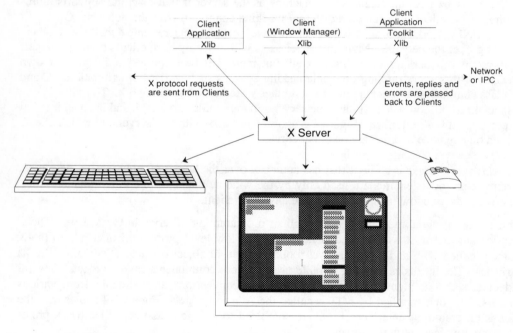

Figure 1-4. The client programming libraries in C

X Protocol Reference Manual

1.2 The X Protocol

The X protocol is the true definition of the X Window System, and any code in any language that implements it is a true implementation of X. It is designed to communicate all the information necessary to operate a window system over a single asynchronous bidirectional stream of 8-bit bytes.

Below the X protocol, any lower layer of network can be used, as long as it is bidirectional and delivers bytes in sequence and unduplicated between a server process and a client process. When the client and server are on the same machine, the connection is typically based on local interprocess communication (IPC) channels; otherwise, a network connection is established between them.

The protocol is designed to be operated asynchronously because this allows much higher performance. Synchronous operating speed is limited by the time required to make a round trip, which on most currently available local area networks is between 5 and 50 milliseconds. This speed is usually much less than the speed of the network in requests without replies. The server also sends events asynchronously, because this allows local polling for applications that must poll continuously for input. An example of such an application would be a game where the display is changing continuously but user input is still sought. Otherwise, applications that must poll for input during continuous drawing would actually be forced to operate synchronously.

Numerous window systems under UNIX use file or channel descriptors to represent windows. This has several disadvantages compared to X's approach of multiplexing all the windows on a single network connection. There is often a limit to the number of such descriptors, and they cannot be shared by clients on different machines and sometimes even on the same machine. Finally, the time order of communications through each descriptor is difficult to guarantee. The multiplexing of requests affecting different windows on the same stream allows the client to control the time order of updates, and similarly, the multiplexing of events on one stream also guarantees that the correct order is preserved.

Normally, clients implement the X protocol using a programming library that interfaces to a single underlying network protocol, typically TCP/IP or DECnet. The sample implementation provided by MIT of the C language client programming library called Xlib uses *sockets* on systems based on Berkeley UNIX.* MIT does not provide a routine for handling networking on systems based on AT&T's System V Release 3 UNIX. AT&T, in its proprietary implementation of Xlib, uses the System V native *streams*, where a protocol module supporting any underlying network protocol can be "pushed" onto a stream, allowing Xlib to use any underlying protocol for which a streams module exists.

---

*The *interfaces* defined in MIT's implementation of Xlib are standard, but the code is not. In other words, hardware vendors are allowed to change and optimize the library code for their systems as long as it provides exactly the same programming interface as MIT's version of Xlib. The same is true of MIT's sample servers and of their implementation of the Xt Intrinsics.

Servers often understand more than one underlying protocol so that they can communicate with clients on more than one type of network at once. For example, the DECwindows server accepts connections from clients using TCP/IP or from clients using DECnet. Currently, these are the only two network protocols commonly supported in X servers.

1.2.1 Message Types

The X protocol specifies four types of messages that can be transferred over the network. Requests are sent from the client to the server, and replies, events, and errors are sent from the server to the client.

- A *request* is generated by the client and sent to the server. A protocol request can carry a wide variety of information, such as a specification for drawing a line or changing the color value in a cell in a colormap or an inquiry about the current size of a window. A protocol request can be any multiple of 4 bytes in length.

- A *reply* is sent from the server to the client in response to certain requests. Not all requests are answered by replies—only the ones that ask for information. Requests that specify drawing, for example, do not generate replies, but requests that inquire about the current size of a window do. Protocol replies can be any multiple of 4 bytes in length, with a minimum of 32 bytes.

- An *event* is sent from the server to the client and contains information about a device action or about a side effect of a previous request. The data contained in events is quite varied because it is the principal method by which clients get information. All events are stored in a 32-byte structure to simplify queueing and handling them.

- An *error* is like an event, but it is handled differently by clients. Errors are sent to an error-handling routine by the client-side programming library. Error messages are the same size as events, to simplify handling them.

A protocol request that requires a reply is called a *round-trip request*. Round-trip requests have to be minimized in client programs because they lower performance when there are network delays. This will be discussed in more detail in the section on client library implementation.

You will notice that all the X protocol message types are designed to have a length in multiples of 4 bytes. This is to simplify implementation of the protocol on architectures that require alignment of values on 16- or 32-bit boundaries. As we will see, 16- and 32-bit values within the messages are always placed on 16- and 32-bit boundaries respectively.

We will define the contents of each of these protocol message types in more detail a little later.

1.2.2 Division of Responsibilities

In the process of designing the X protocol, much thought went into the division of capability between the server and the client, since this determines what information has to be passed back and forth through requests, replies, and events. An excellent source of information about the rationale behind certain choices made in designing the protocol is the article *The X Window System*, by Robert W. Scheifler and Jim Gettys, published in the Association of Computing Machinery journal *Transactions on Graphics*, Vol. 5, No. 2, April 1987. The decisions ultimately reached were based on portability of client programs, ease of client programming, and performance.

First, the server is designed, as much as possible, to hide differences in the underlying hardware from client applications. The server manages windows, does all drawing, and interfaces to the device drivers to get keyboard and pointer input. The server also manages off-screen memory, windows, fonts, cursors, and colormaps. The sample server code written at MIT contains a device-independent part and a device-dependent part. The device-dependent part must be customized for each hardware configuration, and it is here that the characteristics of the hardware are translated into the abstractions used by X such as "colormap."

Having the server responsible for managing the hierarchy and overlapping of windows has few, if any, disadvantages. It would seem quite possible for the client to waste network time by requesting graphics to a window that is not visible, since the client knows nothing of the window position or stacking order. (Such a request would have no effect since X does not preserve the contents of obscured windows.) However, this situation is dealt with by having clients draw only in response to an **Expose** event that announces when an area of a window has become exposed. In X, it is the client's responsibility to send the appropriate requests needed to redraw the contents of the rectangle of a window specified in the **Expose** event. For the rare clients where this responsibility leads to a severe performance penalty, X servers may (but are not required to) have a backing store feature that lets the server maintain window contents regardless of visibility.

There are certain hardware variations that are impossible or unwise to hide in the server. The X server could attempt to insulate the client from screen variations such as screen size, color vs. monochrome, number of colors, etc., but each of these would come at some cost. Hiding the screen size would make it easier to program applications that require graphics of a consistent size independent of the screen resolution, but it would make it harder to identify and manipulate single pixels, and it would add a burden to the server code. Hiding whether the screen is color or monochrome and the number of planes would lessen the load on the client program for simple color use, but it would be harder to manipulate the colormap in powerful ways, or use tricks in color such as overlays. A decision was made to make client programming more complicated in order to make it more powerful, since the goal was to hide this complexity in toolkit libraries anyway.

The server takes steps to make keyboard handling as uniform as possible on different machines, but it cannot completely hide variations in what symbols are actually embossed on the caps of the keys. For example, not all keyboards have Control and Meta keys. X handles this by providing several ways of handling the keyboard at different levels of abstraction. Each physical key has a code assigned by the server's device-dependent layer, which is reported in each key event. The server implementation also provides a table of key combinations and a resulting symbol which is the meaning of that key combination. For example, if the ''a'' key was pressed while the ''Shift'' key was being held, the key symbol in the table would represent ''A''. This table is managed by the server so that it applies to all clients, but the client library often maintains a copy of it so that the client can interpret events locally (quickly). The server does not use the table to interpret events before sending them to the client, which allows the client to interpret the keys in different languages or to use other event-handling techniques if desired (a client might want to treat the keyboard as a musical instrument rather than for text, for example). X supplies a request (**ChangeKeyboardMapping**) for changing the key symbol table, which results in an **MappingNotify** event to be sent to all clients. Clients other than the one that called **ChangeKeyboardMapping** respond to this event by sending a (**GetKeyboardMapping**) request, which gets the updated table.

Some decisions were made purely to simplify (or enhance) client programming. For example, coordinates in drawing requests are interpreted relative to the window being drawn into rather than to the entire screen. This provides a virtual drawing surface or ''window'' and makes client programming easier because the client does not need to continually track the window position and calculate where to draw based on this position. This gives the server the burden of determining where to actually draw graphics on the screen based on window positions. This, in turn, allows the server to support the window hierarchy without necessarily having to report all changes back to the client.

In other cases, decisions were made to increase performance. An example of this is the graphics context. The X *graphics context* (GC) allows the server to cache information about how graphics requests are to be interpreted, so this information need not be sent over the network from the client with every graphics request. This reduction in network traffic results in improved performance, particularly when the network is slow. Also, servers can be designed to cache GCs so that switching between them is fast and efficient. Finally, it is a happy coincidence that the GC usually makes client programming easier, because it reduces the number of parameters needed in drawing calls.

The GC is one of several abstractions X maintains in the server; the most important others are the Window, Pixmap (an off-screen virtual drawing surface that must be copied into a window to become visible), Colormap, and Font. The client refers to each abstraction in protocol requests using a unique integer ID assigned by the server. This ID is a 29-bit integer (high bits are unused to simplify implementation on architectures that employ garbage collection). IDs are chosen by the client-side libraries, but using a specific subrange specified by the server at connection time that guarantees that the IDs will be unique from all other IDs that can be created by other clients using the same server. The fact that IDs are not assigned by the server means that creating an abstraction does not require a reply by the server. This is very important in reducing the startup time of applications because creating each abstraction would otherwise waste at least one round-trip time.

The Window abstraction lets the server manage which parts of the screen are displaying which parts of which window, and lets the server take care of applying the window attributes (such things as the border and background) to each window. The X protocol includes requests that get information about abstractions, so that the client is not completely in the dark. However, not every detail of each abstraction is necessarily accessible from the client side, since some information of limited usefulness was left out of query replies to allow more flexibility in server code design. One example of this is that some of the window attributes cannot be queried (such as bit gravity, which is for redrawing optimization). Another is that the values in GCs cannot be queried at all. Neither the window attributes that cannot be queried nor the GC values are changed by any client other than the one that created them. Therefore, it does not add much burden to clients to require them to keep track of their own parameter settings if they need the information later. Furthermore, programming the server to be able to provide this information places constraints on the server that could affect performance.

1.3 A Sample Session

The following sections describe what happens over the network during a minimal application that creates a window, allocates a color, waits for events, draws into the window, and quits. This example uses three of the four types of X network messages as they would occur in an application. The fourth is the error, which we hope will not occur during the normal operation of an application. How errors are generated and handled and what the network message for an error looks like will be explained after successful operation is described.

Here are the network events that will take place during a successful client session:

- Client opens connection to the server and sends information describing itself.

- Server sends back to client data describing the server or refusing the connection request.

- Client makes a request to create a window. Note that this request has no reply.

- Client makes a request to allocate a color.

- Server sends back a reply describing the allocated color.

- Client makes a request to create a graphics context, for using in later drawing requests.

- Client makes a request identifying the types of events it requires. In this case, **Expose** and **ButtonPress** events.

- Client makes a request to map (display on the screen) the created window.

- Client waits for an **Expose** event before continuing. This sends the accumulated requests to the server.

- Server sends to client an **Expose** event indicating that the window has been displayed.

- Client makes a request to draw a graphic, using graphics context.

- Loop back to wait for an **Expose** event.

We note in this session description that client requests are queued up by the client library before being sent to the server and that the client reading events triggers the sending. This is not actually a required characteristic of client libraries, but it improves performance greatly because it takes advantage of the asynchronous design of the protocol. Xlib works this way. This behavior allows the client to continue running without having to stop to wait for network access, until it would have to wait for an event anyway.

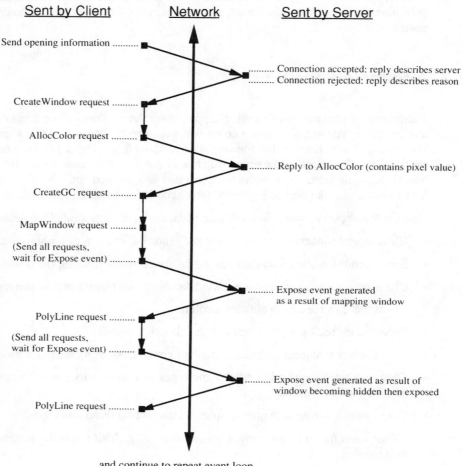

Figure 1-5. A sample X Window System client session.

Note that many of the actions taken by the client in the session must be done in the order shown for the application to work properly. For example, **Expose** events must be selected before the window is mapped, because otherwise no event would arrive to notify the client when to draw. This becomes even more important when a window manager is managing the screen. Many window managers let the user decide on the size and position of a window before allowing it to be mapped, introducing a sizeable delay between the time the client requests mapping the window and when the window actually appears on the screen ready to be drawn into. Only the **Expose** event tells the client when it is time to draw.

Colors are allocated very early in the session before creating the graphics context to optimize the usage of protocol requests. To allocate a color, the client tells the server what color is desired, and the server responds by giving the client a "pixel value," which is a number that identifies the cell in the colormap containing the closest color available (the exact color may not be physically possible on the screen, or all colormap entries may already be in use by other clients). When creating the graphics context, this pixel value can be used to set the foreground color to be used for drawing. It is also possible to create a default graphics context before allocating the color, but then setting the foreground value in the existing graphics context would require an additional, unnecessary request.*

1.3.1 Opening the Connection

The client allows the user to identify the server it wants to connect to by specifying a host and display number. The display number is zero on personal workstations, because there is only one keyboard, pointer, and display connected to a single host, and hence only one server. Multi-user workstations and timesharing systems that support graphics terminals are rare today, but X leaves open the possibility that a single host could support two or more servers by having two or more sets of display, keyboard, and mouse.

The client-side library should provide an easy-to-use method for the user to specify which server to connect to. Under UNIX, Xlib reads the environment variable DISPLAY. The user specifies the server by setting DISPLAY to the host name and server number separated by a colon, for example, *ghost:0*. The networking utilities under Berkeley UNIX translate host names into network addresses using the file */etc/hosts* (or on some systems, the yellow pages daemon).

For TCP connections, displays on a given host are numbered starting from zero, and the server for display N listens and accepts connections on port 6000+N. For DECnet connections, displays on a given host are numbered starting from zero, and the server for display N listens and accepts connections on the object name obtained by concatenating "X$X" with the decimal representation for N, e.g., X$X0 and X$X1.

Once the proper address is known, the client begins sending bytes that describe itself. Then the server sends back information describing itself if the connection is acceptable or describing what went wrong if the connection is refused.

Table 1-1 specifies the data that the client sends. Throughout this chapter, when the type for a certain piece of data is not defined by the protocol, it is not critical and is not shown.

---

*For more information about of the order of operations for most effective client programming, see the *Xlib Programming Manual* (O'Reilly and Associates, Inc., 1988).

Table 1-1. Byte Stream Sent by Client to Open Connection

# of Bytes	Type	Values	Description
1		102 (MSB first) 154 (LSB first)	byte-order
1			unused
2	unsigned integer		protocol-major-version
2	unsigned integer		protocol-minor-version
2		n	length of authorization-protocol-name
2		d	length of authorization-protocol-data
2			unused
n	list of unsigned integers		authorization-protocol-name
p			unused, p=pad(n)
d	list of unsigned integers		authorization-protocol-data
q			unused, q=pad(d)

The first byte of data identifies the byte order employed on the client's machine. The value 102 (ASCII upper case B) means values are transmitted most significant byte first, and the value 154 (ASCII lower case l) means values are transmitted least significant byte first. All 16-bit and 32-bit quantities, except those involving image data, are transferred in both directions using this byte order specified by the client. Image data is an exception and is described at the end of this section.

Next, the client tells the server the version of the protocol it expects the server to implement. The major version is currently 11 and the minor version is 0 (this is true for Release 1, 2, and 3 of X Version 11). The version numbers are an escape hatch in case future revisions of the protocol are necessary. In general, the major version would increment for incompatible changes, and the minor version would increment for small upward-compatible changes. The server returns the protocol version numbers it actually supports, which might not equal the version sent by the client. The server can (but need not) refuse connections from clients that offer a different version than the server supports. A server can (but need not) support more than one version simultaneously.

The authorization name indicates what authorization protocol the client expects the server to use, and the data is specific to that protocol. Specification of valid authorization mechanisms is not part of the core X protocol. (See Section 1.4.5, *Security*.) In the meantime, most servers ignore this information.

The padding and unused bytes are required because each network message generated by X always has a length that is a multiple of 4 bytes, and all 16- and 32-bit quantities are placed in the message such that they are on 16- or 32-bit boundaries. This is done to make implementation of the protocol easier on architectures that require data to be aligned on 16- or 32-bit boundaries. Consequently, lengths of data in the X protocol are always specified in units of 4 bytes.

The server sends back the information shown in Table 1-2 if connection is refused.

Table 1-2. Byte Stream Returned by Server on Failed Connection

# of Bytes	Type	Values	Description
1		0	failed
1		n	length of reason in bytes
2	unsigned integer		protocol-major-version
2	unsigned integer		protocol-minor-version
2		(n+p)/4	length in 4-byte units of "additional data"
n	list of unsigned integers		reason
p			unused, p=pad(n)

The value of the first element is 1 if the connection succeeded or 0 if it failed. The protocol version elements describe the protocol version preferred (or the only one accepted) by the server. (This may be the reason for connection failure if the client expected a different version.) The reason element describes why connection failed. Current servers do not use standard codes for reasons.

Table 1-3 shows the stream of data returned when the connection is successful. The Xlib client programming library stores this information in the `Display` structure, and the pointer to this structure is passed as an argument to most Xlib routines. The routines then access this information internally when necessary. Xlib also provides macros (and function equivalents) for accessing a few of the more frequently used items, so that client programs do not depend on the particular implementation of the structure that contains this information.

You need to know that an X server can support multiple screens to understand the returned connection information. An X server shows information to a single user but perhaps through more than one physical or logical screen. An example of a use for two physical screens would be to be able to debug an application on a color screen and on a monochrome screen at the same time. Both screens are controlled by a single server. The sample server on Sun color systems currently provides two logical screens on a single physical screen, one with the screen acting as monochrome (which is currently much faster), and the other with the screen acting in color. The user switches between the screens by moving the pointer off either side of the screen. No geometry of the screens is defined by the protocol, and how the mouse moves between the various screens depends on the server implementation.

The connection information describes each of the attached screens separately. Since there can be any number of attached screens, there is a section of the connection information that is repeated for each screen. Moreover, each screen can sometimes be used in a variety of ways. For example, a color screen can also be used to display windows in black and white. X calls the attributes describing a particular way of using a screen a *visual*. For each screen, there is information describing the one or more ways that screen can be used.

The concept of the visual has a number of advantages. If you know a certain window is going to be used in black and white even on a color screen (for example, a terminal emulator window), it is much more efficient to treat it that way because it requires handling only 1 bit per pixel instead of up to 24. Some servers can take advantage of this to improve performance dramatically.

As we will see in the **CreateWindow** request, a window is created with a particular visual, and this is a permanent aspect of the created window. Since there may be several different ways of using color on a certain screen, the block of data that describes a visual may be repeated several times for each screen. Each screen description includes the width-in-pixels, height-in-pixels, width-in-millimeters, and height-in-millimeters of the root window (which cannot be changed). This information can be used to tailor client operation according to the screen size and aspect ratio.

Each screen also has a default colormap which contains at least two permanently allocated entries called BlackPixel and WhitePixel, which can be used in implementing a monochrome application on monochrome or color screens. The actual RGB values of BlackPixel and WhitePixel may be settable on some screens and, in any case, may not actually be black and white. The names are intended to convey the expected relative intensity of the colors.

Table 1-3. Byte Stream Returned by Server on Successful Connection

# of Bytes	Type	Values	Description
1		1	success
1			unused
2	unsigned integer		protocol-major-version
2	unsigned integer		protocol-minor-version
2		8+2n+(v+p+m)/4	length in 4-byte units of "additional data"
4	unsigned integer		release-number
4	unsigned integer		resource-id-base
4	unsigned integer		resource-id-mask
4	unsigned integer		motion-buffer-size
2		v	length of vendor
2	unsigned integer		maximum-request-length
1	unsigned integer		number of SCREENs in roots
1		n	number for FORMATs in pixmap-formats
1		0 (LSBFirst) 1 (MSBFirst)	image-byte-order
1		0 (LeastSignificant) 1 (MostSignificant)	bitmap-format-bit-order

# of Bytes	Type	Values	Description
1	unsigned integer		bitmap-format-scanline-unit
1	unsigned integer		bitmap-format-scanline-pad
1	KEYCODE (unsigned integer)		min-keycode
1	KEYCODE (unsigned integer)		max-keycode
4			unused
v	list of unsigned integers		vendor
p			unused, p=pad(v)
8n	LISTofFORMAT		pixmap-formats
m	LISTofSCREEN		roots (m is always a multiple of 4)
FORMAT			
1	unsigned integer		depth
1	unsigned integer		bits-per-pixel
1	unsigned integer		scanline-pad
5			unused
SCREEN			
4	WINDOW		root
4	COLORMAP		default-colormap
4	unsigned integer		white-pixel
4	unsigned integer		black-pixel
4	SETofEVENT		current-input-masks
2	unsigned integer		width-in-pixels
2	unsigned integer		height-in-pixels
2	unsigned integer		width-in-millimeters
2	unsigned integer		height-in-millimeters
2	unsigned integer		min-installed-maps
2	unsigned integer		max-installed-maps
4	VISUALID		root-visual
1		0 (Never) 1 (WhenMapped) 2 (Always)	backing-stores
1	BOOL		save-unders
1	unsigned integer		root-depth
1	unsigned integer		number of DEPTHs in allowed-depths

# of Bytes	Type	Values	Description
n	LISTofDEPTH		allowed-depths (n is always a multiple of 4)
DEPTH			
1	unsigned integer		depth
1			unused
2		n	number of VISUAL-TYPES in visuals
4			unused
24n	LISTofVISUALTYPE		visuals
VISUALTYPE			
4	VISUALID		visual-id
1		0 (StaticGray) 1 (GrayScale) 2 (StaticColor) 3 (PseudoColor) 4 (TrueColor) 5 (DirectColor)	class
1	unsigned integer		bits-per-rgb-value
2	unsigned integer		colormap-entries
4	unsigned integer		red-mask
4	unsigned integer		green-mask
4	unsigned integer		blue-mask
4			unused

All this information describes the server in painstaking detail. It is impossible to describe all of it in detail here, but we will touch on some of the more interesting parts.

The resource-id-mask and resource-id-base elements provide the information necessary for the client to generate IDs that are unique within the client but also unique from IDs generated in other clients. An ID must be unique with respect to the IDs of all other abstractions created by all clients, not just other abstractions of the same type and by the same client, because the server manages them all. The resource-id-mask is a 32-bit value with at least 18 bits set. The client allocates an abstract ID* by choosing a value with some subset of these bits set and ORing it with resource-id-base. To allocate the next ID, normally the client increments its value that is a subset of resource-id-mask. This local allocation of IDs is important because it eliminates the need for round-trip requests when creating abstractions, which speeds the startup time of clients.

---

*In this book, we use the term abstract instead of the term "resource" because resource has a different meaning in programming contexts.

Maximum-request-length specifies the maximum length of a request, in 4-byte units, accepted by the server. This limit might depend on the amount of available memory in the server. This is the maximum value that can appear in the length field of a request. Requests larger than this generate a **BadLength** error, and the server will read and simply discard the entire request. Maximum-request-length will always be at least 4096 (that is, requests of length up to and including 16384 bytes will be accepted by all servers).

X servers are required to swap the bytes of data from machines with different native byte order, in all cases except in image processing. The first byte in the message that opens the connection between the client and the server, sent from the client library, indicates to the server which byte order is native on the host running the client.

Image data is always sent to the server and received from the server using the server's byte order. This is because image data is likely to be voluminous and byte-swapping it expensive. The client is told the server's byte order in the information returned after connecting to the server. The client may then be able to store and operate on the image in the correct format for the server, eliminating the need to swap bytes.

1.3.2 Creating a Window

Once the connection to the server is successfully opened, the first thing most applications do is create one or more windows.

The **CreateWindow** request is more complicated than most X protocol requests, but all requests have the same structure; a block of data consisting of an opcode, some number of fixed length parameters, and sometimes a variable-length parameter. Every request begins with an 8-bit major opcode, followed by a 16-bit length field expressed in units of 4 bytes. The length field defines the total length of the request, including the opcode and length field and must equal the minimum length required to contain the request, or an error is generated. Unused bytes in a request are not required to be zero.

Major opcodes 128 through 255 are reserved for extensions. Each extension is intended to contain multiple requests; all requests within a particular extension would use the same major opcode. Therefore, extension requests typically have an additional minor opcode encoded in the data byte immediately following the length field.

We will describe the fixed- and variable-length components of **CreateWindow** after you have seen the data sent in this request. Table 1-4 shows the byte stream sent by a client to the server to create a window. (Do not be put off by its complexity; most requests are much simpler than this one.)

Table 1-4. The **CreateWindow** *Request*

# of Bytes	Type	Values	Description
1	1		opcode of request
1	unsigned integer		depth
2	8+n		request length
4	WINDOW		client selected ID for window
4	WINDOW		parent's ID
2	signed integer		x (position)
2	signed integer		y
2	unsigned integer		width (size, inside border)
2	unsigned integer		height
2	unsigned integer		border-width
2		0 (**CopyFromParent**) 1 (**InputOutput**) 2 (**InputOnly**)	class
4	VISUALID	(id) 0 (**CopyFromParent**)	visual
4	BITMASK		value-mask (has n 1-bits) for attributes
	#x00000001	background-pixmap	
	#x00000002	background-pixel	
	#x00000004	border-pixmap	
	#x00000008	border-pixel	
	#x00000010	bit-gravity	
	#x00000020	win-gravity	
	#x00000040	backing-store	
	#x00000080	backing-planes	
	#x00000100	backing-pixel	
	#x00000200	override-redirect	
	#x00000400	save-under	
	#x00000800	event-mask	
	#x00001000	do-not-propagate-mask	
	#x00002000	colormap	
	#x00004000	cursor	
4n	LISTofVALUE		value-list
VALUES			
4	PIXMAP	(pixmap) 0 (**None**) 1 (**ParentRelative**)	background-pixmap

Table 1-4. The **CreateWindow** Request (continued)

Introduction to
X Protocol

# of Bytes	Type	Values	Description
4	unsigned integer		background-pixel
4	PIXMAP	(pixmap)	border-pixmap
		0 (**CopyFromParent**)	
4	unsigned integer		border-pixel
1	BITGRAVITY		bit-gravity
1	WINGRAVITY		win-gravity
1		0 (**NotUseful**)	backing-store
		1 (**WhenMapped**)	
		2 (**Always**)	
4	unsigned integer		backing-planes
4	unsigned integer		backing-pixel
1	BOOL		override-redirect
1	BOOL		save-under
4	SETofEVENT		event-mask
4	SETofDEVICEEVENT	do-not-propagate-mask	
4	COLORMAP	(colormap)	colormap
		0 (**CopyFromParent**)	
4	CURSOR	(cursor)	cursor
		0 (**None**)	

The most interesting aspect of **CreateWindow** is that it varies in length according to how much information needs to be transferred. The fixed-length components of **CreateWindow** include the ID of the parent window; the ID the client has chosen for this window; the window size, position, and border width; the window class (**InputOutput** or **InputOnly**); and the window's visual (ID of a server-created abstraction which describes how color should be used in the window). The final component of the fixed-length portion of **Create-Window** is a bitmask which describes which of the optional components are present. Optional components are always bits of information for which the server has a reasonable default for the ones not specified. The bitmask tells the server which items are going to be present in the remainder of the request.

The optional components in **CreateWindow** are the window attributes. The window attributes control:

* The background and border colors or patterns.

* Whether the contents of a window are saved when the window is resized and where the old contents are placed (bit gravity).

* Whether and how subwindows should be automatically moved when the parent is resized (window gravity).

* Whether the window contents should be preserved by the server (backing store).

- Whether the server should save under a temporary window to speed redrawing when this window is unmapped (save under).

- The events that should be delivered to the client when they occur in this window (event mask).

- Events that should not propagate to higher windows in the hierarchy (do-not-propagate-mask).

- Whether the window should be immune to window manager intervention (override-redirect).

- Which colormap should be used to translate pixel values into colors for this window (colormap).

- What cursor should be used in this window (cursor).

1.3.2.1 Selecting Events

The only attribute that every client sets is the event mask.

The server is capable of sending many types of events to the client, each of which contains information about a different user action or side effect of a request. But the client is not always interested in every type of event, and it is wasteful to send them over simply to be thrown away. Therefore, each window has an attribute that controls which events are sent over when they occur in that window.

The event mask can be set in **CreateWindow** or as part of a somewhat simpler request called **ChangeWindowAttributes**. However, if the correct event mask is known when the window is created, it is more efficient to set the event mask at that window creation time rather than with a separate request. Note that the time delay between window creation and setting of the event mask when done in separate requests is not a problem, because events cannot occur in this window yet because it is not yet displayed. Windows do not appear on the screen until they are mapped, which is discussed in Section 1.3.5.

For this sample session, we will select **Expose** and **ButtonPress** events. The **Expose** events are necessary to tell us when our window appears on the screen so we can draw on it, and the **ButtonPress** event will allow us to escape from the closed event handling loop.

1.3.3 A Request with Reply

Some requests require an immediate reply from the server, because the client cannot continue without the information. Most of these requests get information about server abstractions such as windows, fonts, and properties. Others report success or failure of a request whose effects must take place before the client can safely continue. Some requests require replies for both these reasons. Either a particular request has a reply or it does not; there are no requests that sometimes have replies and other times do not. Replies are always immediate.

As an example, we demonstrate here a request that allocates a color. To describe color handling in X completely would take considerable space, and it is unnecessary for a conceptual understanding of the protocol. But you can understand the request and the reply if you understand just a little about color. The client specifies a color by specifying the index of a cell in a server-maintained colormap. This index is called a pixel value. The client has to request from the server the pixel value that represents a certain color, because only the server knows what color is in each cell. The X server is capable of maintaining multiple virtual colormaps, and it can install one or more of them depending on the hardware. Each of these colormaps has an ID and can be read-only or read/write. Read-only colormaps contain cells with preset color values, and these cells can be shared because no client can change them, but often clients will not find the exact color they need in the colormap. Read/write colormaps can have colorcells that are private to a single application and others that are shared among applications. X specifies colors in red, green, and blue values that are each 16-bit numbers.

The **AllocColor** request allocates a read-only color from a colormap. Therefore, it works on any kind of colormap. However, the exact color the client asks for might not be available, so the server has to supply the pixel value of the closest color that exists in the map. At one extreme, if the colormap happened to be monochrome, the closest color allocated will always be either black or white. The reply to **AllocColor** tells the client the pixel value of the closest color available, and the red, green, and blue values of the color stored in that cell. The client can decide whether the red, green, and blue values of the cell are close enough to the requested color to be adequate.

Table 1-5. The AllocColor *Request*

# of Bytes	Type	Values	Description
1		84	opcode
1			unused
2		4	request length
4	COLORMAP		colormap ID
2	unsigned integer		red
2	unsigned integer		green
2	unsigned integer		blue
2			unused

The **AllocColor** request specifies which colormap the client wants to use, and the red, green, and blue values for the desired color. The server replies with the ID of the read-only cell in the colormap that comes closest to the color desired, and the actual red, green, and blue values in that cell.

The reply opcode is always 1; this member in errors is 0 and in core (non-extension) events ranges from 2 to 34. The sequence number is a count kept by the server of the last request processed before sending this information. Everything that the server sends to the client (replies, events, and errors) contains a sequence number field.

Notice that replies, like requests, contain a length field even when they are of fixed length. This makes it easier to write client library code to process the requests and replies correctly because there is no need to look up the length in a table based on the opcode. This is a trade-off that simplifies the client library code in exchange for transferring a few unnecessary bytes over the network.

Table 1-6. Server Reply to AllocColor

# of Bytes	Type	Values	Description
1		1	reply opcode
1			unused
2	unsigned integer		sequence number
4		0	reply length
2	unsigned integer		red
2	unsigned integer		green
2	unsigned integer		blue
2			unused
4	unsigned integer		pixel value
12			unused

As in requests, the length field is expressed in units of 4 bytes. Unused bytes within a reply are not guaranteed to be zero.

The unused field right after the blue field is present to align the pixel field, which is a 32-bit value, with a 32-bit boundary for easier handling on architectures that require either 16- or 32-bit alignment.

Table 1-7 lists all X requests that generate replies. From this table, you should get an idea of the types of requests that require replies. Each of these requests is briefly described in Appendix H, *Alphabetical Listing of Requests*.

Table 1-7. Requests that have Replies

AllocColor	GetSelectionOwner	QueryBestSize
GetAtomName	GetWindowAttributes	QueryColors
GetGeometry	GrabKeyboard	QueryExtension
GetImage	GrabPointer	QueryFont
GetKeyboardControl	InternAtom	QueryKeymap
GetKeyboardMapping	ListExtensions	QueryPointer
GetModifierMapping	ListFonts	QueryTextExtents
GetMotionEvents	ListHosts	QueryTree
GetPointerControl	ListInstalledColormaps	SetModifierMapping
GetPointerMapping	ListProperties	SetPointerMapping
GetProperty	LookupColor	TranslateCoordinates
GetScreenSaver		

1.3.4 Creating a Graphics Context

A graphics context (GC) is an abstraction that controls the server's interpretation of graphics requests. The GC controls line width, how lines connect, how they end, what colors are used, what planes of the display are affected, how the existing contents of the screen are factored into the calculation, and how areas are filled or patterned.

GCs should be created early and set once (if possible) to speed up the loop that responds to user events.

The **CreateGC** request is very similar to the **CreateWindow** request, in that one member of the request is a bitmask, which defines the length and composition of the remainder of the request. Only the members of the GC that are being set to values other than the default take up space in the request.

Since **CreateGC** shows nothing new, we will not show you the detailed contents of the request here.

1.3.5 Mapping a Window

Mapping makes a window eligible for display on the screen. In the simplest case, when the application is alone on the screen, mapping does actually display the window. But more generally, whether the window appears depends on the following:

1. The window must be mapped with **MapWindow**.

2. All of the window's ancestors must be mapped.

3. The window must in a position so that it is not obscured by visible sibling windows or their ancestors. If sibling windows are overlapping, whether or not a window is obscured depends on the stacking order. The stacking order can be manipulated with **Configure-Window**.

4. The client-library request buffer must be flushed. More information on this topic is provided in Section 1.4.1.

5. The initial mapping of a top-level window is a special case, since the window's visibility may be delayed by the window manager. For complicated reasons, a client must wait for the first **Expose** event before assuming that its window is visible and drawing into it.

Table 1-8 shows the request that maps a window, **MapWindow**.

Table 1-8. The MapWindow *Request*

# of Bytes	Type	Values	Description
1		8	opcode of request
1			unused
2		2	request length
4	WINDOW		window

That's a refreshing sight after the connection information and **CreateWindow**! The **MapWindow** request simply sends the ID of the window that is to be marked for display, so that it will be visible when the conditions listed above are met.

1.3.6 The Expose event

From the client's point of view, the only true indication that a window is visible is when the server generates an **Expose** event for it. Only after receiving this **Expose** event can the client begin drawing into the window. The server generates one or more **Expose** events for a window when it meets all the criteria listed above. There may be more than one **Expose** event because each one describes an exposed rectangle, and it may take several such rectangles to describe the areas of a window not covered by overlapping windows.

Table 1-9 shows what the server sends to the client to represent an **Expose** event. Note that all events are exactly 32 bytes long.

Table 1-9. The Expose *Event, as Sent from Server*

# of Bytes	Type	Values	Description
1		12	code
1			unused
2	unsigned integer		sequence number
4	WINDOW		window
2	unsigned integer		x
2	unsigned integer		y
2	unsigned integer		width
2	unsigned integer		height
2	unsigned integer		count
14			unused

The code indicates which type of event this is. The sequence number is the number assigned by the server for the most recently processed request; it is used in tracking errors. The window field specifies which window was exposed, and the x, y, width, and height fields specify the area within that window that was exposed. The count specifies how many more **Expose** events follow that were generated as the result of the same protocol request.

Figure 1-6 shows a window arrangement in which, if window E were raised, four **Expose** events would be generated, to report that the four corners of window E have now become visible.

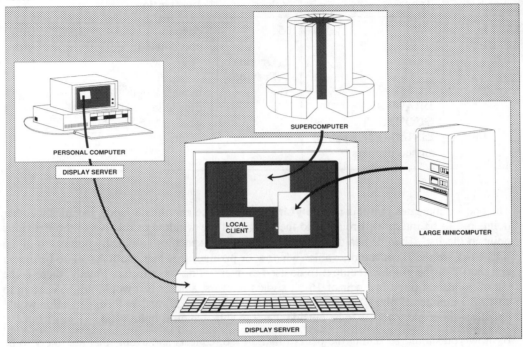

Figure 1-6. Expose events generated when window E is raised.

The X protocol specifies that all the **Expose** events resulting from a single protocol request (in this case, **ConfigureWindow** raising window E) must be contiguous.

In client programs, events are gathered and processed one at a time in a closed loop. **Expose** events will always be processed in these loops (unless the client has no windows). Clients may but need not provide any way to exit, since a separate client (called *xkill* in the standard X distribution) is normally available to kill running programs.

1.3.7 Drawing a Graphic

The **Expose** event says to the client, in effect, "go ahead and draw now." This applies not only to the first time the window is displayed on the screen but also to any later time when the window becomes obscured and then exposed. It applies to redrawing as well as to first-time drawing.

Now let's take a look at the request to draw some lines. The protocol request to draw connected lines is **PolyLine**, shown in Table 1-10.

Table 1-10. The PolyLine *Request*

# of Bytes	Type	Values	Description
1		65	opcode
1			coordinate-mode
		0 (**Origin**)	
		1 (**Previous**)	
2		3+n	request length
4	DRAWABLE		drawable
4	GCONTEXT		gc
4n	LISTofPOINT (pair of signed integers)		points

The opcode indicates that this is a **PolyLine** request. The coordinate-mode specifies whether points are to be interpreted relative to the **Origin** of the window or relative to the **Previous** point in the list. Then comes the request length, which specifies how many points are in the list. Next are the ID of the drawable (window or pixmap) in which the lines are to be drawn and the ID of the graphics context to be used in interpreting the request. Finally, there is the list of points. A point is a pair of 16-bit signed integers, since 8 bits would not be enough to cover the number of pixels on the screen (usually around 1000) and an unsigned value would not allow the x and y values to be outside the drawable, which is quite valid.

By now you should be seeing the pattern that all the requests and events that are likely to be issued during the loop that processes events are normally short, while the requests to setup things before this loop are long. Response to user actions is kept fast by spending the time necessary to setup before the event loop is started.

1.3.8 Closing the Connection

You may have noticed that there seems to be no way to exit this session! Some X clients are actually written this way. They can only be killed by a separate X client (called *xkill*) or by finding the process ID and killing the process from the UNIX shell. Other clients supply a button or command for exiting. Outside termination is acceptable because the client need not do anything to terminate the session properly. There is no request that the client sends to the server that means "I'm about to quit." It is the server's responsibility to be able to clean up after the client dies.

The client library closes the session simply by closing the network connection (with `close` on BSD systems). This is also done automatically by the operating system when the client dies abnormally. The application program itself needs only to free any local structures that may have been created. The server then cleans up after the client by destroying the abstractions the client created.

The X protocol does, however, provide the **SetCloseDownMode** request to modify this behavior so that abstractions created by a client are not immediately destroyed when the client exits. This allows a new invocation of the client to attempt to recover from fatal errors such as a broken network connection that caused an earlier invocation to die before valuable information stored in the server could be saved to disk. A companion to this request is **KillClient**, which is used to kill the preserved abstractions when they are no longer needed.

1.3.9 Errors

We have described how requests, replies, and events operate during a successful client session. But what happens when a parameter does not meet the server's specifications for a given request, or the server cannot allocate enough memory to complete the request? An error message is generated and sent to the client.

Usually errors indicate a client programming error, but they can also occur when the server is unable to allocate enough memory or in other similar situations. Therefore, all clients must be able to handle errors. The definition of "wrong" depends on the particular request. The server does range checking to make sure that the arguments sent with each request are valid, and it also makes sure that each request sent from the client is the length it says it is. The client library does not do range checking because it does not have access to all the information necessary to check ranges (like window depths) and, secondly, because it makes more sense to have the server do it than to have multiple copies of this code in every client.

Although an error message looks much like an event, it is handled differently by the client. Unlike events, which are queued by the client library to be read later, errors are dispatched immediately upon arrival to a routine that processes the error. This routine may be a general routine that simply reports the error before exiting, or it may attempt to recover from the error by correcting the mistake in the request. However, recovery is normally difficult because of the delay between the time when a request is invoked by the application program and when the mistake is detected by the server and the error message is sent to the client. Often a number of other requests will have already been made in the intervening time, and the server will continue to act on these requests even after sending the error to the client. There is no way to "take back" the requests that have already been processed since the error. In any case, the X protocol specifies that the client is not allowed to respond to an error by making requests to the server, such as drawing to the screen, because this might cause a cycle of errors. For these reasons, the normal response to an error is for the client library to print an error message and then exit the client process.

Another form of error occurs when any sort of system call error occurs, such as the connection with a server dying due to a machine crash. These types of errors are detected on the client side, and the client library normally contains a routine for handling them. There is no alternative in this case but to report the error and exit the client process.

Let's continue our client session, but this time make an illegal request and see what happens.

- Client queues a illegal request for the server (just so we can see what happens).

- Client sends the illegal request to the server.

- Server processes the queued requests and sends an error report back to the client. Client processes the error and recovers somehow if the error is not fatal or exits.

As an example, lets say the client sends a request to draw a line to the server but gets the window and GC arguments reversed. The server will return a **BadWindow** error report, as shown in Table 1-11.

Table 1-11. The Error Message, as Sent from Server

# of Bytes	Type	Values	Description
1		0	error (always zero for errors)
1		3	code (**BadWindow**)
2	unsigned integer		sequence number
4	unsigned integer		bad resource id
2	unsigned integer		minor opcode
1	unsigned integer		major opcode
21			unused

Error reports are sent from the server to the client in a package identical to that used for events. This is because errors are so rare that they do not justify separate handling, even though this could save a small amount of network time (21 bytes are sent but not used by every error). They are basically treated just like events all the way to the routine in the client library that receives them. It is at this point that they are sent to the error-handling routine instead of being queued.

The first field is the one used to identify the various event types and is zero for all errors. The code field identifies the type of error that occurred. Error codes 128 through 255 are reserved for extensions. The sequence number, as in events, gives the last request successfully processed just before the error. The sequence number can be used to determine exactly which protocol request caused the error, which, as we will see after discussing how the client library is actually implemented, becomes quite important. The bad-resource-id field gives the value that was unacceptable for all the errors that are caused by invalid values and is unused by the other errors. The major and minor opcodes identify the type of request that caused the error. In the core protocol, the major opcode identifies which protocol request contained the error, and the minor opcode is unused. But for extensions, typically the entire extension will use a particular major opcode, and the minor opcode will identify each request within that extension.

Unused bytes within an error are not guaranteed to be zero.

1.4 Implementing the X Protocol

MIT includes on its distribution tape of the X Window System implementations of the X protocol in a "sample server" for several different machines and in two client side libraries, one for C and the other for Lisp.

This section discusses several issues that come up in porting this code to new machines.

1.4.1 Client Library Implementation

The client programming library that implements the protocol can do several things to improve performance. This section describes how Xlib, the lowest level C language interface to X, handles the network to improve performance. If you can gain access to the source code for Xlib, you can look at how it handles the network by inspecting the files *XConnDis.c* and *XlibInt.c*.

Xlib buffers requests instead of sending them to the server immediately, so that the client program can continue running instead of waiting to gain access to the network. This is possible for several reasons:

- Because most requests are drawing requests that do not require immediate action.

- Because the network stream is reliable, and therefore no confirmation message from the server is necessary to indicate that the request was received.

This grouping of requests by the client before sending them over the network increases the performance of most networks, because it makes the network transactions longer and less numerous, reducing the total overhead involved.

Xlib triggers the sending of the buffer full of requests to the server under four conditions. The most common is when an application calls a blocking Xlib routine to get an event, but no matching event is currently available on Xlib's queue. Because the application must wait for an appropriate event anyway, it makes sense to flush the request buffer. This says to the server, "I need some information; act on these requests and then give it to me right away."

Secondly, some of the client routines get information from the server, requiring an immediate reply. In this case, all the requests in the buffer are sent before waiting for the reply. This says to the server, "I'm waiting for a certain kind of event, so I'll check if you have already sent the event over to me. If not, please act on these requests immediately and then I'll be waiting for an event from you."

The client can also flush the request buffer explicitly (in Xlib with a call to **Xflush**) in situations where no user events are expected. Note that flushing the request buffer does not generate a protocol request, because it is a local instruction to Xlib. This third situation says to the server, "I don't need any information from you now, but I need you to act on these requests immediately." Normally, this is not used because there are enough of the first two types of calls in the client to make the flushes frequent enough.

Xlib also flushes the request buffer when it fills up.

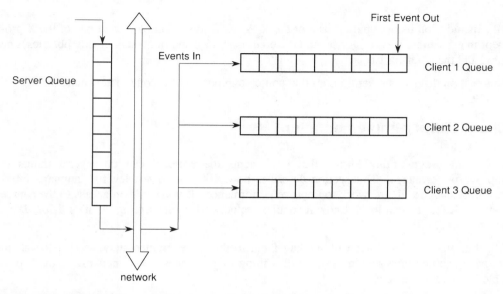

Figure 1-7. *The server's event queue and each client's event queue*

Client-library buffering of requests has important implications for errors. When the client makes an erroneous request, it will not be sent to the server immediately unless the flushing criteria listed above are met. Therefore, the client will continue, queueing additional requests until the flushing criteria are met. Then these requests are sent together to the server. The server then processes each request in turn and detects the error when it attempts to process the bad request, at which point the server sends an error report to the client. The client sends the library error report directly to one of the error-handling routines that reports the error to the user.

In other words, the error does not come to the user's attention until the request buffer is sent, the server processes the requests up to the one containing the error, the server sends the error report to the client, and the client error-handling routine processes it. This delay makes it more difficult to discover which request actually contained the error.

To allow the possibility of the client recovering from the error, the server does not stop itself or disconnect the client after the error. The server goes on processing requests. Therefore, after sending the error, the screen may reflect actions that take place after the error occurred. That is why error reports contain both the sequence number of the last request processed by the server and the opcode of the protocol request that caused the error.

The client library can also make programming easier by providing convenience routines that perform common tasks while hiding the complications in the actual protocol request to be issued. For example, in Xlib, XSetForeground sets the foreground color for drawing in a graphics context. XSetForeground really issues a **ChangeGC** request to the server, but it allows the client to ignore all the other aspects of the GC.

Convenience routines may seem like an invitation for inefficient programming. What if the client sets three different GC values using three convenience routines? This could lead to three round-trip protocol requests when only one would suffice. The solution to this problem is for the library to take advantage of the fact that requests are queued by combining all these similar requests into a single one before sending them to the server. Xlib actually does this: it provides convenience routines for setting all elements of a GC and combines these calls into a single protocol request that is sent just before it is needed by the next drawing call that uses that GC.

1.4.2 Server Implementation

As described earlier, a true X server is any server that accepts X protocol requests and generates replies, errors, and events according to the specifications in the X protocol document. The servers supplied by MIT are known as "sample servers" because no claim is made that they do everything in the best possible way for all machines and cases. In fact, some of the sample servers suffer from poor performance in color because few optimizations were attempted. Building reliability has been the main goal in the first three releases of X Version 11.

The essential tasks of the server are to demultiplex the requests coming in from each client and execute them on the display, and to multiplex keyboard and mouse input back onto the network to the clients. On single-threaded architectures, the server is typically implemented as a single sequential process, using round-robin scheduling among the clients. Although the server might be placed in the kernel of the operating system in an attempt to increase performance, this makes the server much more difficult to maintain and debug. Performance under UNIX does not seem to suffer by having the server run as a process. The number of operating system calls in the server (and the client library) are minimized to improve performance.

The server is typically made up of a device-independent layer and a device-dependent layer. The device-independent layer includes code that is valid for all machines. Even this portion has not been highly tuned even though practically all current servers are based on it. It is primarily designed to be extremely portable between machines. Some improvements can be made by optimizing this code for each machine it is to run on, but the device-dependent layer is where most of the performance improvement can be had. Of course this code will be different for almost every model by every manufacturer.

The server must be designed so that it never trusts clients to provide correct data. It also must be designed so that if it ever has to wait for a response from a client, it must be possible to continue servicing other clients. Without this property, a bad client or a network failure could easily cause the entire display to hang.

The server normally has a buffering mechanism similar to Xlib's for sending data back to clients. According to the protocol specification, all events and errors generated by a single request must be sent contiguously. When the server is processing a request, it queues up all of the events and errors that the request generates (for example, unmapping a window could generate a lot of little exposures) and then tries to send them all. Furthermore, any events caused by executing a request from a given client must be sent to the client before any reply or error is sent.

If the client is a little slow at reading data from the network (usually because the application is doing something complicated, such as garbage collection in Common Lisp), the server can get an error telling it that the network was unable to transmit all of the data. In Release 2 and before, the sample servers would assume that the client was hung and would drop the connection. In Release 3, they keep track of what needs to be sent and wait for the client to be ready for more data (in BSD UNIX this is taken care of by the "writable" mask argument to the `select` system call). This is called delayed writing.

1.4.3 Reducing Network Traffic

X uses several techniques to reduce network traffic. One major technique is to have the server maintain abstractions such as windows, fonts, and graphics contexts and allocate an integer ID number for each one as a nickname to be used by clients. Whenever an operation is to be performed on an abstraction, the ID of the abstraction is specified in the request. This means that instead of an entire structure or string being sent over the network with a request, only a single integer is sent. Remember that since the client and the server may be on separate machines, pointers cannot be used to refer to server-maintained structures (moreover, not all languages allow use of pointers).

The caveat of the abstraction approach is that the client must query the server when it needs information about them, which, as mentioned above, leads to network delays. As it turns out, clients normally do not need to query the server very often, and abstractions greatly simplify programs.

1.4.4 Implementation on Multi-Threaded Architectures

There is nothing in the definition of the X protocol that prevents either the server or the client programming library from using multi-threaded features of the hardware.

For the server, there are obvious opportunities for separating elements of its task among separate processors. One could handle events and another do drawing, as a primitive example. Or perhaps each processor could handle different clients. The task of drawing can also be divided up to increase performance, perhaps along the lines of how the GC separates patterning from selecting pixels and planes to be drawn (which we have not described here).

For clients, the opportunities depend more on the particular characteristics of each application. Depending on the tools that are available on a particular system, the compiler may automatically look for parallelisms to exploit or the application programmer may be able to give the compiler hints.

1.4.5 Security

The X Consortium is right now developing an authorization mechanism for X servers. As you may have noticed, there is provision for one in the X connection procedure.

X does not provide any protection from unauthorized access to individual windows, pixmaps, or other abstractions, once a connection has been made. For example, if an application gets (or guesses) the abstract ID of a window it did not create, using the **QueryTree** request, it can manipulate or even destroy the window. This property was necessary so that window managers could be written independently of the window system. It is a matter of courtesy that applications other than window managers do not attempt this sort of antisocial behavior.

1.4.6 Interclient Communication

The server must provide a means whereby clients operating on the same server can communicate, because the clients may not necessarily be running on the same machine. Otherwise, clients would not be able to communicate directly except by opening a separate network connection between them. This would introduce a operating system dependency in client programs, which is to be avoided.

X calls the base communication mechanism *properties*. Each property has a name and an ID (atom). The name is used by client programs to determine the ID and implies the meaning of the data by convention. For example, the WM_COMMAND atom by convention identifies a property that contains a string describing the command line that invoked an application. The format of the data is not necessarily implied by the property name, but for most of the properties for which conventions currently exist, the type is implied. Colors are an example of a property that might have more than one format. A particular color could be expressed as a string name such as "purple" or as a set of red, green, and blue values. Client applications that wished to set and read this property would have to agree on a code that distinguished the two formats.

Properties are attached to windows. In other words, window A may have the data "blurb" for property USELESS, while window B has data "flub" for the same property. Therefore, a window ID and a property ID uniquely identify a particular piece of data. Protocol requests are defined to set and get the values of this data.

The maximum size of a property is not limited by the maximum protocol request size accepted by the server. The requests that read and write properties provide ways to read and write them in chunks of the maximum request size. Since the length field is a 16-bit value and is in units of 4 bytes, the maximum request size is 262144 bytes. However, the maximum property size is server-dependent and usually depends on the amount of memory available.

There is also a higher level communication procedure called *selections* that uses properties but allows the two parties to communicate back and forth about the format of the data in a particular property. As for the example above for color, selections allow the client that wants to get the property (the requestor) to specify which of the two formats it desires. Then the client that sets the property (the owner) can set it according to the desired format, before indicating to the requestor that the property is ready to be read. There is, of course, also a way to respond when the owner is unable to translate the data into the required format.

1.5 Future Directions

X was meticulously designed not to be limiting in the near future. The extension mechanism allows new features to be built into the server that work at the same performance level as the core X protocol. In practice, extensions are being used by system manufacturers to take advantage of the unique features of their hardware and by the X Consortium to implement and standardize features such as 3-D graphics.

Now that X Version 11 has become widely accepted, development work on it has actually accelerated rather than subsided. The X Consortium at MIT is now very well funded and has a long agenda of improvements and additions that will be made to X. Among the work currently in progress are extensions to support multiple and various input devices, X for Japanese use, multi-buffering and stereo, and PHIGS (3-D graphics).

The lowest levels of X are stable and unlikely to change in incompatible ways. However, there are improvements in performance that can still be made even though the programming interfaces will remain the same.

Part Two:

Protocol Request and Event Reference

Part Two consists of reference pages to each protocol request and event, arranged alphabetically. Each reference page specifies the contents of the request and its reply, if any, the errors that may be generated, a description of what the request does, and the X protocol encoding for the request and reply. Each event reference page is analogous, but includes no reply or error sections.

(continued)...

GraphicsExpose	PolyLine	SetInputFocus
GravityNotify	PolyPoint	SetModifierMapping
ImageText8	PolyRectangle	SetPointerMapping
ImageText16	PolySegment	SetScreenSaver
InstallColormap	PolyText8	SetSelectionOwner
InternAtom	PolyText16	StoreColors
KeymapNotify	PropertyNotify	StoreNamedColor
KeyPress	PutImage	TranslateCoordinates
KeyRelease	QueryBestSize	UngrabButton
KillClient	QueryColors	UngrabKey
LeaveNotify	QueryExtension	UngrabKeyboard
ListExtensions	QueryFont	UngrabPointer
ListFonts	QueryKeymap	UngrabServer
ListFontsWithInfo	QueryPointer	UninstallColorMap
ListHosts	QueryTextExtents	UnmapNotify
ListInstalledColormaps	QueryTree	UnmapSubwindows
ListProperties	RecolorCursor	UnmapWindow
LookupColor	ReparentNotify	VisibilityNotify
MapNotify	ReparentWIndow	WarpPointer
MappingNotify	ResizeRequest	
MapRequest	RotateProperties	
MapSubwindows	SelectionClear	
MapWindow	SelectionNotify	
MotionNotify	SelectionRequest	
NoExpose	SendEvent	
NoOperation	SetAccessControl	
OpenFont	SetClipRectangles	
PolyArc	SetCloseDownMode	
PolyFillArc	SetDashes	
PolyFillRectangle	SetFontPath	

Name

Introduction — guide to contents of reference pages

Request Contents

This section describes the contents of the request packet sent from the client to the server.

Requests are described in the following format:

> **RequestName**
> > *arg1*: type1
> > . . .
> > *argN*: typeN

Each piece of information is listed as a name/type pair. For example, *window*: WINDOW.

This entry identifies what window the request is to apply to, and the information is of type WINDOW. The type WINDOW and all other types represented by capitalized words are described in the Description section of this reference page.

The Request Contents section of the reference pages in the reference section of this document uses the following syntactic conventions:

- The syntax { . . . } encloses a set of alternatives.

- The syntax [. . .] encloses a set of structure components.

- In general, TYPEs are in upper case and **AlternativeValues** use initial capitals and are in bold font.

Reply Contents

If the request has a reply, then this section is present. This section is in the same format as the Request Contents section, but it describes the information sent back from the server to the client in response to this request.

Replies in the Reply Contents sections on the reference pages are described in the following format:

> result1: type1
> . . .
> resultM: typeM

A request with no reply may still report errors.

Event Contents

If the page is describing an event, then this section is present instead of Request Contents and Reply Contents. It describes the contents of the event sent from the server to the client, using the notation described under Request Contents.

Event Contents are described in the following format:

> **EventName**
>> *value1* : type1
>>
>> . . .
>>
>> *valueN*: typeN

Errors

This section lists the errors that may be generated by this request. For example, **Window**. The errors themselves are described in Appendix F, *Errors*. The Description section of request reference pages may also mention what scenario causes each error.

Description

This section describes what the request does and what its reply contains. In the case of events, it describes what information the event contains and when the event is generated. For requests, this section also describes what events may be generated as a side effect.

Types

The reference pages use symbols to represent certain types of data.

A type name of the form LISTofFOO means a counted list of elements of type FOO. The size of the length field may vary (it is not necessarily the same size as a FOO), and in some cases, it may be implicit. It is fully specified in the Encoding portion of each reference page. Except where explicitly noted, zero-length lists are legal.

The types BITMASK and LISTofVALUE are somewhat special. Various requests contain arguments of the form:

> *value-mask*: BITMASK
> *value-list*: LISTofVALUE

These are used to allow the client to specify a subset of a heterogeneous collection of optional arguments. The value-mask specifies which arguments are to be provided; each such argument is assigned a unique bit position. The representation of the BITMASK will typically contain more bits than there are defined arguments. The unused bits in the value-mask must be zero (or the server generates a **Value** error). The value-list contains one value for each bit set to 1 in the mask, from least-significant to most-significant bit in the mask. Each value is represented with four bytes, but the actual value occupies only the least-significant bytes as required. The values of the unused bytes do not matter.

The type OR is of the form "T1 or ... or Tn" meaning the union of the indicated types. A single-element type is given as the element without enclosing braces.

WINDOW:	32-bit value (top three bits guaranteed to be zero)
PIXMAP:	32-bit value (top three bits guaranteed to be zero)
CURSOR:	32-bit value (top three bits guaranteed to be zero)
FONT:	32-bit value (top three bits guaranteed to be zero)
GCONTEXT:	32-bit value (top three bits guaranteed to be zero)

COLORMAP: 32-bit value (top three bits guaranteed to be zero)

DRAWABLE: WINDOW or PIXMAP

FONTABLE: FONT or GCONTEXT

ATOM: 32-bit value (top three bits guaranteed to be zero)

VISUALID: 32-bit value (top three bits guaranteed to be zero)

VALUE: 32-bit quantity (used only in LISTofVALUE)

BYTE: 8-bit value

INT8:   8-bit signed integer

INT16:   16-bit signed integer

INT32:   32-bit signed integer

CARD8:   8-bit unsigned integer

CARD16:   16-bit unsigned integer

CARD32:   32-bit unsigned integer

TIMESTAMP: CARD32

BITGRAVITY: {**Forget**, **Static**, **NorthWest**, **North**, **NorthEast**, **West**, **Center**, **East**, **SouthWest**, **South**, **SouthEast**}

WINGRAVITY: {**Unmap**, **Static**, **NorthWest**, **North**, **NorthEast**, **West**, **Center**, **East**, **SouthWest**, **South**, **SouthEast**}

BOOL: {**True**, **False**}

EVENT: {**KeyPress**, **KeyRelease**, **OwnerGrabButton**, **ButtonPress**, **ButtonRelease**, **EnterWindow**, **LeaveWindow**, **PointerMotion**, **PointerMotionHint**, **Button1Motion**, **Button2Motion**, **Button3Motion**, **Button4Motion**, **Button5Motion**, **ButtonMotion**, **Exposure**, **VisibilityChange**, **StructureNotify**, **ResizeRedirect**, **SubstructureNotify**, **SubstructureRedirect**, **FocusChange**, **PropertyChange**, **ColormapChange**, **KeymapState**}

POINTEREVENT: {**ButtonPress**, **ButtonRelease**, **EnterWindow**, **LeaveWindow**, **PointerMotion**, **PointerMotionHint**, **Button1Motion**, **Button2Motion**, **Button3Motion**, **Button4Motion**, **Button5Motion**, **ButtonMotion**, **KeymapState**}

DEVICEEVENT: {**KeyPress**, **KeyRelease**, **ButtonPress**, **ButtonRelease**, **PointerMotion**, **Button1Motion**, **Button2Motion**, **Button3Motion**, **Button4Motion**, **Button5Motion**, **ButtonMotion**}

KEYSYM: 32-bit value (top three bits guaranteed to be zero)

KEYCODE:	CARD8
BUTTON:	CARD8
KEYMASK:	{**Shift**, **Lock**, **Control**, **Mod1**, **Mod2**, **Mod3**, **Mod4**, **Mod5**}
BUTMASK:	{**Button1**, **Button2**, **Button3**, **Button4**, **Button5**}
KEYBUTMASK:	KEYMASK or BUTMASK
STRING8:	LISTofCARD8
STRING16:	LISTofCHAR2B
CHAR2B:	[byte1, byte2: CARD8]
POINT:	[x, y: INT16]
RECTANGLE:	[x, y: INT16, width, height: CARD16]
ARC:	[x, y: INT16, width, height: CARD16, angle1, angle2: INT16]
HOST:	[family: {**Internet**, **DECnet**, **Chaos**} address: LISTofBYTE]

The [x,y] coordinates of a RECTANGLE specify the upper-left corner.

The primary interpretation of large characters in a STRING16 is that they are composed of two bytes used to index a 2-D matrix; hence, the use of CHAR2B rather than CARD16. This corresponds to the JIS/ISO method of indexing 2-byte characters. It is expected that most large fonts will be defined with 2-byte matrix indexing. For large fonts constructed with linear indexing, a CHAR2B can be interpreted as a 16-bit number by treating byte1 as the most-significant byte. This means that clients should always transmit such 16-bit character values most-significant byte first, as the server will never byte-swap CHAR2B quantities.

The length, format, and interpretation of a HOST address are specific to the family (see **ChangeHosts** request).

Encoding

The encoding section lists the detailed series of bytes that should be sent to represent the request, or that is sent back from the server in the case of replies, and events.

The following four sections describe the protocol format for requests, replies, errors, and events.

Request Format

Every request contains an 8-bit major opcode and a 16-bit length field expressed in units of four bytes. Every request consists of four bytes of a header (containing the major opcode, the length field, and a data byte) followed by zero or more additional bytes of data. The length field defines the total length of the request, including the header. The length field in a request must equal the minimum length required to contain the request. If the specified length is smaller or larger than the required length, an error is generated. Unused bytes in a request are not required to be zero. Major opcodes 128 through 255 are reserved for extensions. Extensions are intended to contain multiple requests, so extension requests typically have an additional minor opcode encoded in the "spare" data byte in the request header. However, the placement and interpretation of this minor opcode and of all other fields in extension requests are not defined by the core protocol. Every request on a given connection is implicitly assigned a sequence number, starting with 1, that is used in replies, errors, and events.

Defined constants are in bold face type in the description column, immediately after their real value in the Value column. For example, the **WarpPointer** request:

# of Bytes	Value	Description
1	41	opcode
1		unused
2	6	request length
4	WINDOW	src-window:
	0	**None**
4	WINDOW	dst-window:
	0	**None**
2	INT16	src-x
2	INT16	src-y
2	CARD16	src-width
2	CARD16	src-height
2	INT16	dst-x
2	INT16	dst-y

Reply Format

Every reply contains a 32-bit length field expressed in units of four bytes. Every reply consists of 32 bytes followed by zero or more additional bytes of data, as specified in the length field. Unused bytes within a reply are not guaranteed to be zero. Every reply also contains the least-significant 16 bits of the sequence number of the corresponding request.

Event Format

Events are 32 bytes long. Unused bytes within an event are not guaranteed to be zero. Every event contains an 8-bit type code. The most-significant bit in this code is set if the event was generated from a **SendEvent** request. Event codes 64 through 127 are reserved for extensions, although the core protocol does not define a mechanism for selecting interest in such events. Every core event (with the exception of **KeymapNotify**) also contains the least-significant 16 bits of the sequence number of the last request issued by the client that was (or is currently being) processed by the server.

Error Format

Error reports are 32 bytes long. Every error includes an 8-bit error code. Error codes 128 through 255 are reserved for extensions. Every error also includes the major and minor opcodes of the failed request and the least-significant 16 bits of the sequence number of the request. For the following errors, the failing resource ID is also returned: **Colormap**, **Cursor**, **Drawable**, **Font**, **GContext**, **IDChoice**, **Pixmap**, and **Window**. For **Atom** errors, the failing atom is returned. For **Value** errors, the failing value is returned. Other core errors return no additional data. Unused bytes within an error are not guaranteed to be zero.

Encoding of Types

In this document, the LISTof notation strictly means some number of repetitions of the FOO encoding; the actual length of the list is encoded elsewhere.

The SETof notation is always represented by a bitmask, with a 1-bit indicating presence in the set.

BITMASK: CARD32

WINDOW: CARD32

PIXMAP: CARD32

CURSOR: CARD32

FONT: CARD32

GCONTEXT: CARD32

COLORMAP: CARD32

DRAWABLE: CARD32

FONTABLE: CARD32

ATOM: CARD32

VISUALID: CARD32

BYTE: 8-bit value

INT8: 8-bit signed integer

INT16: 16-bit signed integer

INT32: 32-bit signed integer

CARD8: 8-bit unsigned integer

CARD16: 16-bit unsigned integer

CARD32: 32-bit unsigned integer

TIMESTAMP: CARD32

BITGRAVITY

0	**Forget**
1	**NorthWest**
2	**North**
3	**NorthEast**
4	**West**
5	**Center**
6	**East**

7	**SouthWest**
8	**South**
9	**SouthEast**
10	**Static**

WINGRAVITY

0	**Unmap**
1	**NorthWest**
2	**North**
3	**NorthEast**
4	**West**
5	**Center**
6	**East**
7	**SouthWest**
8	**South**
9	**SouthEast**
10	**Static**

BOOL

0	**False**
1	**True**

SETofEVENT

#x00000001	**KeyPress**
#x00000002	**KeyRelease**
#x00000004	**ButtonPress**
#x00000008	**ButtonRelease**
#x00000010	**EnterWindow**
#x00000020	**LeaveWindow**
#x00000040	**PointerMotion**
#x00000080	**PointerMotionHint**
#x00000100	**Button1Motion**
#x00000200	**Button2Motion**
#x00000400	**Button3Motion**
#x00000800	**Button4Motion**
#x00001000	**Button5Motion**
#x00002000	**ButtonMotion**
#x00004000	**KeymapState**
#x00008000	**Exposure**
#x00010000	**VisibilityChange**
#x00020000	**StructureNotify**
#x00040000	**ResizeRedirect**
#x00080000	**SubstructureNotify**
#x00100000	**SubstructureRedirect**
#x00200000	**FocusChange**
#x00400000	**PropertyChange**
#x00800000	**ColormapChange**

#x01000000	**OwnerGrabButton**
#xfe000000	unused but must be zero

SETofPOINTEREVENT

encodings are the same as for SETofEVENT, except with

#xffff8003	unused but must be zero

SETofDEVICEEVENT

encodings are the same as for SETofEVENT, except with

#xffffc0b0	unused but must be zero

KEYSYM: CARD32

KEYCODE: CARD8

BUTTON: CARD8

SETofKEYBUTMASK

#x0001	**Shift**
#x0002	**Lock**
#x0004	**Control**
#x0008	**Mod1**
#x0010	**Mod2**
#x0020	**Mod3**
#x0040	**Mod4**
#x0080	**Mod5**
#x0100	**Button1**
#x0200	**Button2**
#x0400	**Button3**
#x0800	**Button4**
#x1000	**Button5**
#xe000	unused but must be zero

SETofKEYMASK

encodings are the same as for SETofKEYBUTMASK, except with

#xff00	unused but must be zero

STRING8: LISTofCARD8

STRING16: LISTofCHAR2B

CHAR2B

1	CARD8	byte1
1	CARD8	byte2

POINT

2	INT16	x
2	INT16	y

RECTANGLE

2	INT16	x
2	INT16	y

2	CARD16	width
2	CARD16	height

ARC

2	INT16	x
2	INT16	y
2	CARD16	width
2	CARD16	height
2	INT16	angle1
2	INT16	angle2

HOST

1		family
	0	**Internet**
	1	**DECnet**
	2	**Chaos**
1		unused
2	n	length of address
n	LISTofBYTE	address
p		unused, p=pad(n)

STR

1	n	length of name in bytes
n	STRING8	name

Encoding Syntax

The Encoding section of the reference pages is in table form, with the contents using the following syntax conventions.

All numbers are in decimal, unless prefixed with #x, in which case they are in hexadecimal (base 16).

For components described in the request, reply, or event contents as:

name: TYPE

the encode-form is:

N   TYPE   name

N is the number of bytes occupied in the data stream, and TYPE is the interpretation of those bytes. For example:

depth: CARD8

becomes:

1   CARD8 depth

For components with a static numeric value the encode-form is:

N   value   name

The value is always interpreted as an N-byte unsigned integer. For example, the first two bytes of a **Window** error are always zero (indicating an error in general) and three (indicating the **Window** error in particular):

```
1               0        Error
1               3        code
```

For components described in the request, reply, or event contents as:

name: { **Name1**, . . . , **NameI** }

the encode-form is:

```
N                          name
              value1 Name1
              . . .
              valueI NameI
```

The value is always interpreted as an N-byte unsigned integer. Note that the size of N is sometimes larger than that strictly required to encode the values. For example:

class: { **InputOutput**, **InputOnly**, **CopyFromParent** }

becomes:

```
2                                        class
          0        CopyFromParent
          1        InputOutput
          2        InputOnly
```

For components described in the request, reply, or event contents as:

NAME: TYPE or **Alternative1** . . . or **AlternativeI**

the encode-form is:

```
N          TYPE                    NAME
          value1   Alternative1
          . . .
          valueI   AlternativeI
```

The alternative values are guaranteed not to conflict with the encoding of TYPE. For example:

destination: WINDOW or **PointerWindow** or **InputFocus**

becomes:

```
4          WINDOW                destination
          0        PointerWindow
          1        InputFocus
```

For components described in the request, reply, or event contents as:

value-mask: BITMASK

the encode-form is:

N	BITMASK	value-mask
	mask1 mask-name1	
	...	
	maskI mask-nameI	

The individual bits in the mask are specified and named, and N is 2 or 4. The most-significant bit in a BITMASK is reserved for use in defining chained (multi-word) bitmasks, as extensions augment existing core requests. The precise interpretation of this bit is not yet defined here, although a probable mechanism is that a 1-bit indicates that another N bytes of bitmask follows, with bits within the overall mask still interpreted from least-significant to most-significant with an N-byte unit, with N-byte units interpreted in stream order, and with the overall mask being byte-swapped in individual N-byte units.

For LISTofVALUE encodings, the request is followed by a table listing an encode-form for each VALUE. The NAME in each encode-form keys to the corresponding BITMASK bit. The encoding of a VALUE always occupies four bytes, but the number of bytes specified in the encoding-form indicates how many of the least-significant bytes are actually used; the remaining bytes are unused and their values do not matter.

In various cases, the number of bytes occupied by a component will be specified by a lower case single-letter variable name instead of a specific numeric value, and often some other component will have its value specified as a simple numeric expression involving these variables. Components specified with such expressions are always interpreted as unsigned integers. The scope of such variables is always just the enclosing request, reply, error, event, or compound type structure. For example:

2	3+n	request length
4n	LISTofPOINT	points

For unused bytes (the values of the bytes are undefined and do no matter), the encode-form is:

N	unused

If the number of unused bytes is variable, the encode-form typically is:

p	unused, p=pad(E)

where E is some expression, and pad(E) is the number of bytes needed to round E up to a multiple of four.

$$pad(E) = (4 - (E \bmod 4)) \bmod 4$$

Connection Setup

Name

Connection Setup

Description

Connection setup opens the connection between a client and a server, over which subsequent requests, replies, events, and errors can be sent.

The client must send an initial byte of data to identify the byte order to be employed. The value of the byte must be octal 102 or 154. The value 102 (ASCII upper case B) means values are transmitted most-significant byte first, and value 154 (ASCII lower case l) means values are transmitted least-significant byte first. Except where explicitly noted in the protocol, all 16-bit and 32-bit quantities sent by the client must be transmitted with this byte order, and all 16-bit and 32-bit quantities returned by the server will be transmitted with this byte order.

Following the byte-order byte, the client sends the following information at connection setup:

protocol-major-version: CARD16
protocol-minor-version: CARD16
authorization-protocol-name: STRING8
authorization-protocol-data: STRING8

The version numbers indicate what version of the protocol the client expects the server to implement.

The authorization name indicates what authorization protocol the client expects the server to use, and the data is specific to that protocol. Specification of valid authorization mechanisms is not part of the core X protocol. A server that implements a different protocol than the client expects or that only implements the host-based mechanism may simply ignore this information. If both name and data strings are empty, this is to be interpreted as "no explicit authorization."

The client receives the following information at connection setup:

success: BOOL
protocol-major-version: CARD16
protocol-minor-version: CARD16
length: CARD16

Length is the amount of additional data to follow, in units of four bytes. The version numbers are an escape hatch in case future revisions of the protocol are necessary. In general, the major version would increment for incompatible changes, and the minor version would increment for small upward compatible changes. Barring changes, the major version will be 11 and the minor version will be 0. The protocol version numbers returned indicate the protocol the server actually supports. This might not equal the version sent by the client. The server can (but need not) refuse connections from clients that offer a different version than the server supports. A server can (but need not) support more than one version simultaneously.

The client receives the following additional data if authorization fails:

 reason: STRING8

The client receives the following additional data if authorization is accepted:

 vendor: STRING8
 release-number: CARD32
 resource-id-base, resource-id-mask: CARD32
 image-byte-order: {**LSBFirst**, **MSBFirst**}
 bitmap-scanline-unit: {8, 16, 32}
 bitmap-scanline-pad: {8, 16, 32}
 bitmap-bit-order: {**LeastSignificant**, **MostSignificant**}
 pixmap-formats: LISTofFORMAT
 roots: LISTofSCREEN
 motion-buffer-size: CARD32
 maximum-request-length: CARD16
 min-keycode, max-keycode: KEYCODE

where:

  FORMAT: [depth: CARD8,
         bits-per-pixel: {1, 4, 8, 16, 24, 32}
         scanline-pad: {8, 16, 32}]

  SCREEN: [root: WINDOW
         width-in-pixels, height-in-pixels: CARD16
         width-in-millimeters, height-in-millimeters: CARD16
         allowed-depths: LISTofDEPTH
         root-depth: CARD8
         root-visual: VISUALID
         default-colormap: COLORMAP
         white-pixel, black-pixel: CARD32
         min-installed-maps, max-installed-maps: CARD16
         backing-stores: {**Never**, **WhenMapped**, **Always**}
         save-unders: BOOL
         current-input-masks: SETofEVENT]

  DEPTH: [depth: CARD8
         visuals: LISTofVISUALTYPE]

VISUALTYPE: [visual-id: VISUALID
                       class: { **StaticGray**, **StaticColor**, **TrueColor**, **GrayScale**,
                       PseudoColor, **DirectColor** }
                       red-mask, green-mask, blue-mask: CARD32
                       bits-per-rgb-value: CARD8
                       colormap-entries: CARD16]

The information that is global to the server is:

- The vendor string gives some identification of the owner of the server implementation. The vendor controls the semantics of the release number.

- The resource-id-mask contains a single contiguous set of bits (at least 18). The client allocates resource IDs for types WINDOW, PIXMAP, CURSOR, FONT, GCONTEXT, and COLORMAP by choosing a value with only some subset of these bits set and ORing it with resource-id-base. Only values constructed in this way can be used to name newly created resources over this connection. Resource IDs never have the top three bits set. The client is not restricted to linear or contiguous allocation of resource IDs. Once an ID has been freed, it can be reused, but this should not be necessary. An ID must be unique with respect to the IDs of all other resources, not just other resources of the same type. However, note that the value spaces of resource identifiers, atoms, visualids, and keysyms are distinguished by context and, as such, are not required to be disjoint; for example, a given numeric value might be both a valid window ID, a valid atom, and a valid keysym.

- Although the server is in general responsible for byte-swapping data to match the client, images are always transmitted and received in formats (including byte order) specified by the server. The byte order for images is given by image-byte-order and applies to each scanline unit in XY format (bitmap format) and to each pixel value in Z format.

- A bitmap is represented in scanline order. Each scanline is padded to a multiple of bits as given by bitmap-scanline-pad. The pad bits are of arbitrary value. The scanline is quantized in multiples of bits as given by bitmap-scanline-unit. The bitmap-scanline-unit is always less than or equal to the bitmap-scanline-pad. Within each unit, the leftmost bit in the bitmap is either the least-significant or the most-significant bit in the unit, as given by bitmap-bit-order. If a pixmap is represented in XY format, each plane is represented as a bitmap, and the planes appear from most-significant to least-significant in bit order with no padding between planes.

- Pixmap-formats contains one entry for each depth value. The entry describes the Z format used to represent images of that depth. An entry for a depth is included if any screen supports that depth, and all screens supporting that depth must support only that Z format for that depth. In Z format, the pixels are in scanline order, left to right within a scanline. The number of bits used to hold each pixel is given by bits-per-pixel. Bits-per-pixel may be larger than strictly required by the depth, in which case the least-significant bits are used to hold the pixmap data, and the values of the unused high-order bits are undefined. When the bits-per-pixel is 4, the order of nibbles in the byte is the same as the image byte-order. When the bits-per-pixel is 1, the format is identical for bitmap format. Each scanline is padded to a multiple of bits as given by scanline-pad. When bits-per-pixel is 1, this will be identical to bitmap-scanline-pad.

- How a pointing device roams the screens is up to the server implementation and is transparent to the protocol. No geometry is defined among screens.

- The server may retain the recent history of pointer motion and do so to a finer granularity than is reported by **MotionNotify** events. The **GetMotionEvents** request makes such history available. The motion-buffer-size gives the approximate size of the history buffer.

- Maximum-request-length specifies the maximum length of a request accepted by the server, in 4-byte units; that is, length is the maximum value that can appear in the length field of a request. Requests larger than this maximum generate a **Length** error, and the server will read and simply discard the entire request. Maximum-request-length will always be at least 4096 (that is, requests of length up to and including 16384 bytes will be accepted by all servers).

- Min-keycode and max-keycode specify the smallest and largest keycode values transmitted by the server. Min-keycode is never less than 8, and max-keycode is never greater than 255. Not all keycodes in this range are required to have corresponding keys.

The information that applies per screen is:

- The allowed-depths specifies what pixmap and window depths are supported. Pixmaps are supported for each depth listed, and windows of that depth are supported if at least one visual type is listed for the depth. A pixmap depth of one is always supported and listed, but windows of depth one might not be supported. A depth of zero is never listed, but zero-depth **InputOnly** windows are always supported.

- Root-depth and root-visual specify the depth and visual type of the root window. Width-in-pixels and height-in-pixels specify the size of the root window (which cannot be changed). The class of the root window is always **InputOutput**. Width-in-millimeters and height-in-millimeters can be used to determine the physical size and the aspect ratio.

- The default-colormap is the one initially associated with the root window. Clients with minimal color requirements creating windows of the same depth as the root may want to allocate from this map by default.

- Black-pixel and white-pixel can be used in implementing a monochrome application. These pixel values are for permanently allocated entries in the default-colormap. The actual RGB values may be settable on some screens and, in any case, may not actually be black and white. The names are intended to convey the expected relative intensity of the colors.

- The border of the root window is initially a pixmap filled with the black-pixel. The initial background of the root window is a pixmap filled with some unspecified two-color pattern using black-pixel and white-pixel.

- Min-installed-maps specifies the number of maps that can be guaranteed to be installed simultaneously (with **InstallColormap**), regardless of the number of entries allocated in each map. Max-installed-maps specifies the maximum number of maps that might possibly be installed simultaneously, depending on their allocations. Multiple static-visual colormaps with identical contents but differing in resource ID should be considered as a single map for the purposes of this number. For the typical case of a single hardware colormap, both values will be 1.

- Backing-stores indicates when the server supports backing stores for this screen, although it may be storage limited in the number of windows it can support at once. If save-unders is **True**, the server can support the save-under mode in **CreateWindow** and **ChangeWindowAttributes**, although again it may be storage limited.

- The current-input-events is what **GetWindowAttributes** would return for the all-event-masks for the root window.

The information that applies per visual-type is:

- A given visual type might be listed for more than one depth or for more than one screen.

- For **PseudoColor**, a pixel value indexes a colormap to produce independent RGB values; the RGB values can be changed dynamically. **GrayScale** is treated in the same way as **PseudoColor** except which primary drives the screen is undefined; thus, the client should always store the same value for red, green, and blue in colormaps. For **DirectColor**, a pixel value is decomposed into separate RGB subfields, and each subfield separately indexes the colormap for the corresponding value. The RGB values can be changed dynamically. **TrueColor** is treated in the same way as **DirectColor** except the colormap has predefined read-only RGB values. These values are server-dependent but provide linear or near-linear increasing ramps in each primary. **StaticColor** is treated in the same way as **PseudoColor** except the colormap has predefined read-only RGB values, which are server-dependent. **StaticGray** is treated in the same way as **StaticColor** except the red, green, and blue values are equal for any single pixel value, resulting in shades of gray. **StaticGray** with a two-entry colormap can be thought of as monochrome.

- The red-mask, green-mask, and blue-mask are only defined for **DirectColor** and **TrueColor**. Each has one contiguous set of bits set to 1 with no intersections. Usually each mask has the same number of bits set to 1.

- The bits-per-rgb-value specifies the log base 2 of the number of distinct color intensity values (individually) of red, green, and blue. This number need not bear any relation to the number of colormap entries. Actual RGB values are always passed in the protocol within a 16-bit spectrum, with 0 being minimum intensity and 65535 being the maximum intensity. On hardware that provides a linear zero-based intensity ramp, the following relationship exists:

```
hw-intensity = protocol-intensity / (65536 / total-hw-intensities)
```

- Colormap entries are indexed from 0. The colormap-entries defines the number of available colormap entries in a newly created colormap. For **DirectColor** and **TrueColor**, this will usually be 2 to the power of the maximum number of bits set to 1 in red-mask, green-mask, and blue-mask.

Encoding

For TCP connections, displays on a given host are numbered starting from 0, and the server for display N listens and accepts connections on port 6000+N. For DECnet connections, displays on a given host are numbered starting from 0, and the server for display N listens and accepts connections on the object name obtained by concatenating "X$X" with the decimal representation of N; for example, X$X0 and X$X1.

Information sent by the client at connection setup:

# Bytes	Value	Description
1		byte-order:
	#x42	MSB first
	#x6C	LSB first
1		unused
2	CARD16	protocol-major-version
2	CARD16	protocol-minor-version
2	n	length of authorization-protocol-name
2	d	length of authorization-protocol-data
2		unused
n	STRING8	authorization-protocol-name
p		unused, p=pad(n)
d	STRING8	authorization-protocol-data
q		unused, q=pad(d)

Except where explicitly noted in the protocol, all 16-bit and 32-bit quantities sent by the client must be transmitted with the specified byte order, and all 16-bit and 32-bit quantities returned by the server will be transmitted with this byte order.

Information received by the client if authorization fails:

# Bytes	Value	Description
1	0	failed
1	n	length of reason in bytes
2	CARD16	protocol-major-version
2	CARD16	protocol-minor-version
2	(n+p)/4	length in 4-byte units of "additional data"
n	STRING8	reason
p		unused, p=pad(n)

Information received by the client if authorization is accepted:

# Bytes	Value	Description
1	1	success
1		unused
2	CARD16	protocol-major-version
2	CARD16	protocol-minor-version
2	8+2n+(v+p+m)/4	length in 4-byte units of ''additional data''
4	CARD32	release-number
4	CARD32	resource-id-base
4	CARD32	resource-id-mask
4	CARD32	motion-buffer-size
2	v	length of vendor
2	CARD16	maximum-request-length
1	CARD8	number of SCREENs in roots
1	n	number for FORMATs in pixmap-formats
1		image-byte-order:
	0	LSBFirst
	1	MSBFirst
1		bitmap-format-bit-order:
	0	LeastSignificant
	1	MostSignificant
1	CARD8	bitmap-format-scanline-unit
1	CARD8	bitmap-format-scanline-pad
1	KEYCODE	min-keycode
1	KEYCODE	max-keycode
4		unused
v	STRING8	vendor
p		unused, p=pad(v)
8n	LISTofFORMAT	pixmap-formats
m	LISTofSCREEN	roots
		(m is always a multiple of 4)

LISTofFORMAT is *n* repetitions of the encoding for FORMAT shown in the table below:

# Bytes	Value	Description
1	CARD8	depth
1	CARD8	bits-per-pixel
1	CARD8	scanline-pad
5		unused

LISTofSCREEN is *n* repetitions of the encoding for SCREEN shown in the table below:

# Bytes	Value	Description
4	WINDOW	root
4	COLORMAP	default-colormap
4	CARD32	white-pixel
4	CARD32	black-pixel
4	SETofEVENT	current-input-masks
2	CARD16	width-in-pixels
2	CARD16	height-in-pixels
2	CARD16	width-in-millimeters
2	CARD16	height-in-millimeters
2	CARD16	min-installed-maps
2	CARD16	max-installed-maps
4	VISUALID	root-visual
1		backing-stores:
	0	Never
	1	WhenMapped
	2	Always
1	BOOL	save-unders
1	CARD8	root-depth
1	CARD8	number of DEPTHs in allowed-depths
n	LISTofDEPTH	allowed-depths
		(n is always a multiple of 4)

LISTofDEPTH is *n* repetitions of the encoding for DEPTH shown in the table below:

# Bytes	Value	Description
1	CARD8	depth
1		unused
2	n	number of VISUALTYPES in visuals
4		unused
24n	LISTofVISUALTYPE	visuals

LISTofVISUALTYPE is *n* repetitions of the encoding for VISUALTYPE shown in the table below:

# Bytes	Value	Description
4	VISUALID	visual-id
1		class:
	0	StaticGray
	1	GrayScale
	2	StaticColor
	3	PseudoColor

# Bytes	Value	Description
	4	TrueColor
	5	DirectColor
1	CARD8	bits-per-rgb-value
2	CARD16	colormap-entries
4	CARD32	red-mask
4	CARD32	green-mask
4	CARD32	blue-mask
4		unused

AllocColor

Name
AllocColor

Request Contents
cmap: COLORMAP
red, green, blue: CARD16

Reply Contents
pixel: CARD32
red, green, blue: CARD16

Errors
Colormap, Alloc

Description
This request allocates a read-only colormap entry corresponding to the closest RGB values provided by the hardware. It also returns the pixel and the RGB values actually used.

Request Encoding

# of Bytes	Value	Description
1	84	opcode
1		unused
2	4	request length
4	COLORMAP	cmap
2	CARD16	red
2	CARD16	green
2	CARD16	blue
2		unused

Reply Encoding

# of Bytes	Value	Description
1	1	reply
1		unused
2	CARD16	sequence number
4	0	reply length
2	CARD16	red
2	CARD16	green
2	CARD16	blue
2		unused

# of Bytes	Value	Description
4	CARD32	pixel
12		unused

AllocColorCells

Name
AllocColorCells

Request Contents
cmap: COLORMAP
colors, planes: CARD16
contiguous: BOOL

Reply Contents
pixels, masks: LISTofCARD32

Errors
Colormap, **Value**, **Alloc**

Description
The number of colors must be positive, and the number of planes must be nonnegative (or a **Value** error results). If C colors and P planes are requested, then C pixels and P masks are returned. No mask will have any bits in common with any other mask or with any of the pixels. By ORing together masks and pixels, $C*2^P$ distinct pixels can be produced; all of these are allocated writable by the request. For **GrayScale** or **PseudoColor**, each mask will have exactly one bit set to 1; for **DirectColor**, each will have exactly three bits set to 1. If contiguous is **True** and if all masks are ORed together, a single contiguous set of bits will be formed for **GrayScale** or **PseudoColor**, and three contiguous sets of bits (one within each pixel subfield) for **DirectColor**. The RGB values of the allocated entries are undefined.

Request Encoding

# of Bytes	Value	Description
1	86	opcode
1	BOOL	contiguous
2	3	request length
4	COLORMAP	cmap
2	CARD16	colors
2	CARD16	planes

Reply Encoding

# of Bytes	Value	Description
1	1	reply
1		unused
2	CARD16	sequence number
4	n+m	reply length

# of Bytes	Value	Description
2	n	number of CARD32s in pixels
2	m	number of CARD32s in masks
20		unused
4n	LISTofCARD32	pixels
4m	LISTofCARD32	masks

AllocColorPlanes

Name

AllocColorPlanes

Request Contents

cmap: COLORMAP
colors, *reds*, *greens*, *blues*: CARD16
contiguous: BOOL

Reply Contents

pixels: LISTofCARD32
red-mask, green-mask, blue-mask: CARD32

Errors

Colormap, **Value**, **Alloc**

Description

The number of colors must be positive, and the reds, greens, and blues must be nonnegative (or a **Value** error results). If C colors, R reds, G greens, and B blues are requested, then C pixels are returned, and the masks have R, G, and B bits set, respectively. If contiguous is **True**, then each mask will have a contiguous set of bits. No mask will have any bits in common with any other mask or with any of the pixels. For **DirectColor**, each mask will lie within the corresponding pixel subfield. By ORing together subsets of masks with pixels, $C*2^{R+G+B}$ distinct pixels can be produced; all of these are allocated by the request. The initial RGB values of the allocated entries are undefined. In the colormap, there are only $C*2^R$ independent red entries, $C*2^G$ independent green entries, and $C*2^B$ independent blue entries. This is true even for **PseudoColor**. When the colormap entry for a pixel value is changed using **StoreColors** or **StoreNamedColor**, the pixel is decomposed according to the masks, and the corresponding independent entries are updated.

Request Encoding

# of Bytes	Value	Description
1	87	opcode
1	BOOL	contiguous
2	4	request length
4	COLORMAP	cmap
2	CARD16	colors
2	CARD16	reds
2	CARD16	greens
2	CARD16	blues

Reply Encoding

# of Bytes	Value	Description
1	1	reply
1		unused
2	CARD16	sequence number
4	n	reply length
2	n	number of CARD32s in pixels
2		unused
4	CARD32	red-mask
4	CARD32	green-mask
4	CARD32	blue-mask
8		unused
4n	LISTofCARD32	pixels

AllocNamedColor

Name
AllocNamedColor

Request Contents
cmap: COLORMAP
name: STRING8

Reply Contents
pixel: CARD32
exact-red, exact-green, exact-blue: CARD16
visual-red, visual-green, visual-blue: CARD16

Errors
Colormap, Name, Alloc

Description
This request looks up the named color with respect to the screen associated with the colormap. Then, it does an **AllocColor** on cmap. The name should use the ISO Latin-1 encoding, and upper case and lower case do not matter. The exact RGB values specify the true values for the color, and the visual values specify the values actually used in the colormap.

Request Encoding

# of Bytes	Value	Description
1	85	opcode
1		unused
2	3+(n+p)/4	request length
4	COLORMAP	cmap
2	n	length of name
2		unused
n	STRING8	name
p		unused, p=pad(n)

Reply Encoding

# of Bytes	Value	Description
1	1	reply
1		unused
2	CARD16	sequence number
4	0	reply length
4	CARD32	pixel
2	CARD16	exact-red
2	CARD16	exact-green

# of Bytes	Value	Description
2	CARD16	exact-blue
2	CARD16	visual-red
2	CARD16	visual-green
2	CARD16	visual-blue
8		unused

Name

AllowEvents

Request Contents

mode: {**AsyncPointer**, **SyncPointer**, **ReplayPointer**, **AsyncKeyboard**, **SyncKeyboard**, **ReplayKeyboard**, **AsyncBoth**, **SyncBoth**}
time: TIMESTAMP or **CurrentTime**

Errors

Value

Description

This request releases some queued events if the client has caused a device to freeze. The request has no effect if the specified time is earlier than the last-grab time of the most recent active grab for the client or if the specified time is later than the current server time.

For **AsyncPointer**, if the pointer is frozen by the client, pointer event processing continues normally. If the pointer is frozen twice by the client on behalf of two separate grabs, **Async-Pointer** thaws for both. **AsyncPointer** has no effect if the pointer is not frozen by the client, but the pointer need not be grabbed by the client.

For **SyncPointer**, if the pointer is frozen and actively grabbed by the client, pointer event processing continues normally until the next **ButtonPress** or **ButtonRelease** event is reported to the client, at which time the pointer again appears to freeze. However, if the reported event causes the pointer grab to be released, then the pointer does not freeze. **SyncPointer** has no effect if the pointer is not frozen by the client or if the pointer is not grabbed by the client.

For **ReplayPointer**, if the pointer is actively grabbed by the client and is frozen as the result of an event having been sent to the client (either from the activation of a **GrabButton** or from a previous **AllowEvents** with mode **SyncPointer** but not from a **GrabPointer**), then the pointer grab is released and that event is completely reprocessed, this time ignoring any passive grabs at or above (towards the root) the grab-window of the grab just released. The request has no effect if the pointer is not grabbed by the client or if the pointer is not frozen as the result of an event.

For **AsyncKeyboard**, if the keyboard is frozen by the client, keyboard event processing continues normally. If the keyboard is frozen twice by the client on behalf of two separate grabs, **AsyncKeyboard** thaws for both. **AsyncKeyboard** has no effect if the keyboard is not frozen by the client, but the keyboard need not be grabbed by the client.

For **SyncKeyboard**, if the keyboard is frozen and actively grabbed by the client, keyboard event processing continues normally until the next **KeyPress** or **KeyRelease** event is reported to the client, at which time the keyboard again appears to freeze. However, if the reported event causes the keyboard grab to be released, then the keyboard does not freeze. **Sync-Keyboard** has no effect if the keyboard is not frozen by the client or if the keyboard is not grabbed by the client.

For **ReplayKeyboard**, if the keyboard is actively grabbed by the client and is frozen as the result of an event having been sent to the client (either from the activation of a **GrabKey** or from a previous **AllowEvents** with mode **SyncKeyboard** but not from a **GrabKeyboard**), then the keyboard grab is released and that event is completely reprocessed, this time ignoring any passive grabs at or above (towards the root) the grab-window of the grab just released. The request has no effect if the keyboard is not grabbed by the client or if the keyboard is not frozen as the result of an event.

For **SyncBoth**, if both pointer and keyboard are frozen by the client, event processing (for both devices) continues normally until the next **ButtonPress**, **ButtonRelease**, **KeyPress**, or **KeyRelease** event is reported to the client for a grabbed device (button event for the pointer, key event for the keyboard), at which time the devices again appear to freeze. However, if the reported event causes the grab to be released, then the devices do not freeze (but if the other device is still grabbed, then a subsequent event for it will still cause both devices to freeze). **SyncBoth** has no effect unless both pointer and keyboard are frozen by the client. If the pointer or keyboard is frozen twice by the client on behalf of two separate grabs, **SyncBoth** thaws for both (but a subsequent freeze for **SyncBoth** will only freeze each device once).

For **AsyncBoth**, if the pointer and the keyboard are frozen by the client, event processing for both devices continues normally. If a device is frozen twice by the client on behalf of two separate grabs, **AsyncBoth** thaws for both. **AsyncBoth** has no effect unless both pointer and keyboard are frozen by the client.

AsyncPointer, **SyncPointer**, and **ReplayPointer** have no effect on processing of keyboard events. **AsyncKeyboard**, **SyncKeyboard**, and **ReplayKeyboard** have no effect on processing of pointer events.

It is possible for both a pointer grab and a keyboard grab to be active simultaneously (by the same or different clients). When a device is frozen on behalf of either grab, no event processing is performed for the device. It is possible for a single device to be frozen because of both grabs. In this case, the freeze must be released on behalf of both grabs before events can again be processed.

Request Encoding

# of Bytes	Value	Description
1	35	opcode
1		mode:
	0	**AsyncPointer**
	1	**SyncPointer**
	2	**ReplayPointer**
	3	**AsyncKeyboard**
	4	**SyncKeyboard**
	5	**ReplayKeyboard**
	6	**AsyncBoth**
	7	**SyncBoth**

# of Bytes	Value	Description
2	2	request length
4	TIMESTAMP	time:
	0	**CurrentTime**

Bell

Name
Bell

Request Contents
percent: INT8

Errors
Value

Description
This request rings the bell on the keyboard at a volume relative to the base volume for the keyboard, if possible. Percent can range from −100 to 100 inclusive (or a **Value** error results). The volume at which the bell is rung when percent is nonnegative is:

```
base - [(base * percent) / 100] + percent
```

When percent is negative, it is:

```
base + [(base * percent) / 100]
```

Request Encoding

# of Bytes	Value	Description
1	104	opcode
1	INT8	percent
2	1	request length

Name
ButtonPress

Event Contents
root, *event*: WINDOW
child: WINDOW or **None**
same-screen: BOOL
root-x, *root-y*, *event-x*, *event-y*: INT16
detail: (See Description.)
state: SETofKEYBUTMASK
time: TIMESTAMP

(Same contents as **MotionNotify**.)

Description
ButtonPress events are sent by the server to the client when the user presses a pointer button. Only clients selecting **ButtonPress** events will receive them. The window member of this event depends on which window the pointer is in when the button is pressed and on the values of the event-mask and do-not-propagate field for that window and its ancestors.

For more information, see **MotionNotify**.

Request Encoding

# of Bytes	Value	Description
1	4	code
1	BUTTON	detail
2	CARD16	sequence number
4	TIMESTAMP	time
4	WINDOW	root
4	WINDOW	event
4	WINDOW	child:
	0	**None**
2	INT16	root-x
2	INT16	root-y
2	INT16	event-x
2	INT16	event-y
2	SETofKEYBUTMASK	state
1	BOOL	same-screen
1		unused

ButtonRelease

Name
ButtonRelease

Event Contents
root, *event*: WINDOW
child: WINDOW or **None**
same-screen: BOOL
root-x, *root-y*, *event-x*, *event-y*: INT16
detail: (See Description.)
state: SETofKEYBUTMASK
time: TIMESTAMP

(Same contents as **MotionNotify**.)

Description
ButtonRelease events are sent by the server to the client when the user presses a pointer button. Only clients selecting **ButtonRelease** events will receive them. The window member of this event depends on which window the pointer is in when the button is pressed and on the values of the event-mask and do-not-propagate field for that window and its ancestors.

For more information, see **MotionNotify**.

Request Encoding

# of Bytes	Value	Description
1	5	code
1	BUTTON	detail
2	CARD16	sequence number
4	TIMESTAMP	time
4	WINDOW	root
4	WINDOW	event
4	WINDOW	child:
	0	**None**
2	INT16	root-x
2	INT16	root-y
2	INT16	event-x
2	INT16	event-y
2	SETofKEYBUTMASK	state
1	BOOL	same-screen
1		unused

Name

ChangeActivePointerGrab

Request Contents

event-mask: SETofPOINTEREVENT
cursor: CURSOR or **None**
time: TIMESTAMP or **CurrentTime**

Errors

Cursor, **Value**

Description

This request changes the specified dynamic parameters if the pointer is actively grabbed by the client and the specified time is no earlier than the last-pointer-grab time and no later than the current server time. The interpretation of event-mask and cursor are the same as in **Grab-Pointer**. This request has no effect on the parameters of any passive grabs established with **GrabButton**.

Request Encoding

# of Bytes	Value	Description
1	30	opcode
1		unused
2	4	request length
4	CURSOR	cursor:
	0	**None**
4	TIMESTAMP	time:
	0	**CurrentTime**
2	SETofPOINTEREVENT	event-mask
2		unused

Name
ChangeGC

Request Contents
gc: GCONTEXT
value-mask: BITMASK
value-list: LISTofVALUE

Errors
GContext, **Pixmap**, **Font**, **Match**, **Value**, **Alloc**

Description
This request changes components in gc. The value-mask and value-list specify which components are to be changed. The values and restrictions are the same as for **CreateGC**.

Changing the clip-mask also overrides any previous **SetClipRectangles** request on the context. Changing dash-offset or dashes overrides any previous **SetDashes** request on the context.

The order in which components are verified and altered is server-dependent. If an error is generated, a subset of the components may have been altered.

Request Encoding

# of Bytes	Value	Description
1	56	opcode
1		unused
2	3+n	request length
4	GCONTEXT	gc
4	BITMASK	value-mask (has n bits set to 1)
		(Encodings are the same as for **CreateGC**.)
4n	LISTofVALUE	value-list
		(Encodings are the same as for **CreateGC**.)

ChangeHosts

Name
ChangeHosts

Request Contents
mode: {**Insert**, **Delete**}
host: HOST

Errors
Access, **Value**

Description
This request adds or removes the specified host from the access control list. When the access control mechanism is enabled and a host attempts to establish a connection to the server, the host must be in this list, or the server will refuse the connection.

The client must reside on the same host as the server and/or have been granted permission by a server-dependent method to execute this request (or an **Access** error results).

An initial access control list can usually be specified, typically by naming a file that the server reads at startup and reset.

The following address families are defined. A server is not required to support these families and may support families not listed here. Use of an unsupported family, an improper address format, or an improper address length within a supported family results in a **Value** error.

For the Internet family, the address must be four bytes long. The address bytes are in standard order; the server performs no automatic swapping on the address bytes. For a Class A address, the network number is the first byte in the address and the host number is the remaining three bytes, most-significant byte first. For a Class B address, the network number is the first two bytes and the host number is the last two bytes, each most-significant byte first. For a Class C address, the network number is the first three bytes, most-significant byte first, and the last byte is the host number.

For the DECnet family, the server performs no automatic swapping on the address bytes. A Phase IV address is two bytes long: the first byte contains the least-significant eight bits of the node number, and the second byte contains the most-significant two bits of the node number in the least-significant two bits of the byte and the area in the most significant six bits of the byte.

For the Chaos family, the address must be two bytes long. The host number is always the first byte in the address, and the subnet number is always the second byte. The server performs no automatic swapping on the address bytes.

Request Encoding

# of Bytes	Value	Description
1	109	opcode
1		mode:
	0	**Insert**
	1	**Delete**
2	2+(n+p)/4	request length
1		family:
	0	**Internet**
	1	**DECnet**
	2	**Chaos**
1		unused
2	CARD16	length of address
n	LISTofCARD8	address
p		unused, p=pad(n)

ChangeKeyboardControl

Name
ChangeKeyboardControl

Request Contents
value-mask: BITMASK
value-list: LISTofVALUE

Errors
Match, Value

Description
This request controls various aspects of the keyboard. The value-mask and value-list specify which controls are to be changed. The possible values are:

Control	Type
key-click-percent	INT8
bell-percent	INT8
bell-pitch	INT16
bell-duration	INT16
led	CARD8
led-mode	{**On, Off**}
key	KEYCODE
auto-repeat-mode	{**On, Off, Default**}

The key-click-percent sets the volume for key clicks between 0 (off) and 100 (loud) inclusive, if possible. Setting to –1 restores the default. Other negative values generate a **Value** error.

The bell-percent sets the base volume for the bell between 0 (off) and 100 (loud) inclusive, if possible. Setting to –1 restores the default. Other negative values generate a **Value** error.

The bell-pitch sets the pitch (specified in Hz) of the bell, if possible. Setting to –1 restores the default. Other negative values generate a **Value** error.

The bell-duration sets the duration of the bell (specified in milliseconds), if possible. Setting to –1 restores the default. Other negative values generate a **Value** error.

If both led-mode and led are specified, then the state of that LED is changed, if possible. If only led-mode is specified, then the state of all LEDs are changed, if possible. At most 32 LEDs, numbered from one, are supported. No standard interpretation of LEDs is defined. It is a **Match** error if an led is specified without an led-mode.

If both auto-repeat-mode and key are specified, then the auto-repeat mode of that key is changed, if possible. If only auto-repeat-mode is specified, then the global auto-repeat mode for the entire keyboard is changed, if possible, without affecting the per-key settings. It is a

Match error if a key is specified without an auto-repeat-mode. Each key has an individual mode of whether or not it should auto-repeat and a default setting for that mode. In addition, there is a global mode of whether auto-repeat should be enabled or not and a default setting for that mode. When the global mode is **On**, keys should obey their individual auto-repeat modes. When the global mode is **Off**, no keys should auto-repeat. An auto-repeating key generates alternating **KeyPress** and **KeyRelease** events. When a key is used as a modifier, it is desirable for the key not to auto-repeat, regardless of the auto-repeat setting for that key.

A bell generator connected with the console but not directly on the keyboard is treated as if it were part of the keyboard.

The order in which controls are verified and altered is server-dependent. If an error is generated, a subset of the controls may have been altered.

Request Encoding

# of Bytes	Value	Description
1	102	opcode
1		unused
2	2+n	request length
4	BITMASK	value-mask (has n bits set to 1):
	#x0001	key-click-percent
	#x0002	bell-percent
	#x0004	bell-pitch
	#x0008	bell-duration
	#x0010	led
	#x0020	led-mode
	#x0040	key
	#x0080	auto-repeat-mode
4n	LISTofVALUE	value-list

LISTofVALUE is *n* repetitions of the encoding for VALUE shown in the table below:

# of Bytes	Value	Description
1	INT8	key-click-percent
1	INT8	bell-percent
2	INT16	bell-pitch
2	INT16	bell-duration
1	CARD8	led
1		led-mode:
	0	**Off**
	1	**On**

# of Bytes	Value	Description
1	KEYCODE	key
1		auto-repeat-mode:
	0	**Off**
	1	**On**
	2	**Default**

ChangeKeyboardMapping

Name
ChangeKeyboardMapping

Request Contents
first-keycode : KEYCODE
keysyms-per-keycode : CARD8
keysyms : LISTofKEYSYM

Errors
Value, **Alloc**

Description
This request defines the symbols for the specified number of keycodes, starting with the specified keycode. The symbols for keycodes outside this range remained unchanged. The number of elements in the keysyms list must be a multiple of keysyms-per-keycode (or a **Length** error results). The first-keycode must be greater than or equal to min-keycode as returned in the connection setup (or a **Value** error results) and:

```
first-keycode + (keysyms-length / keysyms-per-keycode) - 1
```

must be less than or equal to max-keycode as returned in the connection setup (or a **Value** error results). KEYSYM number N (counting from zero) for keycode K has an index (counting from zero) of:

```
(K - first-keycode) * keysyms-per-keycode + N
```

in keysyms. The keysyms-per-keycode can be chosen arbitrarily by the client to be large enough to hold all desired symbols. A special KEYSYM value of **NoSymbol** should be used to fill in unused elements for individual keycodes. It is legal for **NoSymbol** to appear in nontrailing positions of the effective list for a keycode.

This request generates a **MappingNotify** event.

There is no requirement that the server interpret this mapping; it is merely stored for reading and writing by clients (see Appendix E, *Keyboards and Pointers*).

Request Encoding

# of Bytes	Value	Description
1	100	opcode
1	n	keycode-count
2	2+nm	request length
1	KEYCODE	first-keycode
1	m	keysyms-per-keycode
2		unused
4nm	LISTofKEYSYM	keysyms

ChangePointerControl

Name

ChangePointerControl

Request Contents

do-acceleration, *do-threshold*: BOOL
acceleration-numerator, *acceleration-denominator* : INT16
threshold: INT16

Errors

Value

Description

This request defines how the pointer moves. The acceleration is a multiplier for movement expressed as a fraction. For example, specifying 3/1 means the pointer moves three times as fast as normal. The fraction can be rounded arbitrarily by the server. Acceleration only takes effect if the pointer moves more than threshold number of pixels at once and only applies to the amount beyond the threshold. Setting a value to –1 restores the default. Other negative values generate a **Value** error, as does a zero value for acceleration-denominator.

Request Encoding

# of Bytes	Value	Description
1	105	opcode
1		unused
2	3	request length
2	INT16	acceleration-numerator
2	INT16	acceleration-denominator
2	INT16	threshold
1	BOOL	do-acceleration
1	BOOL	do-threshold

ChangeProperty

Name

ChangeProperty

Request Contents

window: WINDOW
property, *type*: ATOM
format: {8, 16, 32}
mode: {**Replace**, **Prepend**, **Append**}
data: LISTofINT8 or LISTofINT16 or LISTofINT32

Errors

Window, Atom, Value, Match, Alloc

Description

This request alters the property for the specified window. The type is uninterpreted by the server. The format specifies whether the data should be viewed as a list of 8-bit, 16-bit, or 32-bit quantities so that the server can correctly byte-swap as necessary.

If the mode is **Replace**, the previous property value is discarded. If the mode is **Prepend** or **Append**, then the type and format must match the existing property value (or a **Match** error results). If the property is undefined, it is treated as defined with the correct type and format with zero-length data. For **Prepend**, the data is tacked on to the beginning of the existing data, and for **Append**, it is tacked on to the end of the existing data.

This request generates a **PropertyNotify** event on the window.

The lifetime of a property is not tied to the storing client. Properties remain until explicitly deleted, until the window is destroyed, or until server reset (see Appendix A, *Connection Close*).

The maximum size of a property is server-dependent and may vary dynamically.

Request Encoding

# of Bytes	Value	Description
1	18	opcode
1		mode:
	0	**Replace**
	1	**Prepend**
	2	**Append**
2	6+(n+p)/4	request length
4	WINDOW	window
4	ATOM	property
4	ATOM	type
1	CARD8	format
3		unused

# of Bytes	Value	Description
4	CARD32	length of data in format units
		(= n for format = 8)
		(= n/2 for format = 16)
		(= n/4 for format = 32)
n	LISTofBYTE	data
		(n is a multiple of 2 for format = 16)
		(n is a multiple of 4 for format = 32)
p		unused, p=pad(n)

ChangeSaveSet

Name

ChangeSaveSet

Request Contents

window: WINDOW
mode: {**Insert, Delete**}

Errors

Window, Match, Value

Description

This request adds or removes the specified window from the client's save-set. The window must have been created by some other client (or a **Match** error results). For further information about the use of the save-set, see Appendix A, *Connection Close*.

When windows are destroyed, the server automatically removes them from the save-set.

Request Encoding

# of Bytes	Value	Description
1	6	opcode
1		mode:
	0	**Insert**
	1	**Delete**
2	2	request length
4	WINDOW	window

ChangeWindowAttributes

Name

ChangeWindowAttributes

Request Contents

window: WINDOW
value-mask: BITMASK
value-list: LISTofVALUE

Errors

Window, Pixmap, Colormap, Cursor, Match, Value, Access

Description

The value-mask and value-list specify which attributes are to be changed. The values and restrictions are the same as for **CreateWindow**.

Setting a new background, whether by background-pixmap or background-pixel, overrides any previous background. Setting a new border, whether by border-pixel or border-pixmap, overrides any previous border.

Changing the background does not cause the window contents to be changed. Setting the border or changing the background such that the border tile origin changes causes the border to be repainted. Changing the background of a root window to **None** or **ParentRelative** restores the default background pixmap. Changing the border of a root window to **CopyFromParent** restores the default border pixmap.

Changing the win-gravity does not affect the current position of the window.

Changing the backing-store of an obscured window to **WhenMapped** or **Always** or changing the backing-planes, backing-pixel, or save-under of a mapped window may have no immediate effect.

Multiple clients can select input on the same window; their event-masks are disjoint. When an event is generated, it will be reported to all interested clients. However, only one client at a time can select for **SubstructureRedirect**, only one client at a time can select for **Resize-Redirect**, and only one client at a time can select for **ButtonPress**. An attempt to violate these restrictions results in an **Access** error.

There is only one do-not-propagate-mask for a window, not one per client.

Changing the colormap of a window (by defining a new map, not by changing the contents of the existing map) generates a **ColormapNotify** event. Changing the colormap of a visible window might have no immediate effect on the screen (see **InstallColormap** request).

Changing the cursor of a root window to **None** restores the default cursor.

The order in which attributes are verified and altered is server-dependent. If an error is generated, a subset of the attributes may have been altered.

Request Encoding

# of Bytes	Value	Description
1	2	opcode
1		unused
2	3+n	request length
4	WINDOW	window
4	BITMASK	value-mask (has n bits set to 1)
		(Encodings are the same as for **CreateWindow**.)
4n	LISTofVALUE	value-list
		(Encodings are the same as for **CreateWindow**.)

CirculateNotify

Name

CirculateNotify

Event Contents

event, *window*: WINDOW
place: { **Top**, **Bottom** }

Description

This event is reported to clients selecting **StructureNotify** on the window and to clients selecting **SubstructureNotify** on the parent. It is generated when the window is actually restacked from a **CirculateWindow** request. The event is the window on which the event was generated, and the window is the window that is restacked. If place is **Top**, the window is now on top of all siblings. Otherwise, it is below all siblings.

Request Encoding

# of Bytes	Value	Description
1	26	code
1		unused
2	CARD16	sequence number
4	WINDOW	event
4	WINDOW	window
4	WINDOW	unused
1		place:
	0	**Top**
	1	**Bottom**
15		unused

CirculateRequest

Name

CirculateRequest

Event Contents

parent, *window*: WINDOW
place: { **Top**, **Bottom** }

Description

This event is reported to the client selecting **StructureRedirect** on the parent and is generated when a **CirculateWindow** request is issued on the parent and a window actually needs to be restacked. The window specifies the window to be restacked, and the place specifies what the new position in the stacking order should be.

Request Encoding

# of Bytes	Value	Description
1	27	code
1		unused
2	CARD16	sequence number
4	WINDOW	parent
4	WINDOW	window
4		unused
1		place:
	0	**Top**
	1	**Bottom**
15		unused

CirculateWindow

Name
CirculateWindow

Request Contents
window: WINDOW
direction: { **RaiseLowest**, **LowerHighest** }

Errors
Window, **Value**

Description
If some other client has selected **Substructure**Redirect on the window, then a **CirculateRe-quest** event is generated, and no further processing is performed. Otherwise, the following is performed, and then a **CirculateNotify** event is generated if the window is actually restacked.

For **RaiseLowest**, **CirculateWindow** raises the lowest mapped child (if any) that is occluded by another child to the top of the stack. For **LowerHighest**, **CirculateWindow** lowers the highest mapped child (if any) that occludes another child to the bottom of the stack. Exposure processing is performed on formerly obscured windows.

Request Encoding

# of Bytes	Value	Description
1	13	opcode
1		direction:
	0	**RaiseLowest**
	1	**LowerHighest**
2	2	request length
4	WINDOW	window

ClearArea

Name
ClearArea

Request Contents
window: WINDOW
x, y: INT16
width, height: CARD16
exposures: BOOL

Errors
Window, Value, Match

Description
The x and y coordinates are relative to the window's origin and specify the upper-left corner of the rectangle. If width is zero, it is replaced with the current width of the window minus x. If height is zero, it is replaced with the current height of the window minus y. If the window has a defined background tile, the rectangle is tiled with a plane-mask of all ones and function of **Copy** and a subwindow-mode of **ClipByChildren**. If the window has background **None**, the contents of the window are not changed. In either case, if exposures is **True**, then one or more exposure events are generated for regions of the rectangle that are either visible or being retained in a backing store.

It is a **Match** error to use an **InputOnly** window in this request.

Request Encoding

# of Bytes	Value	Description
1	61	opcode
1	BOOL	exposures
2	4	request length
4	WINDOW	window
2	INT16	x
2	INT16	y
2	CARD16	width
2	CARD16	height

ClientMessage

Name

ClientMessage

Event Contents

window: WINDOW
type: ATOM
format: {8, 16, 32}
data: LISTofINT8 or LISTofINT16 or LISTofINT32

Description

This event is only generated by clients using **SendEvent**. The type specifies how the data is to be interpreted by the receiving client; the server places no interpretation on the type or the data. The format specifies whether the data should be viewed as a list of 8-bit, 16-bit, or 32-bit quantities, so that the server can correctly byte-swap, as necessary. The data always consists of either 20 8-bit values or 10 16-bit values or 5 32-bit values, although particular message types might not make use of all of these values.

Request Encoding

# of Bytes	Value	Description
1	33	code
1	CARD8	format
2	CARD16	sequence number
4	WINDOW	window
4	ATOM	type
20		data

CloseFont

Name

CloseFont

Request Contents

font : FONT

Errors

Font

Description

This request deletes the association between the resource ID and the font. The font itself will be freed when no other resource references it.

Request Encoding

# of Bytes	Value	Description
1	46	opcode
1		unused
2	2	request length
4	FONT	font

ColormapNotify

Name

ColormapNotify

Event Contents

window: WINDOW
colormap: COLORMAP or **None**
new: BOOL
state: {**Installed**, **Uninstalled**}

Description

This event is reported to clients selecting **ColormapChange** on the window. It is generated with value **True** for new when the colormap attribute of the window is changed and is generated with value **False** for new when the colormap of a window is installed or uninstalled. In either case, the state indicates whether the colormap is currently installed.

Request Encoding

# of Bytes	Value	Description
1	32	code
1		unused
2	CARD16	sequence number
4	WINDOW	window
4	COLORMAP	colormap:
	0	**None**
1	BOOL	new
1		state:
	0	**Uninstalled**
	1	**Installed**
18		unused

ConfigureNotify

Name

ConfigureNotify

Event Contents

event, *window*: WINDOW
x, *y*: INT16
width, *height*, *border-width*: CARD16
above-sibling: WINDOW or **None**
override-redirect: BOOL

Description

This event is reported to clients selecting **StructureNotify** on the window and to clients selecting **SubstructureNotify** on the parent. It is generated when a **ConfigureWindow** request actually changes the state of the window. The event is the window on which the event was generated, and the window is the window that is changed. The x and y coordinates are relative to the new parent's origin and specify the position of the upper-left outer corner of the window. The width and height specify the inside size, not including the border. If above-sibling is **None**, then the window is on the bottom of the stack with respect to siblings. Otherwise, the window is immediately on top of the specified sibling. The override-redirect flag is from the window's attribute.

Request Encoding

# of Bytes	Value	Description
1	22	code
1		unused
2	CARD16	sequence number
4	WINDOW	event
4	WINDOW	window
4	WINDOW	above-sibling:
	0	**None**
2	INT16	x
2	INT16	y
2	CARD16	width
2	CARD16	height
2	CARD16	border-width
1	BOOL	override-redirect
5		unused

ConfigureRequest

Name

ConfigureRequest

Event Contents

parent, *window*: WINDOW
x, *y*: INT16
width, *height*, *border-width*: CARD16
sibling: WINDOW or **None**
stack-mode: { **Above**, **Below**, **TopIf**, **BottomIf**, **Opposite** }
value-mask: BITMASK

Description

This event is reported to the client selecting **SubstructureRedirect** on the parent and is generated when a **ConfigureWindow** request is issued on the window by some other client. The value-mask indicates which components were specified in the request. The value-mask and the corresponding values are reported as given in the request. The remaining values are filled in from the current geometry of the window, except in the case of sibling and stack-mode, which are reported as **None** and **Above** (respectively) if not given in the request.

Request Encoding

# of Bytes	Value	Description
1	23	code
1		stack-mode:
	0	**Above**
	1	**Below**
	2	**TopIf**
	3	**BottomIf**
	4	**Opposite**
2	CARD16	sequence number
4	WINDOW	parent
4	WINDOW	window
4	WINDOW	sibling:
	0	**None**
2	INT16	x
2	INT16	y
2	CARD16	width
2	CARD16	height
2	CARD16	border-width
2	BITMASK	value-mask:
	#x0001	x
	#x0002	y
	#x0004	width
	#x0008	height

# of Bytes	Value	Description
	#x0010	border-width
	#x0020	sibling
	#x0040	stack-mode
4		unused

ConfigureWindow

Name
ConfigureWindow

Request Contents
window: WINDOW
value-mask: BITMASK
value-list: LISTofVALUE

Errors
Window, **Match**, **Value**

Description
This request changes the configuration of the window. The value-mask and value-list specify which values are to be given. The possible values are:

Attribute	Type
x	INT16
y	INT16
width	CARD16
height	CARD16
border-width	CARD16
sibling	WINDOW
stack-mode	{**Above**, **Below**, **TopIf**, **BottomIf**, **Opposite**}

The x and y coordinates are relative to the parent's origin and specify the position of the upper-left outer corner of the window. The width and height specify the inside size, not including the border, and must be nonzero (or a **Value** error results). Those values not specified are taken from the existing geometry of the window. Note that changing just the border-width leaves the outer-left corner of the window in a fixed position but moves the absolute position of the window's origin. It is a **Match** error to attempt to make the border-width of an **InputOnly** window nonzero.

If the override-redirect attribute of the window is **False** and some other client has selected **SubstructureRedirect** on the parent, a **ConfigureRequest** event is generated, and no further processing is performed. Otherwise, the following is performed.

If some other client has selected **ResizeRedirect** on the window and the inside width or height of the window is being changed, a **ResizeRequest** event is generated, and the current inside width and height are used instead. Note that the override-redirect attribute of the window has no effect on **ResizeRedirect** and that **SubstructureRedirect** on the parent has precedence over **ResizeRedirect** on the window.

The geometry of the window is changed as specified, the window is restacked among siblings, and a **ConfigureNotify** event is generated if the state of the window actually changes. If the inside width or height of the window has actually changed, then children of the window are affected, according to their win-gravity. Exposure processing is performed on formerly obscured windows (including the window itself and its inferiors if regions of them were obscured but now are not). Exposure processing is also performed on any new regions of the window (as a result of increasing the width or height) and on any regions where window contents are lost.

If the inside width or height of a window is not changed but the window is moved or its border is changed, then the contents of the window are not lost but move with the window. Changing the inside width or height of the window causes its contents to be moved or lost, depending on the bit-gravity of the window. It also causes children to be reconfigured, depending on their win-gravity. For a change of width and height of W and H, we define the [x,y] pairs as:

Direction	Deltas
NorthWest	[0, 0]
North	[W/2, 0]
NorthEast	[W, 0]
West	[0, H/2]
Center	[W/2, H/2]
East	[W, H/2]
SouthWest	[0, H]
South	[W/2, H]
SouthEast	[W, H]

When a window with one of these bit-gravities is resized, the corresponding pair defines the change in position of each pixel in the window. When a window with one of these win-gravities has its parent window resized, the corresponding pair defines the change in position of the window within the parent. This repositioning generates a **GravityNotify** event. **GravityNotify** events are generated after the **ConfigureNotify** event is generated.

A gravity of **Static** indicates that the contents or origin should not move relative to the origin of the root window. If the change in size of the window is coupled with a change in position of [X,Y], then for bit-gravity, the change in position of each pixel is [–X,–Y] and, for win-gravity, the change in position of a child when its parent is so resized is [–X,–Y]. Note that **Static** gravity still only takes effect when the width or height of the window is changed, not when the window is simply moved.

A bit-gravity of **Forget** indicates that the window contents are always discarded after a size change, even if backing-store or save-under has been requested. The window is tiled with its background (except, if no background is defined, the existing screen contents are not altered), and zero or more exposure events are generated. A server may also ignore the specified bit-gravity and use **Forget** instead.

A win-gravity of **Unmap** is like **NorthWest**, but the child is also unmapped when the parent is resized, and an **UnmapNotify** event is generated. **UnmapNotify** events are generated after the **ConfigureNotify** event is generated.

If a sibling and a stack-mode are specified, the window is restacked as follows:

Above   The window is placed just above the sibling.

Below   The window is placed just below the sibling.

TopIf   If the sibling occludes the window, then the window is placed at the top of the stack.

BottomIf   If the window occludes the sibling, then the window is placed at the bottom of the stack.

Opposite   If the sibling occludes the window, then the window is placed at the top of the stack. Otherwise, if the window occludes the sibling, then the window is placed at the bottom of the stack.

If a stack-mode is specified but no sibling is specified, the window is restacked as follows:

Above   The window is placed at the top of the stack.

Below   The window is placed at the bottom of the stack.

TopIf   If any sibling occludes the window, then the window is placed at the top of the stack.

BottomIf   If the window occludes any sibling, then the window is placed at the bottom of the stack.

Opposite   If any sibling occludes the window, then the window is placed at the top of the stack. Otherwise, if the window occludes any sibling, then the window is placed at the bottom of the stack.

It is a **Match** error if a sibling is specified without a stack-mode or if the window is not actually a sibling.

Note that the computations for **BottomIf**, **TopIf**, and **Opposite** are performed with respect to the window's final geometry (as controlled by the other arguments to the request), not to its initial geometry.

Attempts to configure a root window have no effect.

Request Encoding

# of Bytes	Value	Description
1	12	opcode
1		unused
2	3+n	request length
4	WINDOW	window
2	BITMASK	value-mask (has n bits set to 1):
	#x0001	x
	#x0002	y

# of Bytes	Value	Description
	#x0004	width
	#x0008	height
	#x0010	border-width
	#x0020	sibling
	#x0040	stack-mode
2		unused
4n	LISTofVALUE	value-list

LISTofVALUE is *n* repetitions of the encoding for VALUE shown in the table below:

# of Bytes	Value	Description
2	INT16	x
2	INT16	y
2	CARD16	width
2	CARD16	height
2	CARD16	border-width
4	WINDOW	sibling
1		stack-mode:
	0	**Above**
	1	**Below**
	2	**TopIf**
	3	**BottomIf**
	4	**Opposite**

Name

ConvertSelection

Request Contents

selection, *target*: ATOM
property: ATOM or **None**
requestor: WINDOW
time: TIMESTAMP or **CurrentTime**

Errors

Atom, **Window**

Description

If the specified selection has an owner, the server sends a **SelectionRequest** event to that owner. If no owner for the specified selection exists, the server generates a **SelectionNotify** event to the requestor with property **None**. The arguments are passed on unchanged in either event.

Request Encoding

# of Bytes	Value	Description
1	24	opcode
1		unused
2	6	request length
4	WINDOW	requestor
4	ATOM	selection
4	ATOM	target
4	ATOM	property:
	0	**None**
4	TIMESTAMP	time:
	0	**CurrentTime**

CopyArea

Name
CopyArea

Request Contents
src-drawable, *dst-drawable* : DRAWABLE
gc : GCONTEXT
src-x, *src-y* : INT16
width, *height* : CARD16
dst-x, *dst-y* : INT16

Errors
Drawable, **GContext**, **Match**

Description
This request combines the specified rectangle of src-drawable with the specified rectangle of dst-drawable. The src-x and src-y coordinates are relative to src-drawable's origin. The dst-x and dst-y are relative to dst-drawable's origin, each pair specifying the upper-left corner of the rectangle. The src-drawable must have the same root and the same depth as dst-drawable (or a **Match** error results).

If regions of the source rectangle are obscured and have not been retained in backing store or if regions outside the boundaries of the source drawable are specified, then those regions are not copied, but the following occurs on all corresponding destination regions that are either visible or retained in backing-store. If the dst-drawable is a window with a background other than **None**, these corresponding destination regions are tiled (with plane-mask of all ones and function **Copy**) with that background. Regardless of tiling and whether the destination is a window or a pixmap, if graphics-exposures in gc is **True**, then **GraphicsExpose** events for all corresponding destination regions are generated.

If graphics-exposures is **True** but no **GraphicsExpose** events are generated, then a **NoExpose** event is generated.

GC components: function, plane-mask, subwindow-mode, graphics-exposures, clip-x-origin, clip-y-origin, clip-mask.

Request Encoding

# of Bytes	Value	Description
1	62	opcode
1		unused
2	7	request length
4	DRAWABLE	src-drawable
4	DRAWABLE	dst-drawable
4	GCONTEXT	gc
2	INT16	src-x
2	INT16	src-y

# of Bytes	Value	Description
2	INT16	dst-x
2	INT16	dst-y
2	CARD16	width
2	CARD16	height

CopyColormapAndFree

Name

CopyColormapAndFree

Request Contents

mid, *src-cmap*: COLORMAP

Errors

IDChoice, **Colormap**, **Alloc**

Description

This request creates a colormap of the same visual type and for the same screen as src-cmap, and it associates identifier mid with it. It also moves all of the client's existing allocations from src-cmap to the new colormap with their color values intact and their read-only or writable characteristics intact, and it frees those entries in src-cmap. Color values in other entries in the new colormap are undefined. If src-cmap was created by the client with alloc **All** (see **CreateColormap** request), then the new colormap is also created with alloc **All**, all color values for all entries are copied from src-cmap, and then all entries in src-cmap are freed. If src-cmap was not created by the client with alloc **All**, then the allocations to be moved are all those pixels and planes that have been allocated by the client using either **AllocColor**, **Alloc-NamedColor**, **AllocColorCells**, or **AllocColorPlanes** and that have not been freed since they were allocated.

Request Encoding

# of Bytes	Value	Description
1	80	opcode
1		unused
2	3	request length
4	COLORMAP	mid
4	COLORMAP	src-cmap

Name
CopyGC

Request Contents
src-gc, *dst-gc*: GCONTEXT
value-mask: BITMASK

Errors
GContext, Value, Match, Alloc

Description
This request copies components from src-gc to dst-gc. The value-mask specifies which components to copy, as for **CreateGC**. The two gcontexts must have the same root and the same depth (or a **Match** error results).

Request Encoding

# of Bytes	Value	Description
1	57	opcode
1		unused
2	4	request length
4	GCONTEXT	src-gc
4	GCONTEXT	dst-gc
4	BITMASK	value-mask
		(Encodings are the same as for **CreateGC**.)

CopyPlane

Name
CopyPlane

Request Contents
src-drawable, *dst-drawable*: DRAWABLE
gc: GCONTEXT
src-x, *src-y*: INT16
width, *height*: CARD16
dst-x, *dst-y*: INT16
bit-plane: CARD32

Errors
Drawable, **GContext**, **Value**, **Match**

Description
The src-drawable must have the same root as dst-drawable (or a **Match** error results), but it need not have the same depth. The bit-plane must have exactly one bit set to 1, and the value of bit-plane must be less than 2^n, where n is the depth of src-drawable (or a **Value** error results). Effectively, a pixmap of the same depth as dst-drawable and with size specified by the source region is formed using the foreground/background pixels in gc (foreground everywhere the bit-plane in src-drawable contains a bit set to 1, background everywhere the bit-plane contains a bit set to 0), and the equivalent of a **CopyArea** is performed, with all the same exposure semantics. This can also be thought of as using the specified region of the source bit-plane as a stipple with a fill-style of **OpaqueStippled** for filling a rectangular area of the destination.

GC components: function, plane-mask, foreground, background, subwindow-mode, graphics-exposures, clip-x-origin, clip-y-origin, clip-mask

Request Encoding

# of Bytes	Value	Description
1	63	opcode
1		unused
2	8	request length
4	DRAWABLE	src-drawable
4	DRAWABLE	dst-drawable
4	GCONTEXT	gc
2	INT16	src-x
2	INT16	src-y
2	INT16	dst-x
2	INT16	dst-y

# of Bytes	Value	Description
2	CARD16	width
2	CARD16	height
4	CARD32	bit-plane

CreateColormap

Name

CreateColormap

Request Contents

mid: COLORMAP
visual: VISUALID
window: WINDOW
alloc: {**None**, **All**}

Errors

IDChoice, **Window**, **Value**, **Match**, **Alloc**

Description

This request creates a colormap of the specified visual type for the screen on which the window resides and associates the identifier mid with it. The visual type must be one supported by the screen (or a **Match** error results). The initial values of the colormap entries are undefined for classes **GrayScale**, **PseudoColor**, and **DirectColor**. For **StaticGray**, **StaticColor**, and **TrueColor**, the entries will have defined values, but those values are specific to the visual and are not defined by the core protocol. For **StaticGray**, **StaticColor**, and **TrueColor**, alloc must be specified as **None** (or a **Match** error results). For the other classes, if alloc is **None**, the colormap initially has no allocated entries, and clients can allocate entries.

If alloc is **All**, then the entire colormap is "allocated" writable. The initial values of all allocated entries are undefined. For **GrayScale** and **PseudoColor**, the effect is as if an **AllocColorCells** request returned all pixel values from zero to N–1, where N is the colormap-entries value in the specified visual. For **DirectColor**, the effect is as if an **AllocColorPlanes** request returned a pixel value of zero and red-mask, green-mask, and blue-mask values containing the same bits as the corresponding masks in the specified visual. However, in all cases, none of these entries can be freed with **FreeColors**.

Request Encoding

# of Bytes	Value	Description
1	78	opcode
1		alloc:
	0	**None**
	1	**All**
2	4	request length
4	COLORMAP	mid
4	WINDOW	window
4	VISUALID	visual

CreateCursor

Name
CreateCursor

Request Contents
cid: CURSOR
source: PIXMAP
mask: PIXMAP or **None**
fore-red, fore-green, fore-blue: CARD16
back-red, back-green, back-blue: CARD16
x, y: CARD16

Errors
IDChoice, **Pixmap**, **Match**, **Alloc**

Description
This request creates a cursor and associates identifier cid with it. The foreground and background RGB values must be specified, even if the server only has a **StaticGray** or **GrayScale** screen. The foreground is used for the bits set to 1 in the source, and the background is used for the bits set to 0. Both source and mask (if specified) must have depth one (or a **Match** error results), but they can have any root. The mask pixmap defines the shape of the cursor. That is, the bits set to 1 in the mask define which source pixels will be displayed, and where the mask has bits set to 0, the corresponding bits of the source pixmap are ignored. If no mask is given, all pixels of the source are displayed. The mask, if present, must be the same size as the source (or a **Match** error results). The x and y coordinates define the hotspot relative to the source's origin and must be a point within the source (or a **Match** error results).

The components of the cursor may be transformed arbitrarily to meet display limitations.

The pixmaps can be freed immediately if no further explicit references to them are to be made.

Subsequent drawing in the source or mask pixmap has an undefined effect on the cursor. The server might or might not make a copy of the pixmap.

Request Encoding

# of Bytes	Value	Description
1	93	opcode
1		unused
2	8	request length
4	CURSOR	cid
4	PIXMAP	source
4	PIXMAP	mask:
	0	**None**
2	CARD16	fore-red
2	CARD16	fore-green
2	CARD16	fore-blue

# of Bytes	Value	Description
2	CARD16	back-red
2	CARD16	back-green
2	CARD16	back-blue
2	CARD16	x
2	CARD16	y

Name
CreateGC

Request Contents
cid: GCONTEXT
drawable: DRAWABLE
value-mask: BITMASK
value-list: LISTofVALUE

Errors
IDChoice, **Drawable**, **Pixmap**, **Font**, **Match**, **Value**, **Alloc**

Description
This request creates a graphics context and assigns the identifier cid to it. The gcontext can be used with any destination drawable having the same root and depth as the specified drawable; use with other drawables results in a **Match** error.

The value-mask and value-list specify which components are to be explicitly initialized. The context components are:

Component	Type
function	{ **Clear**, **And**, **AndReverse**, **Copy**, **AndInverted**, **NoOp**, **Xor**, **Or**, **Nor**, **Equiv**, **Invert**, **OrReverse**, **CopyInverted**, **OrInverted**, **Nand**, **Set** }
plane-mask	CARD32
foreground	CARD32
background	CARD32
line-width	CARD16
line-style	{ **Solid**, **OnOffDash**, **DoubleDash** }
cap-style	{ **NotLast**, **Butt**, **Round**, **Projecting** }
join-style	{ **Miter**, **Round**, **Bevel** }
fill-style	{ **Solid**, **Tiled**, **OpaqueStippled**, **Stippled** }
fill-rule	{ **EvenOdd**, **Winding** }
arc-mode	{ **Chord**, **PieSlice** }
tile	PIXMAP
stipple	PIXMAP
tile-stipple-x-origin	INT16
tile-stipple-y-origin	INT16
font	FONT
subwindow-mode	{ **ClipByChildren**, **IncludeInferiors** }
graphics-exposures	BOOL
clip-x-origin	INT16
clip-y-origin	INT16

Component	Type
clip-mask	PIXMAP or **None**
dash-offset	CARD16
dashes	CARD8

In graphics operations, given a source and destination pixel, the result is computed bitwise on corresponding bits of the pixels; that is, a Boolean operation is performed in each bit plane. The plane-mask restricts the operation to a subset of planes, so the result is:

```
((src FUNC dst) AND plane-mask) OR (dst AND (NOT plane-mask))
```

Range checking is not performed on the values for foreground, background, or plane-mask. They are simply truncated to the appropriate number of bits.

The meanings of the functions are:

Function	Operation
Clear	0
And	src AND dst
AndReverse	src AND (NOT dst)
Copy	src
AndInverted	(NOT src) AND dst
NoOp	dst
Xor	src XOR dst
Or	src OR dst
Nor	(NOT src) AND (NOT dst)
Equiv	(NOT src) XOR dst
Invert	NOT dst
OrReverse	src OR (NOT dst)
CopyInverted	NOT src
OrInverted	(NOT src) OR dst
Nand	(NOT src) OR (NOT dst)
Set	1

The line-width is measured in pixels and can be greater than or equal to one, a wide line, or to the special value zero, a thin line.

Wide lines are drawn centered on the path described by the graphics request. Unless otherwise specified by the join or cap style, the bounding box of a wide line with endpoints [x1,y1], [x2,y2] and width w is a rectangle with vertices at the following real coordinates:

```
[x1-(w*sn/2),y1+(w*cs/2)], [x1+(w*sn/2),y1-(w*cs/2)],
[x2-(w*sn/2),y2+(w*cs/2)], [x2+(w*sn/2),y2-(w*cs/2)]
```

The sn is the sine of the angle of the line and cs is the cosine of the angle of the line. A pixel is part of the line (and hence drawn) if the center of the pixel is fully inside the bounding box, which is viewed as having infinitely thin edges. If the center of the pixel is exactly on the bounding box, it is part of the line if and only if the interior is immediately to its right (x increasing direction). Pixels with centers on a horizontal edge are a special case and are part of the line if and only if the interior or the boundary is immediately below (y increasing direction) and if the interior or the boundary is immediately to the right (x increasing direction). Note that this description is a mathematical model describing the pixels that are drawn for a wide line and does not imply that trigonometry is required to implement such a model. Real or fixed point arithmetic is recommended for computing the corners of the line endpoints for lines greater than one pixel in width.

Thin lines (zero line-width) are ''one pixel wide'' lines drawn using an unspecified, device-dependent algorithm. There are only two constraints on this algorithm. First, if a line is drawn unclipped from [x1,y1] to [x2,y2] and another line is drawn unclipped from [x1+dx,y1+dy] to [x2+dx,y2+dy], then a point [x,y] is touched by drawing the first line if and only if the point [x+dx,y+dy] is touched by drawing the second line. Second, the effective set of points comprising a line cannot be affected by clipping. Thus, a point is touched in a clipped line if and only if the point lies inside the clipping region and the point would be touched by the line when drawn unclipped.

Note that a wide line drawn from [x1,y1] to [x2,y2] always draws the same pixels as a wide line drawn from [x2,y2] to [x1,y1], not counting cap-style and join-style. Implementors are encouraged to make this property true for thin lines, but it is not required. A line-width of zero may differ from a line-width of one in which pixels are drawn. In general, drawing a thin line will be faster than drawing a wide line of width one, but thin lines may not mix well aesthetically with wide lines because of the different drawing algorithms. If it is desirable to obtain precise and uniform results across all displays, a client should always use a line-width of one, rather than a line-width of zero.

The line-style defines which sections of a line are drawn:

Solid   The full path of the line is drawn.

DoubleDash   The full path of the line is drawn but the even dashes are filled differently than the odd dashes (see fill-style), with Butt cap-style used where even and odd dashes meet.

OnOffDash   Only the even dashes are drawn, and cap-style applies to all internal ends of the individual dashes (except **NotLast** is treated as **Butt**).

The cap-style defines how the endpoints of a path are drawn:

NotLast   The result is equivalent to **Butt**, except that for a line-width of zero the final endpoint is not drawn.

Butt   The result is square at the endpoint (perpendicular to the slope of the line) with no projection beyond.

Round   The result is a circular arc with its diameter equal to the line-width, centered on the endpoint; it is equivalent to **Butt** for line-width zero.

Projecting The result is square at the end but the path continues beyond the endpoint for a distance equal to half the line-width; it is equivalent to **Butt** for line-width zero.

The join-style defines how corners are drawn for wide lines:

Miter The outer edges of the two lines extend to meet at an angle. However, if the angle is less than 11 degrees, a **Bevel** join-style is used instead.

Round The result is a circular arc with a diameter equal to the line-width, centered on the joinpoint.

Bevel The result is **Butt** endpoint styles, and then the triangular ''notch'' is filled.

For a line with coincident endpoints (x1=x2,y1=y2), when the cap-style is applied to both endpoints, the semantics depends on the line-width and the cap-style:

NotLast thin This is device-dependent, but the desired effect is that nothing is drawn.

Butt thin This is device-dependent, but the desired effect is that a single pixel is drawn.

Round thin This is the same as **Butt**/thin.

Projecting thin This is the same as **Butt**/thin.

Butt wide Nothing is drawn.

Round wide The closed path is a circle, centered at the endpoint and with a diameter equal to the line-width.

Projecting wide The closed path is a square, aligned with the coordinate axes, centered at the endpoint and with sides equal to the line-width.

For a line with coincident endpoints (x1=x2,y1=y2), when the join-style is applied at one or both endpoints, the effect is as if the line was removed from the overall path. However, if the total path consists of (or is reduced to) a single point joined with itself, the effect is the same as when the cap-style is applied at both endpoints.

The tile/stipple and clip origins are interpreted relative to the origin of whatever destination drawable is specified in a graphics request.

The tile pixmap must have the same root and depth as the gcontext (or a **Match** error results). The stipple pixmap must have depth one and must have the same root as the gcontext (or a **Match** error results). For fill-style **Stippled** (but not fill-style **OpaqueStippled**), the stipple pattern is tiled in a single plane and acts as an additional clip mask to be ANDed with the clip-mask. Any size pixmap can be used for tiling or stippling, although some sizes may be faster to use than others.

The fill-style defines the contents of the source for line, text, and fill requests. For all text and fill requests (for example, **PolyText8**, **PolyText16**, **PolyFillRectangle**, **FillPoly**, and

PolyFillArc) as well as for line requests with line-style **Solid**, (for example, **PolyLine**, **PolySegment**, **PolyRectangle**, **PolyArc**) and for the even dashes for line requests with line-style **OnOffDash** or **DoubleDash**:

Solid	Foreground.
Tiled	Tile.
OpaqueStippled	A tile with the same width and height as stipple but with background everywhere stipple has a zero and with foreground everywhere stipple has a one.
Stippled	Foreground masked by stipple.

For the odd dashes for line requests with line-style **DoubleDash**:

Solid	Background.
Tiled	Same as for even dashes.
OpaqueStippled	Same as for even dashes.
Stippled	Background masked by stipple.

The dashes value allowed here is actually a simplified form of the more general patterns that can be set with **SetDashes**. Specifying a value of N here is equivalent to specifying the two element list [N,N] in **SetDashes**. The value must be nonzero (or a **Value** error results). The meaning of dash-offset and dashes are explained in the **SetDashes** request.

The clip-mask restricts writes to the destination drawable. Only pixels where the clip-mask has bits set to 1 are drawn. Pixels are not drawn outside the area covered by the clip-mask or where the clip-mask has bits set to 0. The clip-mask affects all graphics requests, but it does not clip sources. The clip-mask origin is interpreted relative to the origin of whatever destination drawable is specified in a graphics request. If a pixmap is specified as the clip-mask, it must have depth 1 and have the same root as the gcontext (or a **Match** error results). If clip-mask is **None**, then pixels are always drawn, regardless of the clip origin. The clip-mask can also be set with the **SetClipRectangles** request.

For **ClipByChildren**, both source and destination windows are additionally clipped by all viewable **InputOutput** children. For **IncludeInferiors**, neither source nor destination window is clipped by inferiors. This will result in including subwindow contents in the source and drawing through subwindow boundaries of the destination. The use of **IncludeInferiors** with a source or destination window of one depth with mapped inferiors of differing depth is not illegal, but the semantics is undefined by the core protocol.

The fill-rule defines what pixels are inside (that is, are drawn) for paths given in **FillPoly** requests. **EvenOdd** means a point is inside if an infinite ray with the point as origin crosses the path an odd number of times. For **Winding**, a point is inside if an infinite ray with the point as origin crosses an unequal number of clockwise- and counterclockwise-directed path segments. A clockwise-directed path segment is one that crosses the ray from left to right as observed from the point. A counter-clockwise segment is one that crosses the ray from right to left as observed from the point. The case where a directed line segment is coincident with the ray is uninteresting because one can simply choose a different ray that is not coincident with a segment.

For both fill rules, a point is infinitely small and the path is an infinitely thin line. A pixel is inside if the center point of the pixel is inside and the center point is not on the boundary. If the center point is on the boundary, the pixel is inside if and only if the polygon interior is immediately to its right (x increasing direction). Pixels with centers along a horizontal edge are a special case and are inside if and only if the polygon interior is immediately below (y increasing direction).

The arc-mode controls filling in the **PolyFillArc** request.

The graphics-exposures flag controls **GraphicsExpose** event generation for **CopyArea** and **CopyPlane** requests (and any similar requests defined by extensions).

The default component values are:

Component	Default
function	**Copy**
plane-mask	All ones
foreground	0
background	1
line-width	0
line-style	**Solid**
cap-style	**Butt**
join-style	**Miter**
fill-style	**Solid**
fill-rule	**EvenOdd**
arc-mode	**PieSlice**
tile	Pixmap of unspecified size filled with foreground pixel (that is, client specified pixel if any, else 0) (subsequent changes to foreground do not affect this pixmap)
stipple	Pixmap of unspecified size filled with ones
tile-stipple-x-origin	0
tile-stipple-y-origin	0
font	Server-dependent font
subwindow-mode	**ClipByChildren**
graphics-exposures	**True**
clip-x-origin	0
clip-y-origin	0
clip-mask	**None**
dash-offset	0
dashes	4 (that is, the list [4,4])

Storing a pixmap in a gcontext might or might not result in a copy being made. If the pixmap is later used as the destination for a graphics request, the change might or might not be reflected in the gcontext. If the pixmap is used simultaneously in a graphics request as both a destination and a tile or stipple, the results are not defined.

It is quite likely that some amount of gcontext information will be cached in display hardware and that such hardware can only cache a small number of gcontexts. Given the number and complexity of components, clients should view switching between gcontexts with nearly identical state as significantly more expensive than making minor changes to a single gcontext.

Request Encoding

# of Bytes	Value	Description
1	55	opcode
1		unused
2	4+n	request length
4	GCONTEXT	cid
4	DRAWABLE	drawable
4	BITMASK	value-mask (has n bits set to 1):
	#x00000001	function
	#x00000002	plane-mask
	#x00000004	foreground
	#x00000008	background
	#x00000010	line-width
	#x00000020	line-style
	#x00000040	cap-style
	#x00000080	join-style
	#x00000100	fill-style
	#x00000200	fill-rule
	#x00000400	tile
	#x00000800	stipple
	#x00001000	tile-stipple-x-origin
	#x00002000	tile-stipple-y-origin
	#x00004000	font
	#x00008000	subwindow-mode
	#x00010000	graphics-exposures
	#x00020000	clip-x-origin
	#x00040000	clip-y-origin
	#x00080000	clip-mask
	#x00100000	dash-offset
	#x00200000	dashes
	#x00400000	arc-mode
4n	LISTofVALUE	value-list

LISTofVALUE is *n* repetitions of the encoding for VALUE shown in the table below:

# of Bytes	Value	Description
1		function:
	0	**Clear**
	1	**And**
	2	**AndReverse**
	3	**Copy**
	4	**AndInverted**
	5	**NoOp**
	6	**Xor**
	7	**Or**
	8	**Nor**
	9	**Equiv**
	10	**Invert**
	11	**OrReverse**
	12	**CopyInverted**
	13	**OrInverted**
	14	**Nand**
	15	**Set**
4	CARD32	plane-mask
4	CARD32	foreground
4	CARD32	background
2	CARD16	line-width
1		line-style:
	0	**Solid**
	1	**OnOffDash**
	2	**DoubleDash**
1		cap-style:
	0	**NotLast**
	1	**Butt**
	2	**Round**
	3	**Projecting**
1		join-style:
	0	**Miter**
	1	**Round**
	2	**Bevel**
1		fill-style:
	0	**Solid**
	1	**Tiled**
	2	**Stippled**
	3	**OpaqueStippled**

# of Bytes	Value	Description
1		fill-rule:
	0	**EvenOdd**
	1	**Winding**
4	PIXMAP	tile
4	PIXMAP	stipple
2	INT16	tile-stipple-x-origin
2	INT16	tile-stipple-y-origin
4	FONT	font
1		subwindow-mode:
	0	**ClipByChildren**
	1	**IncludeInferiors**
1	BOOL	graphics-exposures
2	INT16	clip-x-origin
2	INT16	clip-y-origin
4	PIXMAP	clip-mask:
	0	**None**
2	CARD16	dash-offset
1	CARD8	dashes
1		arc-mode:
	0	**Chord**
	1	**PieSlice**

CreateGlyphCursor

Name

CreateGlyphCursor

Request Contents

cid : CURSOR
source-font : FONT
mask-font : FONT or **None**
source-char, *mask-char* : CARD16
fore-red, *fore-green*, *fore-blue* : CARD16
back-red, *back-green*, *back-blue* : CARD16

Errors

IDChoice , **Font** , **Value** , **Alloc**

Description

This request is similar to **CreateCursor** , except the source and mask bitmaps are obtained from the specified font glyphs. The source-char must be a defined glyph in source-font, and if mask-font is given, mask-char must be a defined glyph in mask-font (or a **Value** error results). The mask font and character are optional. The origins of the source and mask (if it is defined) glyphs are positioned coincidently and define the hotspot. The source and mask need not have the same bounding box metrics, and there is no restriction on the placement of the hotspot relative to the bounding boxes. If no mask is given, all pixels of the source are displayed. Note that source-char and mask-char are CARD16, not CHAR2B. For 2-byte matrix fonts, the 16-bit value should be formed with byte1 in the most-significant byte and byte2 in the least-significant byte.

The components of the cursor may be transformed arbitrarily to meet display limitations.

The fonts can be freed immediately if no further explicit references to them are to be made.

Request Encoding

# of Bytes	Value	Description
1	94	**CreateGlyphCursor**
1		unused
2	8	request length
4	CURSOR	cid
4	FONT	source-font
4	FONT	mask-font:
	0	**None**
2	CARD16	source-char
2	CARD16	mask-char
2	CARD16	fore-red
2	CARD16	fore-green
2	CARD16	fore-blue

# of Bytes	Value	Description
2	CARD16	back-red
2	CARD16	back-green
2	CARD16	back-blue

CreateNotify

Name
CreateNotify

Event Contents
parent, *window*: WINDOW
x, *y*: INT16
width, *height*, *border-width*: CARD16
override-redirect: BOOL

Description
This event is reported to clients selecting **SubstructureNotify** on the parent and is generated when the window is created. The arguments are as in the **CreateWindow** request.

Request Encoding

# of Bytes	Value	Description
1	16	code
1		unused
2	CARD16	sequence number
4	WINDOW	parent
4	WINDOW	window
2	INT16	x
2	INT16	y
2	CARD16	width
2	CARD16	height
2	CARD16	border-width
1	BOOL	override-redirect
9		unused

Name

CreatePixmap

Request Contents

pid: PIXMAP
drawable: DRAWABLE
depth: CARD8
width, *height*: CARD16

Errors

IDChoice, **Drawable**, **Value**, **Alloc**

Description

This request creates a pixmap and assigns the identifier pid to it. The width and height must be nonzero (or a **Value** error results). The depth must be one of the depths supported by the root of the specified drawable (or a **Value** error results). The initial contents of the pixmap are undefined.

It is legal to pass an **InputOnly** window as a drawable to this request.

Request Encoding

# of Bytes	Value	Description
1	53	opcode
1	CARD8	depth
2	4	request length
4	PIXMAP	pid
4	DRAWABLE	drawable
2	CARD16	width
2	CARD16	height

Name

CreateWindow

Request Contents

wid, parent: WINDOW
class: {**InputOutput, InputOnly, CopyFromParent**}
depth: CARD8
visual: VISUALID or **CopyFromParent**
x, y: INT16
width, height, border-width: CARD16
value-mask: BITMASK
value-list: LISTofVALUE

Errors

IDChoice, Window, Pixmap, Colormap, Cursor, Match, Value, Alloc

Description

This request creates an unmapped window and assigns the identifier wid to it.

A class of **CopyFromParent** means the class is taken from the parent. A depth of zero for class **InputOutput** or **CopyFromParent** means the depth is taken from the parent. A visual of **CopyFromParent** means the visual type is taken from the parent. For class **InputOutput**, the visual type and depth must be a combination supported for the screen (or a **Match** error results). The depth need not be the same as the parent, but the parent must not be of class **InputOnly** (or a **Match** error results). For class **InputOnly**, the depth must be zero (or a **Match** error results), and the visual must be one supported for the screen (or a **Match** error results). However, the parent can have any depth and class.

The server essentially acts as if **InputOnly** windows do not exist for the purposes of graphics requests, exposure processing, and **VisibilityNotify** events. An **InputOnly** window cannot be used as a drawable (as a source or destination for graphics requests). **InputOnly** and **Input-Output** windows act identically in other respects—properties, grabs, input control, and so on.

The window is placed on top in the stacking order with respect to siblings. The x and y coordinates are relative to the parent's origin and specify the position of the upper-left outer corner of the window (not the origin). The width and height specify the inside size (not including the border) and must be nonzero (or a **Value** error results). The border-width for an **InputOnly** window must be zero (or a **Match** error results).

The value-mask and value-list specify attributes of the window that are to be explicitly initialized. The possible values are:

Attribute	Type
background-pixmap	PIXMAP or **None** or **ParentRelative**
background-pixel	CARD32
border-pixmap	PIXMAP or **CopyFromParent**
border-pixel	CARD32
bit-gravity	BITGRAVITY
win-gravity	WINGRAVITY
backing-store	{ **NotUseful**, **WhenMapped**, **Always** }
backing-planes	CARD32
backing-pixel	CARD32
save-under	BOOL
event-mask	SETofEVENT
do-not-propagate-mask	SETofDEVICEEVENT
override-redirect	BOOL
colormap	COLORMAP or **CopyFromParent**
cursor	CURSOR or **None**

The default values when attributes are not explicitly initialized are:

Attribute	Default
background-pixmap	**None**
border-pixmap	**CopyFromParent**
bit-gravity	**Forget**
win-gravity	**NorthWest**
backing-store	**NotUseful**
backing-planes	All ones
backing-pixel	Zero
save-under	**False**
event-mask	{ } (empty set)
do-not-propagate-mask	{ } (empty set)
override-redirect	**False**
colormap	**CopyFromParent**
cursor	**None**

Only the following attributes are defined for **InputOnly** windows:

- win-gravity

- event-mask

- do-not-propagate-mask

- override-redirect

- cursor

It is a **Match** error to specify any other attributes for **InputOnly** windows.

If background-pixmap is given, it overrides the default background-pixmap. The background pixmap and the window must have the same root and the same depth (or a **Match** error results). Any size pixmap can be used, although some sizes may be faster than others. If background **None** is specified, the window has no defined background. If background **ParentRelative** is specified, the parent's background is used, but the window must have the same depth as the parent (or a **Match** error results). If the parent has background **None**, then the window will also have background **None**. A copy of the parent's background is not made. The parent's background is reexamined each time the window background is required. If background-pixel is given, it overrides the default background-pixmap and any background-pixmap given explicitly, and a pixmap of undefined size filled with background-pixel is used for the background. Range checking is not performed on the background-pixel value; it is simply truncated to the appropriate number of bits. For a **ParentRelative** background, the background tile origin always aligns with the parent's background tile origin. Otherwise, the background tile origin is always the window origin.

When no valid contents are available for regions of a window and either the regions are visible or the server is maintaining backing store, the server automatically tiles the regions with the window's background unless the window has a background of **None**. If the background is **None**, the previous screen contents from other windows of the same depth as the window are simply left in place if the contents come from the parent of the window or an inferior of the parent; otherwise, the initial contents of the exposed regions are undefined. Exposure events are then generated for the regions, even if the background is **None**.

The border tile origin is always the same as the background tile origin. If border-pixmap is given, it overrides the default border-pixmap. The border pixmap and the window must have the same root and the same depth (or a **Match** error results). Any size pixmap can be used, although some sizes may be faster than others. If **CopyFromParent** is given, the parent's border pixmap is copied (subsequent changes to the parent's border attribute do not affect the child), but the window must have the same depth as the parent (or a **Match** error results). The pixmap might be copied by sharing the same pixmap object between the child and parent or by making a complete copy of the pixmap contents. If border-pixel is given, it overrides the default border-pixmap and any border-pixmap given explicitly, and a pixmap of undefined size filled with border-pixel is used for the border. Range checking is not performed on the border-pixel value; it is simply truncated to the appropriate number of bits.

Output to a window is always clipped to the inside of the window, so that the border is never affected.

The bit-gravity defines which region of the window should be retained if the window is resized, and win-gravity defines how the window should be repositioned if the parent is resized (see **ConfigureWindow** request).

A backing-store of **WhenMapped** advises the server that maintaining contents of obscured regions when the window is mapped would be beneficial. A backing-store of **Always** advises the server that maintaining contents even when the window is unmapped would be beneficial. In this case, the server may generate an exposure event when the window is created. A value of **NotUseful** advises the server that maintaining contents is unnecessary, although a server may still choose to maintain contents while the window is mapped. Note that if the server maintains contents, then the server should maintain complete contents, not just the region within the parent boundaries, even if the window is larger than its parent. While the server maintains contents, exposure events will not normally be generated, but the server may stop maintaining contents at any time.

If save-under is **True**, the server is advised that when this window is mapped, saving the contents of windows it obscures would be beneficial.

When the contents of obscured regions of a window are being maintained, regions obscured by noninferior windows are included in the destination (and source, when the window is the source) of graphics requests, but regions obscured by inferior windows are not included.

The backing-planes indicates (with bits set to 1) which bit planes of the window hold dynamic data that must be preserved in backing-stores and during save-unders. The backing-pixel specifies what value to use in planes not covered by backing-planes. The server is free to save only the specified bit planes in the backing-store or save-under and regenerate the remaining planes with the specified pixel value. Any bits beyond the specified depth of the window in these values are simply ignored.

The event-mask defines which events the client is interested in for this window (or for some event types, inferiors of the window). The do-not-propagate-mask defines which events should not be propagated to ancestor windows when no client has the event type selected in this window.

The override-redirect specifies whether map and configure requests on this window should override a **SubstructureRedirect** on the parent, typically to inform a window manager not to tamper with the window.

The colormap specifies the colormap that best reflects the true colors of the window. Servers capable of supporting multiple hardware colormaps may use this information, and window managers may use it for **InstallColormap** requests. The colormap must have the same visual type as the window (or a **Match** error results). If **CopyFromParent** is specified, the parent's colormap is copied (subsequent changes to the parent's colormap attribute do not affect the child). However, the window must have the same visual type as the parent (or a **Match** error results), and the parent must not have a colormap of **None** (or a **Match** error results). For an explanation of **None**, see **FreeColormap** request. The colormap is copied by sharing the colormap object between the child and the parent, not by making a complete copy of the colormap contents.

If a cursor is specified, it will be used whenever the pointer is in the window. If **None** is specified, the parent's cursor will be used when the pointer is in the window, and any change in the parent's cursor will cause an immediate change in the displayed cursor.

This request generates a **CreateNotify** event.

The background and border pixmaps and the cursor may be freed immediately if no further explicit references to them are to be made.

Subsequent drawing into the background or border pixmap has an undefined effect on the window state. The server might or might not make a copy of the pixmap.

Request Encoding

# of Bytes	Value	Description
1	1	opcode
1	CARD8	depth
2	8+n	request length
4	WINDOW	wid
4	WINDOW	parent
2	INT16	x
2	INT16	y
2	CARD16	width
2	CARD16	height
2	CARD16	border-width
2		class:
	0	**CopyFromParent**
	1	**InputOutput**
	2	**InputOnly**
4	VISUALID	visual:
	0	**CopyFromParent**
4	BITMASK	value-mask (has n bits set to 1):
	#x00000001	background-pixmap
	#x00000002	background-pixel
	#x00000004	border-pixmap
	#x00000008	border-pixel
	#x00000010	bit-gravity
	#x00000020	win-gravity
	#x00000040	backing-store
	#x00000080	backing-planes
	#x00000100	backing-pixel
	#x00000200	override-redirect
	#x00000400	save-under
	#x00000800	event-mask
	#x00001000	do-not-propagate-mask
	#x00002000	colormap
	#x00004000	cursor
4n	LISTofVALUE	value-list

LISTofVALUE is *n* repetitions of the encoding for VALUE shown in the table below:

# of Bytes	Value	Description
4	PIXMAP	background-pixmap:
	0	**None**
	1	**ParentRelative**
4	CARD32	background-pixel
4	PIXMAP	border-pixmap:
	0	**CopyFromParent**
4	CARD32	border-pixel
1	BITGRAVITY	bit-gravity
1	WINGRAVITY	win-gravity
1		backing-store:
	0	**NotUseful**
	1	**WhenMapped**
	2	**Always**
4	CARD32	backing-planes
4	CARD32	backing-pixel
1	BOOL	override-redirect
1	BOOL	save-under
4	SETofEVENT	event-mask
4	SETofDEVICEEVENT	do-not-propagate-mask
4	COLORMAP	colormap:
	0	**CopyFromParent**
4	CURSOR	cursor:
	0	**None**

DeletePsroperty

Name
DeleteProperty

Request Contents
window: WINDOW
property: ATOM

Errors
Window, Atom

Description
This request deletes the property from the specified window if the property exists and generates a **PropertyNotify** event on the window unless the property does not exist.

Request Encoding

# of Bytes	Value	Description
1	19	opcode
1		unused
2	3	request length
4	WINDOW	window
4	ATOM	property

Name

DestroyNotify

Event Contents

event, window: WINDOW

Description

This event is reported to clients selecting **StructureNotify** on the window and to clients selecting **SubstructureNotify** on the parent. It is generated when the window is destroyed. The event is the window on which the event was generated, and the window is the window that is destroyed.

The ordering of the **DestroyNotify** events is such that, for any given window, **DestroyNotify** is generated on all inferiors of the window before being generated on the window itself. The ordering among siblings and across subhierarchies is not otherwise constrained.

Request Encoding

# of Bytes	Value	Description
1	17	code
1		unused
2	CARD16	sequence number
4	WINDOW	event
4	WINDOW	window
20		unused

DestroySubwindows

Name

DestroySubwindows

Request Contents

window: WINDOW

Errors

Window

Description

This request performs a **DestroyWindow** request on all children of the window, in bottom-to-top stacking order.

Request Encoding

# of Bytes	Value	Description
1	5	opcode
1		unused
2	2	request length
4	WINDOW	window

DestroyWindow

Name
DestroyWindow

Request Contents
window: WINDOW

Errors
Window

Description
If the argument window is mapped, an **UnmapWindow** request is performed automatically. The window and all inferiors are then destroyed, and a **DestroyNotify** event is generated for each window. The ordering of the **DestroyNotify** events is such that, for any given window, **DestroyNotify** is generated on all inferiors of the window before being generated on the window itself. The ordering among siblings and across subhierarchies is not otherwise constrained.

Normal exposure processing on formerly obscured windows is performed.

If the window is a root window, this request has no effect.

Request Encoding

# of Bytes	Value	Description
1	4	opcode
1		unused
2	2	request length
4	WINDOW	window

EnterNotify

Name

EnterNotify

Event Contents

root, *event* : WINDOW
child : WINDOW or **None**
same-screen : BOOL
root-x, *root-y*, *event-x*, *event-y* : INT16
mode : { **Normal**, **Grab**, **Ungrab** }
detail : { **Ancestor**, **Virtual**, **Inferior**, **Nonlinear**, **NonlinearVirtual** }
focus : BOOL
state : SETofKEYBUTMASK
time : TIMESTAMP

(Same contents as **LeaveNotify**.)

Description

EnterNotify events are sent from the server to the client when the user moves the pointer into a window.

For more information, see **LeaveNotify**.

Request Encoding

# of Bytes	Value	Description
1	7	code
1		detail:
	0	**Ancestor**
	1	**Virtual**
	2	**Inferior**
	3	**Nonlinear**
	4	**NonlinearVirtual**
2	CARD16	sequence number
4	TIMESTAMP	time
4	WINDOW	root
4	WINDOW	event
4	WINDOW	child:
	0	**None**
2	INT16	root-x
2	INT16	root-y
2	INT16	event-x
2	INT16	event-y
2	SETofKEYBUTMASK	state

# of Bytes	Value	Description
1		mode:
	0	**Normal**
	1	**Grab**
	2	**Ungrab**
1		same-screen, focus:
	#x01	focus (1 is True, 0 is False)
	#x02	same-screen (1 is True, 0 is False)
	#xfc	unused

Expose

Name

Expose

Event Contents

window: WINDOW
x, y, width, height: CARD16
count: CARD16

Description

This event is reported to clients selecting **Exposure** on the window. It is generated when no valid contents are available for regions of a window, and either the regions are visible, the regions are viewable and the server is (perhaps newly) maintaining backing store on the window, or the window is not viewable but the server is (perhaps newly) honoring window's backing-store attribute of **Always** or **WhenMapped**. The regions are decomposed into an arbitrary set of rectangles, and an **Expose** event is generated for each rectangle.

For a given action causing exposure events, the set of events for a given window are guaranteed to be reported contiguously. If count is zero, then no more **Expose** events for this window follow. If count is nonzero, then at least that many more **Expose** events for this window follow (and possibly more).

The x and y coordinates are relative to window's origin and specify the upper-left corner of a rectangle. The width and height specify the extent of the rectangle.

Expose events are never generated on **InputOnly** windows.

All **Expose** events caused by a hierarchy change are generated after any hierarchy event caused by that change (for example, **UnmapNotify**, **MapNotify**, **ConfigureNotify**, **Gravity-Notify**, **CirculateNotify**). All **Expose** events on a given window are generated after any **VisibilityNotify** event on that window, but it is not required that all **Expose** events on all windows be generated after all **Visibility** events on all windows. The ordering of **Expose** events with respect to **FocusOut**, **EnterNotify**, and **LeaveNotify** events is not constrained.

Request Encoding

# of Bytes	Value	Description
1	12	code
1		unused
2	CARD16	sequence number
4	WINDOW	window
2	CARD16	x
2	CARD16	y
2	CARD16	width
2	CARD16	height

# of Bytes	Value	Description
2	CARD16	count
14		unused

FillPoly

Name
FillPoly

Request Contents
drawable: DRAWABLE
gc: GCONTEXT
shape: {**Complex**, **Nonconvex**, **Convex**}
coordinate-mode: {**Origin**, **Previous**}
points: LISTofPOINT

Errors
Drawable, **GContext**, **Match**, **Value**

Description
This request fills the region closed by the specified path. The path is closed automatically if the last point in the list does not coincide with the first point. No pixel of the region is drawn more than once.

The first point is always relative to the drawable's origin. The rest are relative either to that origin or to the previous point, depending on the coordinate-mode.

The shape parameter may be used by the server to improve performance. **Complex** means the path may self-intersect.

Nonconvex means the path does not self-intersect but the shape is not wholly convex. If known by the client, specifying **Nonconvex** over **Complex** may improve performance. If **Nonconvex** is specified for a self-intersecting path, the graphics results are undefined.

Convex means the path is wholly convex. If known by the client, specifying **Convex** can improve performance. If **Convex** is specified for a path that is not convex, the graphics results are undefined.

GC components: function, plane-mask, fill-style, fill-rule, subwindow-mode, clip-x-origin, clip-y-origin, clip-mask

GC mode-dependent components: foreground, background, tile, stipple, tile-stipple-x-origin, tile-stipple-y-origin

Request Encoding

# of Bytes	Value	Description
1	69	opcode
1		unused
2	4+n	request length
4	DRAWABLE	drawable
4	GCONTEXT	gc

# of Bytes	Value	Description
1		shape:
	0	**Complex**
	1	**Nonconvex**
	2	**Convex**
1		coordinate-mode:
	0	**Origin**
	1	**Previous**
2		unused
4n	LISTofPOINT	points

FocusIn

Name
FocusIn

Event Contents
event: WINDOW
mode: {**Normal**, **WhileGrabbed**, **Grab**, **Ungrab**}
detail: {**Ancestor**, **Virtual**, **Inferior**, **Nonlinear**, **NonlinearVirtual**, **Pointer**,
   PointerRoot, **None**}

(Same contents as **FocusOut**.)

Description
FocusIn events are sent from the server to the client when the keyboard focus is transferred
from one window to another. The window field in **FocusIn** events specifies the window that
gained the keyboard focus.

For more information, see **FocusOut**.

Request Encoding

# of Bytes	Value	Description
1	9	code
1		detail:
	0	**Ancestor**
	1	**Virtual**
	2	**Inferior**
	3	**Nonlinear**
	4	**NonlinearVirtual**
	5	**Pointer**
	6	**PointerRoot**
	7	**None**
2	CARD16	sequence number
4	WINDOW	event
1		mode:
	0	**Normal**
	1	**Grab**
	2	**Ungrab**
	3	**WhileGrabbed**
23		unused

Name

FocusOut

Event Contents

event: WINDOW
mode: {**Normal**, **WhileGrabbed**, **Grab**, **Ungrab**}
detail: {**Ancestor**, **Virtual**, **Inferior**, **Nonlinear**, **NonlinearVirtual**, **Pointer**,
　　PointerRoot, **None**}

Description

FocusIn and FocusOut events are generated when the keyboard focus window changes and are reported to clients selecting **FocusChange** on the window. Events generated by **SetInput-Focus** when the keyboard is not grabbed have mode **Normal**. Events generated by **SetInput-Focus** when the keyboard is grabbed have mode **WhileGrabbed**. Events generated when a keyboard grab activates have mode **Grab**, and events generated when a keyboard grab deactivates have mode **Ungrab**.

All **FocusOut** events caused by a window unmap are generated after any **UnmapNotify** event, but the ordering of **FocusOut** with respect to generated **EnterNotify**, **LeaveNotify**, **VisibilityNotify**, and **Expose** events is not constrained.

Normal and **WhileGrabbed** events are generated as follows.

When the focus moves from window A to window B, A is an inferior of B, and the pointer is in window P:

- **FocusOut** with detail **Ancestor** is generated on A.

- **FocusOut** with detail **Virtual** is generated on each window between A and B exclusive (in order).

- **FocusIn** with detail **Inferior** is generated on B.

- If P is an inferior of B but P is not A or an inferior of A or an ancestor of A, **FocusIn** with detail **Pointer** is generated on each window below B down to and including P (in order).

When the focus moves from window A to window B, B is an inferior of A, and the pointer is in window P:

- If P is an inferior of A but P is not an inferior of B or an ancestor of B, **FocusOut** with detail **Pointer** is generated on each window from P up to but not including A (in order).

- **FocusOut** with detail **Inferior** is generated on A.

- **FocusIn** with detail **Virtual** is generated on each window between A and B exclusive (in order).

- **FocusIn** with detail **Ancestor** is generated on B.

When the focus moves from window A to window B, window C is their least common ancestor, and the pointer is in window P:

- If P is an inferior of A, **FocusOut** with detail **Pointer** is generated on each window from P up to but not including A (in order).

- **FocusOut** with detail **Nonlinear** is generated on A.

- **FocusOut** with detail **NonlinearVirtual** is generated on each window between A and C exclusive (in order).

- **FocusIn** with detail **NonlinearVirtual** is generated on each window between C and B exclusive (in order).

- **FocusIn** with detail **Nonlinear** is generated on B.

- If P is an inferior of B, **FocusIn** with detail **Pointer** is generated on each window below B down to and including P (in order).

When the focus moves from window A to window B on different screens and the pointer is in window P:

- If P is an inferior of A, **FocusOut** with detail **Pointer** is generated on each window from P up to but not including A (in order).

- **FocusOut** with detail **Nonlinear** is generated on A.

- If A is not a root window, **FocusOut** with detail **NonlinearVirtual** is generated on each window above A up to and including its root (in order).

- If B is not a root window, **FocusIn** with detail **NonlinearVirtual** is generated on each window from B's root down to but not including B (in order).

- **FocusIn** with detail **Nonlinear** is generated on B.

- If P is an inferior of B, **FocusIn** with detail **Pointer** is generated on each window below B down to and including P (in order).

When the focus moves from window A to **PointerRoot** (or **None**) and the pointer is in window P:

- If P is an inferior of A, **FocusOut** with detail **Pointer** is generated on each window from P up to but not including A (in order).

- **FocusOut** with detail **Nonlinear** is generated on A.

- If A is not a root window, **FocusOut** with detail **NonlinearVirtual** is generated on each window above A up to and including its root (in order).

- **FocusIn** with detail **PointerRoot** (or **None**) is generated on all root windows.

- If the new focus is **PointerRoot**, **FocusIn** with detail **Pointer** is generated on each window from P's root down to and including P (in order).

When the focus moves from **PointerRoot** (or **None**) to window A and the pointer is in window P:

*   If the old focus is **PointerRoot**, **FocusOut** with detail **Pointer** is generated on each window from P up to and including P's root (in order).

*   **FocusOut** with detail **PointerRoot** (or **None**) is generated on all root windows.

*   If A is not a root window, **FocusIn** with detail **NonlinearVirtual** is generated on each window from A's root down to but not including A (in order).

*   **FocusIn** with detail **Nonlinear** is generated on A.

*   If P is an inferior of A, **FocusIn** with detail **Pointer** is generated on each window below A down to and including P (in order).

When the focus moves from **PointerRoot** to **None** (or vice versa) and the pointer is in window P:

*   If the old focus is **PointerRoot**, **FocusOut** with detail **Pointer** is generated on each window from P up to and including P's root (in order).

*   **FocusOut** with detail **PointerRoot** (or **None**) is generated on all root windows.

*   **FocusIn** with detail **None** (or **PointerRoot**) is generated on all root windows.

*   If the new focus is **PointerRoot**, **FocusIn** with detail **Pointer** is generated on each window from P's root down to and including P (in order).

When a keyboard grab activates (but before generating any actual **KeyPress** event that activates the grab), G is the grab-window for the grab, and F is the current focus:

*   **FocusIn** and **FocusOut** events with mode **Grab** are generated (as for **Normal** above) as if the focus were to change from F to G.

When a keyboard grab deactivates (but after generating any actual **KeyRelease** event that deactivates the grab), G is the grab-window for the grab, and F is the current focus:

*   **FocusIn** and **FocusOut** events with mode **Ungrab** are generated (as for **Normal** above) as if the focus were to change from G to F.

Request Encoding

# of Bytes	Value	Description
1	10	code
1		detail:
	0	**Ancestor**
	1	**Virtual**
	2	**Inferior**
	3	**Nonlinear**
	4	**NonlinearVirtual**
	5	**Pointer**

# of Bytes	Value	Description
	6	**PointerRoot**
	7	**None**
2	CARD16	sequence number
4	WINDOW	event
1		mode:
	0	**Normal**
	1	**Grab**
	2	**Ungrab**
	3	**WhileGrabbed**
23		unused

Name

ForceScreenSaver

Request Contents

mode: { **Activate** , **Reset** }

Errors

Value

Description

If the mode is **Activate** and screen-saver is currently deactivated, then screen-saver is activated (even if screen-saver has been disabled with a timeout value of zero). If the mode is **Reset** and screen-saver is currently enabled, then screen-saver is deactivated (if it was activated), and the activation timer is reset to its initial state as if device input had just been received.

Request Encoding

# of Bytes	Value	Description
1	115	opcode
1		mode:
	0	**Reset**
	1	**Activate**
2	1	request length

Name

FreeColormap

Request Contents

cmap: COLORMAP

Errors

Colormap

Description

This request deletes the association between the resource ID and the colormap and frees the colormap storage. If the colormap is an installed map for a screen, it is uninstalled (see **UninstallColormap** request). If the colormap is defined as the colormap for a window (by means of **CreateWindow** or **ChangeWindowAttributes**), the colormap for the window is changed to **None**, and a **ColormapNotify** event is generated. The protocol does not define the colors displayed for a window with a colormap of **None**.

This request has no effect on a default colormap for a screen.

Request Encoding

# of Bytes	Value	Description
1	79	opcode
1		unused
2	2	request length
4	COLORMAP	cmap

Name

FreeColors

Request Contents

cmap: COLORMAP
pixels: LISTofCARD32
plane-mask: CARD32

Errors

Colormap, Access, Value

Description

The plane-mask should not have any bits in common with any of the pixels. The set of all pixels is produced by ORing together subsets of plane-mask with the pixels. The request frees all of these pixels that were allocated by the client (using **AllocColor**, **AllocNamedColor**, **AllocColorCells**, and **AllocColorPlanes**). Note that freeing an individual pixel obtained from **AllocColorPlanes** may not actually allow it to be reused until all of its related pixels are also freed.

All specified pixels that are allocated by the client in cmap are freed, even if one or more pixels produce an error. A **Value** error is generated if a specified pixel is not a valid index into cmap, and an **Access** error is generated if a specified pixel is not allocated by the client (that is, is unallocated or is only allocated by another client). If more than one pixel is in error, it is arbitrary as to which pixel is reported.

Request Encoding

# of Bytes	Value	Description
1	88	opcode
1		unused
2	3+n	request length
4	COLORMAP	cmap
4	CARD32	plane-mask
4n	LISTofCARD32	pixels

FreeCursor

Name
FreeCursor

Request Contents
cursor: CURSOR

Errors
Cursor

Description
This request deletes the association between the resource ID and the cursor. The cursor storage will be freed when no other resource references it.

Request Encoding

# of Bytes	Value	Description
1	95	opcode
1		unused
2	2	request length
4	CURSOR	cursor

Name
FreeGC

Request Contents
gc: GCONTEXT

Errors
GContext

Description
This request deletes the association between the resource ID and the gcontext and destroys the gcontext.

Request Encoding

# of Bytes	Value	Description
1	60	opcode
1		unused
2	2	request length
4	GCONTEXT	gc

FreePixmap

Name
FreePixmap

Request Contents
pixmap: PIXMAP

Errors
Pixmap

Description
This request deletes the association between the resource ID and the pixmap. The pixmap storage will be freed when no other resource references it.

Request Encoding

# of Bytes	Value	Description
1	54	opcode
1		unused
2	2	request length
4	PIXMAP	pixmap

GetAtomName

Name
GetAtomName

Request Contents
atom: ATOM

Reply Contents
name: STRING8

Errors
Atom

Description
This request returns the name for the given atom.

Request Encoding

# of Bytes	Value	Description
1	17	opcode
1		unused
2	2	request length
4	ATOM	atom

Reply Encoding

# of Bytes	Value	Description
1	1	reply
1		unused
2	CARD16	sequence number
4	(n+p)/4	reply length
2	n	length of name
22		unused
n	STRING8	name
p		unused, p=pad(n)

GetFontPath

Name

GetFontPath

Request Contents

Opcode and request length only.

Reply Contents

path: LISTofSTRING8

Errors

This request has no errors.

Description

This request returns the current search path for fonts.

Request Encoding

# of Bytes	Value	Description
1	52	opcode
1		unused
2	1	request list

Reply Encoding

# of Bytes	Value	Description
1	1	reply
1		unused
2	CARD16	sequence number
4	(n+p)/4	reply length
2	CARD16	number of STRs in path
22		unused
n	LISTofSTR	path
p		unused, p=pad(n)

Name

GetGeometry

Request Contents

drawable : DRAWABLE

Reply Contents

root: WINDOW
depth: CARD8
x, y: INT16
width, height, border-width: CARD16

Errors

Drawable

Description

This request returns the root and current geometry of the drawable. The depth is the number of bits per pixel for the object. The x, y, and border-width will always be zero for pixmaps. For a window, the x and y coordinates specify the upper-left outer corner of the window relative to its parent's origin, and the width and height specify the inside size, not including the border.

It is legal to pass an **InputOnly** window as a drawable to this request.

Request Encoding

# of Bytes	Value	Description
1	14	opcode
1		unused
2	2	request length
4	DRAWABLE	drawable

Reply Encoding

# of Bytes	Value	Description
1	1	reply
1	CARD8	depth
2	CARD16	sequence number
4	0	reply length
4	WINDOW	root
2	INT16	x
2	INT16	y

# of Bytes	Value	Description
2	CARD16	width
2	CARD16	height
2	CARD16	border-width
10		unused

Name
GetImage

Request Contents
drawable: DRAWABLE
x, y: INT16
width, height: CARD16
plane-mask: CARD32
format: { **XYPixmap, ZPixmap** }

Reply Contents
depth: CARD8
visual: VISUALID or **None**
data: LISTofBYTE

Errors
Drawable, Value, Match

Description
This request returns the contents of the given rectangle of the drawable in the given format. The x and y coordinates are relative to the drawable's origin and define the upper-left corner of the rectangle. If **XYPixmap** is specified, only the bit planes specified in plane-mask are transmitted, with the planes appearing from most-significant to least-significant in bit order. If **ZPixmap** is specified, then bits in all planes not specified in plane-mask are transmitted as zero. Range checking is not performed on plane-mask; extraneous bits are simply ignored. The returned depth is as specified when the drawable was created and is the same as a depth component in a FORMAT structure (in the connection setup), not a bits-per-pixel component. If the drawable is a window, its visual type is returned. If the drawable is a pixmap, the visual is **None**.

If the drawable is a pixmap, then the given rectangle must be wholly contained within the pixmap (or a **Match** error results). If the drawable is a window, the window must be viewable, and it must be the case that, if there were no inferiors or overlapping windows, the specified rectangle of the window would be fully visible on the screen and wholly contained within the outside edges of the window (or a **Match** error results). Note that the borders of the window can be included and read with this request. If the window has a backing store, then the backing-store contents are returned for regions of the window that are obscured by noninferior windows; otherwise, the returned contents of such obscured regions are undefined. Also undefined are the returned contents of visible regions of inferiors of different depth than the specified window. The pointer cursor image is not included in the contents returned.

This request is not general-purpose in the same sense as other graphics-related requests. It is intended specifically for rudimentary hardcopy support.

Request Encoding

# of Bytes	Value	Description
1	73	opcode
1		format:
	1	**XYPixmap**
	2	**ZPixmap**
2	5	request length
4	DRAWABLE	drawable
2	INT16	x
2	INT16	y
2	CARD16	width
2	CARD16	height
4	CARD32	plane-mask

Reply Encoding

# of Bytes	Value	Description
1	1	reply
1	CARD8	depth
2	CARD16	sequence number
4	(n+p)/4	reply length
4	VISUALID	visual:
	0	**None**
20		unused
n	LISTofBYTE	data
p		unused, p=pad(n)

GetInputFocus

Name
GetInputFocus

Request Contents
Opcode and request length only.

Reply Contents
focus: WINDOW or **PointerRoot** or **None**
revert-to: {**Parent**, **PointerRoot**, **None**}

Errors
This request has no errors.

Description
This request returns the current focus state.

Request Encoding

# of Bytes	Value	Description
1	43	opcode
1		unused
2	1	request length

Reply Encoding

# of Bytes	Value	Description
1	1	reply
1		revert-to:
	0	**None**
	1	**PointerRoot**
	2	**Parent**
2	CARD16	sequence number
4	0	reply length
4	WINDOW	focus:
	0	**None**
	1	**PointerRoot**
20		unused

GetKeyboardControl

Name

GetKeyboardControl

Request Contents

Opcode and request length only.

Reply Contents

key-click-percent: CARD8
bell-percent: CARD8
bell-pitch: CARD16
bell-duration: CARD16
led-mask: CARD32
global-auto-repeat: {**On**, **Off**}
auto-repeats: LISTofCARD8

Errors

This request has no errors.

Description

This request returns the current control values for the keyboard. For the LEDs, the least-significant bit of led-mask corresponds to LED one, and each one bit in led-mask indicates an LED that is lit. The auto-repeats is a bit vector; each one bit indicates that auto-repeat is enabled for the corresponding key. The vector is represented as 32 bytes. Byte N (from 0) contains the bits for keys 8N to 8N+7, with the least-significant bit in the byte representing key 8N.

Request Encoding

# of Bytes	Value	Description
1	103	opcode
1		unused
2	1	request length

Reply Encoding

# of Bytes	Value	Description
1	1	reply
1		global-auto-repeat:
	0	**Off**
	1	**On**
2	CARD16	sequence number
4	5	reply length
4	CARD32	led-mask

# of Bytes	Value	Description
1	CARD8	key-click-percent
1	CARD8	bell-percent
2	CARD16	bell-pitch
2	CARD16	bell-duration
2		unused
32	LISTofCARD8	auto-repeats

GetKeyboardMapping

Name
GetKeyboardMapping

Request Contents
first-keycode : KEYCODE
count : CARD8

Reply Contents
keysyms-per-keycode: CARD8
keysyms: LISTofKEYSYM

Errors
Value

Description
This request returns the symbols for the specified number of keycodes, starting with the specified keycode. The first-keycode must be greater than or equal to min-keycode as returned in the connection setup (or a **Value** error results), and:

```
first-keycode + count - 1
```

must be less than or equal to max-keycode as returned in the connection setup (or a **Value** error results). The number of elements in the keysyms list is:

```
count * keysyms-per-keycode
```

and KEYSYM number N (counting from zero) for keycode K has an index (counting from zero) of:

```
(K - first-keycode) * keysyms-per-keycode + N
```

in keysyms. The keysyms-per-keycode value is chosen arbitrarily by the server to be large enough to report all requested symbols. A special KEYSYM value of **NoSymbol** is used to fill in unused elements for individual keycodes.

Request Encoding

# of Bytes	Value	Description
1	101	opcode
1		unused
2	2	request length
1	KEYCODE	first-keycode
1	CARD8	count
2		unused

Reply Encoding

# of Bytes	Value	Description
1	1	reply
1	n	keysyms-per-keycode
2	CARD16	sequence number
4	nm	reply length
		(m = count field from the request)
24		unused
4nm	LISTofKEYSYM	keysyms

GetModifierMapping

Name

GetModifierMapping

Request Contents

Opcode and request length only.

Reply Contents

keycodes-per-modifier: CARD8
keycodes: LISTofKEYCODE

Errors

This request has no errors.

Description

This request returns the keycodes of the keys being used as modifiers. The number of keycodes in the list is 8*keycodes-per-modifier. The keycodes are divided into eight sets, with each set containing keycodes-per-modifier elements. The sets are assigned to the modifiers **Shift**, **Lock**, **Control**, **Mod1**, **Mod2**, **Mod3**, **Mod4**, and **Mod5**, in order. The keycodes-per-modifier value is chosen arbitrarily by the server; zeros are used to fill in unused elements within each set. If only zero values are given in a set, the use of the corresponding modifier has been disabled. The order of keycodes within each set is chosen arbitrarily by the server.

Request Encoding

# of Bytes	Value	Description
1	119	opcode
1		unused
2	1	request length

Reply Encoding

# of Bytes	Value	Description
1	1	reply
1	n	keycodes-per-modifier
2	CARD16	sequence number
4	2n	reply length
24		unused
8n	LISTofKEYCODE	keycodes

GetMotionEvents

Name
GetMotionEvents

Request Contents
start, *stop*: TIMESTAMP or **CurrentTime**
window: WINDOW

Reply Contents
events: LISTofTIMECOORD

where:

TIMECOORD: [x, y: INT16
time: TIMESTAMP]

Errors
Window

Description
This request returns all events in the motion history buffer that fall between the specified start and stop times (inclusive) and that have coordinates that lie within (including borders) the specified window at its present placement. The x and y coordinates are reported relative to the origin of the window.

If the start time is later than the stop time or if the start time is in the future, no events are returned. If the stop time is in the future, it is equivalent to specifying **CurrentTime**.

Request Encoding

# of Bytes	Value	Description
1	39	opcode
1		unused
2	4	request length
4	WINDOW	window
4	TIMESTAMP	start:
	0	**CurrentTime**
4	TIMESTAMP	stop:
	0	**CurrentTime**

Reply Encoding

# of Bytes	Value	Description
1	1	reply
1		unused
2	CARD16	sequence number
4	2n	reply length
4	n	number of TIMECOORDs in events
20		unused
8n	LISTofTIMECOORD	events

LISTofTIMECOORD is *n* repetitions of the encoding for TIMECOORD shown in the table below:

# of Bytes	Value	Description
4	TIMESTAMP	time
2	CARD16	x
2	CARD16	y

GetPointerControl

Name

GetPointerControl

Request Contents

Opcode and request length only.

Reply Contents

acceleration-numerator, acceleration-denominator: CARD16
threshold: CARD16

Errors

This request has no errors.

Description

This request returns the current acceleration and threshold for the pointer.

Request Encoding

# of Bytes	Value	Description
1	106	opcode
1		unused
2	1	request length

Reply Encoding

# of Bytes	Value	Description
1	1	reply
1		unused
2	CARD16	sequence number
4	0	reply length
2	CARD16	acceleration-numerator
2	CARD16	acceleration-denominator
2	CARD16	threshold
18		unused

GetPointerMapping

Name

GetPointerMapping

Request Contents

Opcode and request length only.

Reply Contents

map: LISTofCARD8

Errors

This request has no errors.

Description

This request returns the current mapping of the pointer. Elements of the list are indexed starting from one. The length of the list indicates the number of physical buttons.

The nominal mapping for a pointer is the identity mapping:

```
map[i] = i
```

Request Encoding

# of Bytes	Value	Description
1	117	opcode
1		unused
2	1	request length

Reply Encoding

# of Bytes	Value	Description
1	1	reply
1	n	length of map
2	CARD16	sequence number
4	(n+p)/4	reply length
24		unused
n	LISTofCARD8	map
p		unused, p=pad(n)

Name

GetProperty

Request Contents

window: WINDOW
property: ATOM
type: ATOM or **AnyPropertyType**
long-offset, *long-length*: CARD32
delete: BOOL

Reply Contents

type: ATOM or **None**
format: {0, 8, 16, 32}
bytes-after: CARD32
value: LISTofINT8 or LISTofINT16 or LISTofINT32

Errors

Window, **Atom**, **Value**

Description

If the specified property does not exist for the specified window, then the return type is **None**, the format and bytes-after are zero, and the value is empty. The delete argument is ignored in this case. If the specified property exists but its type does not match the specified type, then the return type is the actual type of the property, the format is the actual format of the property (never zero), the bytes-after is the length of the property in bytes (even if the format is 16 or 32), and the value is empty. The delete argument is ignored in this case. If the specified property exists and either **AnyPropertyType** is specified or the specified type matches the actual type of the property, then the return type is the actual type of the property, the format is the actual format of the property (never zero), and the bytes-after and value are as follows, given:

N = actual length of the stored property in bytes
(even if the format is 16 or 32)
I = 4 * long-offset
T = $N - I$
L = MINIMUM (T, 4 * long-length)
A = $N - (I + L)$

The returned value starts at byte index I in the property (indexing from 0), and its length in bytes is L. However, it is a **Value** error if long-offset is given such that L is negative. The value of bytes-after is A, giving the number of trailing unread bytes in the stored property. If delete is **True** and the bytes-after is zero, the property is also deleted from the window, and a **PropertyNotify** event is generated on the window.

Request Encoding

# of Bytes	Value	Description
1	20	opcode
1	BOOL	delete
2	6	request length
4	WINDOW	window
4	ATOM	property
4	ATOM 0	type: **AnyPropertyType**
4	CARD32	long-offset
4	CARD32	long-length

Reply Encoding

# of Bytes	Value	Description
1	1	reply
1	CARD8	format
2	CARD16	sequence number
4	(n+p)/4	reply length
4	ATOM 0	type: **None**
4	CARD32	bytes-after
4	CARD32	length of value in format units (= 0 for format = 0) (= n for format = 8) (= n/2 for format = 16) (= n/4 for format = 32)
12		unused
n	LISTofBYTE	value (n is zero for format = 0) (n is a multiple of 2 for format = 16) (n is a multiple of 4 for format = 32)
p		unused, p=pad(n)

GetScreenSaver

Name

GetScreenSaver

Request Contents

Opcode and request length only.

Reply Contents

timeout, interval: CARD16
prefer-blanking: {**Yes**, **No**}
allow-exposures: {**Yes**, **No**}

Errors

This request has no errors.

Description

This request returns the current screen-saver control values.

Request Encoding

# of Bytes	Value	Description
1	108	opcode
1		unused
2	1	request length

Reply Encoding

# of Bytes	Value	Description
1	1	reply
1		unused
2	CARD16	sequence number
4	0	reply length
2	CARD16	timeout
2	CARD16	interval
1		prefer-blanking:
	0	**No**
	1	**Yes**
1		allow-exposures:
	0	**No**
	1	**Yes**
18		unused

GetSelectionOwner

Name

GetSelectionOwner

Request Contents

selection : ATOM

Reply Contents

owner: WINDOW or **None**

Errors

Atom

Description

This request returns the current owner window of the specified selection, if any. If **None** is returned, then there is no owner for the selection.

Request Encoding

# of Bytes	Value	Description
1	23	opcode
1		unused
2	2	request length
4	ATOM	selection

Reply Encoding

# of Bytes	Value	Description
1	1	reply
1		unused
2	CARD16	sequence number
4	0	reply length
4	WINDOW	owner:
	0	**None**
20		unused

GetWindowAttributes

Name

GetWindowAttributes

Request Contents

window: WINDOW

Reply Contents

visual: VISUALID
class: {**InputOutput**, **InputOnly**}
bit-gravity: BITGRAVITY
win-gravity: WINGRAVITY
backing-store: {**NotUseful**, **WhenMapped**, **Always**}
backing-planes: CARD32
backing-pixel: CARD32
save-under: BOOL
colormap: COLORMAP or **None**
map-is-installed: BOOL
map-state: {**Unmapped**, **Unviewable**, **Viewable**}
all-event-masks, your-event-mask: SETofEVENT
do-not-propagate-mask: SETofDEVICEEVENT
override-redirect: BOOL

Errors

Window

Description

This request returns the current attributes of the window. A window is **Unviewable** if it is mapped but some ancestor is unmapped. All-event-masks is the inclusive-OR of all event masks selected on the window by clients. Your-event-mask is the event mask selected by the querying client.

Request Encoding

# of Bytes	Value	Description
1	3	opcode
1		unused
2	2	request length
4	WINDOW	window

Reply Encoding

# of Bytes	Value	Description
1	1	reply
1		backing-store:
	0	**NotUseful**
	1	**WhenMapped**
	2	**Always**
2	CARD16	sequence number
4	3	reply length
4	VISUALID	visual
2		class:
	1	**InputOutput**
	2	**InputOnly**
1	BITGRAVITY	bit-gravity
1	WINGRAVITY	win-gravity
4	CARD32	backing-planes
4	CARD32	backing-pixel
1	BOOL	save-under
1	BOOL	map-is-installed
1		map-state:
	0	**Unmapped**
	1	**Unviewable**
	2	**Viewable**
1	BOOL	override-redirect
4	COLORMAP	colormap:
	0	**None**
4	SETofEVENT	all-event-masks
4	SETofEVENT	your-event-mask
2	SETofDEVICEEVENT	do-not-propagate-mask
2		unused

Name

GrabButton

Request Contents

modifiers: SETofKEYMASK or **AnyModifier**
button: BUTTON or **AnyButton**
grab-window: WINDOW
owner-events: BOOL
event-mask: SETofPOINTEREVENT
pointer-mode, *keyboard-mode*: {**Synchronous**, **Asynchronous**}
confine-to: WINDOW or **None**
cursor: CURSOR or **None**

Errors

Cursor, **Window**, **Value**, **Access**

Description

This request establishes a passive grab. In the future, the pointer is actively grabbed as
described in **GrabPointer**, the last-pointer-grab time is set to the time at which the button was
pressed (as transmitted in the **ButtonPress** event), and the **ButtonPress** event is reported if all
of the following conditions are true:

- The pointer is not grabbed and the specified button is logically pressed when the specified modifier keys are logically down, and no other buttons or modifier keys are logically
  down.

- The grab-window contains the pointer.

- The confine-to window (if any) is viewable.

- A passive grab on the same button/key combination does not exist on any ancestor of
  grab-window.

The interpretation of the remaining arguments is the same as for **GrabPointer**. The active
grab is terminated automatically when the logical state of the pointer has all buttons released,
independent of the logical state of modifier keys. Note that the logical state of a device (as
seen by means of the protocol) may lag the physical state if device event processing is frozen.

This request overrides all previous passive grabs by the same client on the same button/key
combinations on the same window. A modifier of **AnyModifier** is equivalent to issuing the
request for all possible modifier combinations (including the combination of no modifiers). It is
not required that all specified modifiers have currently assigned keycodes. A button of **Any-
Button** is equivalent to issuing the request for all possible buttons. Otherwise, it is not required
that the button specified currently be assigned to a physical button.

An **Access** error is generated if some other client has already issued a **GrabButton** request
with the same button/key combination on the same window. When using **AnyModifier** or

AnyButton, the request fails completely (no grabs are established), and an **Access** error is generated if there is a conflicting grab for any combination. The request has no effect on an active grab.

Request Encoding

# of Bytes	Value	Description
1	28	opcode
1	BOOL	owner-events
2	6	request length
4	WINDOW	grab-window
2	SETofPOINTEREVENT	event-mask
1		pointer-mode:
	0	**Synchronous**
	1	**Asynchronous**
1		keyboard-mode:
	0	**Synchronous**
	1	**Asynchronous**
4	WINDOW	confine-to:
	0	**None**
4	CURSOR	cursor:
	0	**None**
1	BUTTON	button:
	0	**AnyButton**
1		unused
2	SETofKEYMASK	modifiers:
	#x8000	**AnyModifier**

Name
GrabKey

Request Contents
key: KEYCODE or **AnyKey**
modifiers: SETofKEYMASK or **AnyModifier**
grab-window: WINDOW
owner-events: BOOL
pointer-mode, *keyboard-mode*: { **Synchronous**, **Asynchronous** }

Errors
Window, **Value**, **Access**

Description
This request establishes a passive grab on the keyboard. In the future, the keyboard is actively grabbed as described in **GrabKeyboard**, the last-keyboard-grab time is set to the time at which the key was pressed (as transmitted in the **KeyPress** event), and the **KeyPress** event is reported if all of the following conditions are true:

- The keyboard is not grabbed and the specified key (which can itself be a modifier key) is logically pressed when the specified modifier keys are logically down, and no other modifier keys are logically down.

- Either the grab-window is an ancestor of (or is) the focus window or the grab-window is a descendent of the focus window and contains the pointer.

- A passive grab on the same key combination does not exist on any ancestor of grab-window.

The interpretation of the remaining arguments is the same as for **GrabKeyboard**. The active grab is terminated automatically when the logical state of the keyboard has the specified key released, independent of the logical state of modifier keys. Note that the logical state of a device (as seen by means of the protocol) may lag the physical state if device event processing is frozen.

This request overrides all previous passive grabs by the same client on the same key combinations on the same window. A modifier of **AnyModifier** is equivalent to issuing the request for all possible modifier combinations (including the combination of no modifiers). It is not required that all modifiers specified have currently assigned keycodes. A key of **AnyKey** is equivalent to issuing the request for all possible keycodes. Otherwise, the key must be in the range specified by min-keycode and max-keycode in the connection setup (or a **Value** error results).

An **Access** error is generated if some other client has issued a **GrabKey** with the same key combination on the same window. When using **AnyModifier** or **AnyKey**, the request fails completely (no grabs are established), and an **Access** error is generated if there is a conflicting grab for any combination.

Request Encoding

# of Bytes	Value	Description
1	33	opcode
1	BOOL	owner-events
2	4	request length
4	WINDOW	grab-window
2	SETofKEYMASK	modifiers:
	#x8000	**AnyModifier**
1	KEYCODE	key:
	0	**AnyKey**
1		pointer-mode:
	0	**Synchronous**
	1	**Asynchronous**
1		keyboard-mode:
	0	**Synchronous**
	1	**Asynchronous**
3		unused

GrabKeyboard

Name
GrabKeyboard

Request Contents
grab-window: WINDOW
owner-events: BOOL
pointer-mode, *keyboard-mode*: {**Synchronous**, **Asynchronous**}
time: TIMESTAMP or **CurrentTime**

Reply Contents
status: {**Success**, **AlreadyGrabbed**, **Frozen**, **InvalidTime**, **NotViewable**}

Errors
Window, **Value**

Description
This request actively grabs control of the keyboard. Further key events are reported only to the grabbing client. This request overrides any active keyboard grab by this client.

If owner-events is **False**, all generated key events are reported with respect to grab-window. If owner-events is **True** and if a generated key event would normally be reported to this client, it is reported normally. Otherwise, the event is reported with respect to the grab-window. Both **KeyPress** and **KeyRelease** events are always reported, independent of any event selection made by the client.

If keyboard-mode is **Asynchronous**, keyboard event processing continues normally. If the keyboard is currently frozen by this client, then processing of keyboard events is resumed. If keyboard-mode is **Synchronous**, the state of the keyboard (as seen by means of the protocol) appears to freeze. No further keyboard events are generated by the server until the grabbing client issues a releasing **AllowEvents** request or until the keyboard grab is released. Actual keyboard changes are not lost while the keyboard is frozen. They are simply queued for later processing.

If pointer-mode is **Asynchronous**, pointer event processing is unaffected by activation of the grab. If pointer-mode is **Synchronous**, the state of the pointer (as seen by means of the protocol) appears to freeze. No further pointer events are generated by the server until the grabbing client issues a releasing **AllowEvents** request or until the keyboard grab is released. Actual pointer changes are not lost while the pointer is frozen. They are simply queued for later processing.

This request generates **FocusIn** and **FocusOut** events.

The request fails with status **AlreadyGrabbed** if the keyboard is actively grabbed by some other client. The request fails with status **Frozen** if the keyboard is frozen by an active grab of another client. The request fails with status **NotViewable** if grab-window is not viewable. The request fails with status **InvalidTime** if the specified time is earlier than the last-keyboard-grab time or later than the current server time. Otherwise, the last-keyboard-grab time is set to the specified time with **CurrentTime** replaced by the current server time.

Request Encoding

# of Bytes	Value	Description
1	31	opcode
1	BOOL	owner-events
2	4	request length
4	WINDOW	grab-window
4	TIMESTAMP	time:
	0	**CurrentTime**
1		pointer-mode:
	0	**Synchronous**
	1	**Asynchronous**
1		keyboard-mode:
	0	**Synchronous**
	1	**Asynchronous**
2		unused

Reply Encoding

# of Bytes	Value	Description
1	1	reply
1		status:
	0	**Success**
	1	**AlreadyGrabbed**
	2	**InvalidTime**
	3	**NotViewable**
	4	**Frozen**
2	CARD16	sequence number
4	0	reply length
24		unused

GrabPointer

Name
GrabPointer

Request Contents
grab-window: WINDOW
owner-events: BOOL
event-mask: SETofPOINTEREVENT
pointer-mode, *keyboard-mode*: {**Synchronous**, **Asynchronous**}
confine-to: WINDOW or **None**
cursor: CURSOR or **None**
time: TIMESTAMP or **CurrentTime**

Reply Contents
status: {**Success**, **AlreadyGrabbed**, **Frozen**, **InvalidTime**, **NotViewable**}

Errors
Cursor, **Window**, **Value**

Description
This request actively grabs control of the pointer. Further pointer events are only reported to the grabbing client. The request overrides any active pointer grab by this client.

If owner-events is **False**, all generated pointer events are reported with respect to grab-window and are only reported if selected by event-mask. If owner-events is **True** and a generated pointer event would normally be reported to this client, it is reported normally. Otherwise, the event is reported with respect to the grab-window and is only reported if selected by event-mask. For either value of owner-events, unreported events are simply discarded.

If pointer-mode is **Asynchronous**, pointer event processing continues normally. If the pointer is currently frozen by this client, then processing of pointer events is resumed. If pointer-mode is **Synchronous**, the state of the pointer (as seen by means of the protocol) appears to freeze, and no further pointer events are generated by the server until the grabbing client issues a releasing **AllowEvents** request or until the pointer grab is released. Actual pointer changes are not lost while the pointer is frozen. They are simply queued for later processing.

If keyboard-mode is **Asynchronous**, keyboard event processing is unaffected by activation of the grab. If keyboard-mode is **Synchronous**, the state of the keyboard (as seen by means of the protocol) appears to freeze, and no further keyboard events are generated by the server until the grabbing client issues a releasing **AllowEvents** request or until the pointer grab is released. Actual keyboard changes are not lost while the keyboard is frozen. They are simply queued for later processing.

If a cursor is specified, then it is displayed regardless of what window the pointer is in. If no cursor is specified, then when the pointer is in grab-window or one of its subwindows, the normal cursor for that window is displayed. Otherwise, the cursor for grab-window is displayed.

If a confine-to window is specified, then the pointer will be restricted to stay contained in that window. The confine-to window need have no relationship to the grab-window. If the pointer is not initially in the confine-to window, then it is warped automatically to the closest edge (and enter/leave events are generated normally) just before the grab activates. If the confine-to window is subsequently reconfigured, the pointer will be warped automatically as necessary to keep it contained in the window.

This request generates **EnterNotify** and **LeaveNotify** events.

The request fails with status **AlreadyGrabbed** if the pointer is actively grabbed by some other client. The request fails with status **Frozen** if the pointer is frozen by an active grab of another client. The request fails with status **NotViewable** if grab-window or confine-to window is not viewable or if the confine-to window lies completely outside the boundaries of the root window. The request fails with status **InvalidTime** if the specified time is earlier than the last-pointer-grab time or later than the current server time. Otherwise, the last-pointer-grab time is set to the specified time, with **CurrentTime** replaced by the current server time.

Request Encoding

# of Bytes	Value	Description
1	26	opcode
1	BOOL	owner-events
2	6	request length
4	WINDOW	grab-window
2	SETofPOINTEREVENT	event-mask
1		pointer-mode:
	0	**Synchronous**
	1	**Asynchronous**
1		keyboard-mode:
	0	**Synchronous**
	1	**Asynchronous**
4	WINDOW	confine-to:
	0	**None**
4	CURSOR	cursor:
	0	**None**
4	TIMESTAMP	time:
	0	**CurrentTime**

Reply Encoding

# of Bytes	Value	Description
1	1	reply
1		status:
	0	**Success**
	1	**AlreadyGrabbed**
	2	**InvalidTime**

# of Bytes	Value	Description
	3	**NotViewable**
	4	**Frozen**
2	CARD16	sequence number
4	0	reply length
24		unused

GrabServer

Name

GrabServer

Request Contents

Opcode and request length only.

Errors

This request has no errors.

Description

This request disables processing of requests and close-downs on all connections other than the one this request arrived on.

Request Encoding

# of Bytes	Value	Description
1	36	opcode
1		unused
2	1	request length

GraphicsExpose

Name
GraphicsExpose

Event Contents
drawable: DRAWABLE
x, y, width, height: CARD16
count: CARD16
major-opcode: CARD8
minor-opcode: CARD16

Description
This event is reported to clients selecting graphics-exposures in a graphics context and is generated when a destination region could not be computed due to an obscured or out-of-bounds source region. All of the regions exposed by a given graphics request are guaranteed to be reported contiguously. If count is zero, then no more **GraphicsExpose** events for this window follow. If count is nonzero, then at least that many more **GraphicsExpose** events for this window follow (and possibly more).

The x and y coordinates are relative to drawable's origin and specify the upper-left corner of a rectangle. The width and height specify the extent of the rectangle.

The major and minor opcodes identify the graphics request used. For the core protocol, major-opcode is always **CopyArea** or **CopyPlane**, and minor-opcode is always zero.

Request Encoding

# of Bytes	Value	Description
1	13	code
1		unused
2	CARD16	sequence number
4	DRAWABLE	drawable
2	CARD16	x
2	CARD16	y
2	CARD16	width
2	CARD16	height
2	CARD16	minor-opcode
2	CARD16	count
1	CARD8	major-opcode
11		unused

GravityNotify

Name
GravityNotify

Event Contents
event, *window*: WINDOW
x, *y*: INT16

Description
This event is reported to clients selecting **SubstructureNotify** on the parent and to clients selecting **StructureNotify** on the window. It is generated when a window is moved because of a change in size of the parent. The event is the window on which the event was generated, and the window is the window that is moved. The x and y coordinates are relative to the new parent's origin and specify the position of the upper-left outer corner of the window.

Request Encoding

# of Bytes	Value	Description
1	24	code
1		unused
2	CARD16	sequence number
4	WINDOW	event
4	WINDOW	window
2	INT16	x
2	INT16	y
16		unused

Name
ImageText8

Request Contents
drawable: DRAWABLE
gc: GCONTEXT
x, y: INT16
string: STRING8

Errors
Drawable, GContext, Match

Description
The x and y coordinates are relative to the drawable's origin and specify the baseline starting position (the initial character origin). The effect is first to fill a destination rectangle with the background pixel defined in gc and then to paint the text with the foreground pixel. The upper-left corner of the filled rectangle is at:

```
[x,y - font-ascent]
```

the width is:

```
overall-width
```

and the height is:

```
font-ascent + font-descent
```

The overall-width, font-ascent, and font-descent are as they would be returned by a **Query-TextExtents** call using gc and string.

The function and fill-style defined in gc are ignored for this request. The effective function is **Copy**, and the effective fill-style **Solid**.

For fonts defined with 2-byte matrix indexing, each STRING8 byte is interpreted as a byte2 value of a CHAR2B with a byte1 value of zero.

GC components: plane-mask, foreground, background, font, subwindow-mode, clip-x-origin, clip-y-origin, clip-mask

Request Encoding

# of Bytes	Value	Description
1	76	opcode
1	n	length of string
2	4+(n+p)/4	request length
4	DRAWABLE	drawable
4	GCONTEXT	gc

# of Bytes	Value	Description
2	INT16	x
2	INT16	y
n	STRING8	string
p		unused, p=pad(n)

Name
ImageText16

Request Contents
drawable: DRAWABLE
gc: GCONTEXT
x, y: INT16
string: STRING16

Errors
Drawable, **GContext**, **Match**

Description
This request is similar to **ImageText8**, except 2-byte (or 16-bit) characters are used. For fonts defined with linear indexing rather than 2-byte matrix indexing, the server will interpret each CHAR2B as a 16-bit number that has been transmitted most-significant byte first (that is, byte1 of the CHAR2B is taken as the most-significant byte).

Request Encoding

# of Bytes	Value	Description
1	77	opcode
1	n	number of CHAR2Bs in string
2	4+(2n+p)/4	request length
4	DRAWABLE	drawable
4	GCONTEXT	gc
2	INT16	x
2	INT16	y
2n	STRING16	string
p		unused, p=pad(2n)

InstallColormap

Name

InstallColormap

Request Contents

cmap: COLORMAP

Errors

Colormap

Description

This request makes this colormap an installed map for its screen. All windows associated with this colormap immediately display with true colors. As a side effect, additional colormaps might be implicitly installed or uninstalled by the server. Which other colormaps get installed or uninstalled is server-dependent except that the required list must remain installed.

If cmap is not already an installed map, a **ColormapNotify** event is generated on every window having cmap as an attribute. In addition, for every other colormap that is installed or uninstalled as a result of the request, a **ColormapNotify** event is generated on every window having that colormap as an attribute.

At any time, there is a subset of the installed maps that are viewed as an ordered list and are called the required list. The length of the required list is at most M, where M is the min-installed-maps specified for the screen in the connection setup. The required list is maintained as follows. When a colormap is an explicit argument to **InstallColormap**, it is added to the head of the list; the list is truncated at the tail, if necessary, to keep the length of the list to at most M. When a colormap is an explicit argument to **UninstallColormap** and it is in the required list, it is removed from the list. A colormap is not added to the required list when it is installed implicitly by the server, and the server cannot implicitly uninstall a colormap that is in the required list.

Initially the default colormap for a screen is installed (but is not in the required list).

Request Encoding

# of Bytes	Value	Description
1	81	opcode
1		unused
2	2	request length
4	COLORMAP	cmap

Name
InternAtom

Request Contents
name : STRING8
only-if-exists : BOOL

Reply Contents
atom: ATOM or **None**

Errors
Value, **Alloc**

Description
This request returns the atom for the given name. If only-if-exists is **False**, then the atom is created if it does not exist. The string should use the ISO Latin-1 encoding. Upper case and lower case matter.

The lifetime of an atom is not tied to the interning client. Atoms remained defined until server reset (see Appendix A, *Connection Close*).

Request Encoding

# of Bytes	Value	Description
1	16	opcode
1	BOOL	only-if-exists
2	2+(n+p)/4	request length
2	n	length of name
2		unused
n	STRING8	name
p		unused, p=pad(n)

Reply Encoding

# of Bytes	Value	Description
1	1	reply
1		unused
2	CARD16	sequence number
4	0	reply length

# of Bytes	Value	Description
4	ATOM 0	atom: **None**
20		unused

Name

KeymapNotify

Event Contents

keys: LISTofCARD8

Description

The value is a bit vector as described in **QueryKeymap**. This event is reported to clients selecting **KeymapState** on a window and is generated immediately after every **EnterNotify** and **FocusIn**.

Request Encoding

# of Bytes	Value	Description
1	11	code
31	LISTofCARD8	keys (byte for keycodes 0-7 is omitted)

KeyPress

Name

KeyPress

Event Contents

root, *event* : WINDOW
child : WINDOW or **None**
same-screen : BOOL
root-x, *root-y*, *event-x*, *event-y* : INT16
detail : (See Description.)
state : SETofKEYBUTMASK
time : TIMESTAMP

(Same contents as **MotionNotify** .)

Description

KeyPress events are sent by the server to the client when the user presses a keyboard key. Only clients selecting **KeyPress** events will receive them. The window member of this event depends on which window the pointer is in when the button is pressed and on the values of the event-mask and do-not-propagate field for that window and its ancestors.

For more information, see **MotionNotify** .

Request Encoding

# of Bytes	Value	Description
1	2	code
1	KEYCODE	detail
2	CARD16	sequence number
4	TIMESTAMP	time
4	WINDOW	root
4	WINDOW	event
4	WINDOW	child:
	0	**None**
2	INT16	root-x
2	INT16	root-y
2	INT16	event-x
2	INT16	event-y
2	SETofKEYBUTMASK	state
1	BOOL	same-screen
1		unused

Name

KeyRelease

Event Contents

root, *event* : WINDOW
child : WINDOW or **None**
same-screen : BOOL
root-x, *root-y*, *event-x*, *event-y* : INT16
detail : (See Description.)
state : SETofKEYBUTMASK
time : TIMESTAMP

(Same contents as **MotionNotify** .)

Description

KeyRelease events are sent by the server to the client when the user presses a keyboard key. Only clients selecting **KeyRelease** events will receive them. The window member of this event depends on which window the pointer is in when the button is released and on the values of the event-mask and do-not-propagate field for that window and its ancestors.

For more information, see **MotionNotify** .

Request Encoding

# of Bytes	Value	Description
1	3	code
1	KEYCODE	detail
2	CARD16	sequence number
4	TIMESTAMP	time
4	WINDOW	root
4	WINDOW	event
4	WINDOW	child:
	0	**None**
2	INT16	root-x
2	INT16	root-y
2	INT16	event-x
2	INT16	event-y
2	SETofKEYBUTMASK	state
1	BOOL	same-screen
1		unused

KillClient

Name
KillClient

Request Contents
resource: CARD32 or **AllTemporary**

Errors
Value

Description
If a valid resource is specified, **KillClient** forces a close-down of the client that created the resource. If the client has already terminated in either **RetainPermanent** mode or **Retain-Temporary** mode, all of the client's resources are destroyed (see Appendix A, *Connection Close*). If **AllTemporary** is specified, then the resources of all clients that have terminated in **RetainTemporary** are destroyed.

Request Encoding

# of Bytes	Value	Description
1	113	opcode
1		unused
2	2	request length
4	CARD32	resource:
	0	**AllTemporary**

Name
LeaveNotify

Event Contents
root, *event*: WINDOW
child: WINDOW or **None**
same-screen: BOOL
root-x, *root-y*, *event-x*, *event-y*: INT16
mode: {**Normal**, **Grab**, **Ungrab**}
detail: {**Ancestor**, **Virtual**, **Inferior**, **Nonlinear**, **NonlinearVirtual**}
focus: BOOL
state: SETofKEYBUTMASK
time: TIMESTAMP

Description
If pointer motion or window hierarchy change causes the pointer to be in a different window than before, **EnterNotify** and **LeaveNotify** events are generated instead of a **MotionNotify** event. Only clients selecting **EnterWindow** on a window receive **EnterNotify** events, and only clients selecting **LeaveNotify** receive **LeaveNotify** events. The pointer position reported in the event is always the final position, not the initial position of the pointer. The root is the root window for this position, and root-x and root-y are the pointer coordinates relative to root's origin at the time of the event. Event is the event window. If the event window is on the same screen as root, then event-x and event-y are the pointer coordinates relative to the event window's origin. Otherwise, event-x and event-y are zero. In a **LeaveNotify** event, if a child of the event window contains the initial position of the pointer, then the child component is set to that child. Otherwise, it is **None**. For an **EnterNotify** event, if a child of the event window contains the final pointer position, then the child component is set to that child. Otherwise, it is **None**. If the event window is the focus window or an inferior of the focus window, then focus is **True**. Otherwise, focus is **False**.

Normal pointer motion events have mode **Normal**. Pseudo-motion events when a grab activates have mode **Grab**, and pseudo-motion events when a grab deactivates have mode **Ungrab**.

All **EnterNotify** and **LeaveNotify** events caused by a hierarchy change are generated after any hierarchy event caused by that change (that is, **UnmapNotify**, **MapNotify**, **ConfigureNotify**, **GravityNotify**, **CirculateNotify**), but the ordering of **EnterNotify** and **LeaveNotify** events with respect to **FocusOut**, **VisibilityNotify**, and **Expose** events is not constrained.

Normal events are generated as follows.

When the pointer moves from window A to window B and A is an inferior of B:

• **LeaveNotify** with detail **Ancestor** is generated on A.

- **LeaveNotify** with detail **Virtual** is generated on each window between A and B exclusive (in that order).

- **EnterNotify** with detail **Inferior** is generated on B.

When the pointer moves from window A to window B and B is an inferior of A:

- **LeaveNotify** with detail **Inferior** is generated on A.

- **EnterNotify** with detail **Virtual** is generated on each window between A and B exclusive (in that order).

- **EnterNotify** with detail **Ancestor** is generated on B.

When the pointer moves from window A to window B and window C is their least common ancestor:

- **LeaveNotify** with detail **Nonlinear** is generated on A.

- **LeaveNotify** with detail **NonlinearVirtual** is generated on each window between A and C exclusive (in that order).

- **EnterNotify** with detail **NonlinearVirtual** is generated on each window between C and B exclusive (in that order).

- **EnterNotify** with detail **Nonlinear** is generated on B.

When the pointer moves from window A to window B on different screens:

- **LeaveNotify** with detail **Nonlinear** is generated on A.

- If A is not a root window, **LeaveNotify** with detail **NonlinearVirtual** is generated on each window above A up to and including its root (in order).

- If B is not a root window, **EnterNotify** with detail **NonlinearVirtual** is generated on each window from B's root down to but not including B (in order).

- **EnterNotify** with detail **Nonlinear** is generated on B.

When a pointer grab activates (but after any initial warp into a confine-to window and before generating any actual **ButtonPress** event that activates the grab), G is the grab-window for the grab, and P is the window the pointer is in:

- **EnterNotify** and **LeaveNotify** events with mode **Grab** are generated (as for **Normal** above) as if the pointer were to suddenly warp from its current position in P to some position in G. However, the pointer does not warp, and the pointer position is used as both the initial and final positions for the events.

When a pointer grab deactivates (but after generating any actual **ButtonRelease** event that deactivates the grab), G is the grab-window for the grab, and P is the window the pointer is in:

- **EnterNotify** and **LeaveNotify** events with mode **Ungrab** are generated (as for **Normal** above) as if the pointer were to suddenly warp from some position in G to its current position in P. However, the pointer does not warp, and the current pointer position is used as both the initial and final positions for the events.

Request Encoding

# of Bytes	Value	Description
1	8	code
1		detail:
	0	**Ancestor**
	1	**Virtual**
	2	**Inferior**
	3	**Nonlinear**
	4	**NonlinearVirtual**
2	CARD16	sequence number
4	TIMESTAMP	time
4	WINDOW	root
4	WINDOW	event
4	WINDOW	child:
	0	**None**
2	INT16	root-x
2	INT16	root-y
2	INT16	event-x
2	INT16	event-y
2	SETofKEYBUTMASK	state
1		mode:
	0	**Normal**
	1	**Grab**
	2	**Ungrab**
1		same-screen, focus:
	#x01	focus (1 is True, 0 is False)
	#x02	same-screen (1 is True, 0 is False)
	#xfc	unused

ListExtensions

Name

ListExtensions

Request Contents

Opcode and request length only.

Reply Contents

names: LISTofSTRING8

Errors

This request has no errors.

Description

This request returns a list of all extensions supported by the server.

Request Encoding

# of Bytes	Value	Description
1	99	opcode
1		unused
2	1	request length

Reply Encoding

# of Bytes	Value	Description
1	1	reply
1	CARD8	number of STRs in names
2	CARD16	sequence number
4	(n+p)/4	reply length
24		unused
n	LISTofSTR	names
p		unused, p=pad(n)

ListFonts

Name

ListFonts

Request Contents

pattern: STRING8
max-names: CARD16

Reply Contents

names: LISTofSTRING8

Errors

This request has no errors.

Description

This request returns a list of available font names (as controlled by the font search path; see **SetFontPath** request) that match the pattern. At most, max-names names will be returned. The pattern should use the ISO Latin-1 encoding, and upper case and lower case do not matter. In the pattern, the "?" character (octal value 77) will match any single character, and the "*" character (octal value 52) will match any number of characters. The returned names are in lower case.

Request Encoding

# of Bytes	Value	Description
1	49	opcode
1		unused
2	2+(n+p)/4	request length
2	CARD16	max-names
2	n	length of pattern
n	STRING8	pattern
p		unused, p=pad(n)

Reply Encoding

# of Bytes	Value	Description
1	1	reply
1		unused
2	CARD16	sequence number
4	(n+p)/4	reply length
2	CARD16	number of STRs in names

# of Bytes	Value	Description
22		unused
n	LISTofSTR	names
p		unused, p=pad(n)

Name

ListFontsWithInfo

Request Contents

pattern: STRING8
max-names: CARD16

Reply Contents

name: STRING8
info: FONTINFO
replies-hint: CARD32

where:

FONTINFO: [draw-direction: {**LeftToRight**, **RightToLeft**}
min-char-or-byte2, max-char-or-byte2: CARD16
min-byte1, max-byte1: CARD8
all-chars-exist: BOOL
default-char: CARD16
min-bounds: CHARINFO
max-bounds: CHARINFO
font-ascent: INT16
font-descent: INT16
properties: LISTofFONTPROP]

Errors

This request has no errors.

Description

This request is similar to **ListFonts**, but it also returns information about each font. The information returned for each font is identical to what **QueryFont** would return except that the per-character metrics are not returned. Note that this request can generate multiple replies. With each reply, replies-hint may provide an indication of how many more fonts will be returned. This number is a hint only and may be larger or smaller than the number of fonts actually returned. A zero value does not guarantee that no more fonts will be returned. After the font replies, a reply with a zero-length name is sent to indicate the end of the reply sequence.

This request has one reply for each font queried (and it is the only request with multiple replies).

Request Encoding

# of Bytes	Value	Description
1	50	opcode
1		unused
2	2+(n+p)/4	request length

# of Bytes	Value	Description
2	CARD16	max-names
2	n	length of pattern
n	STRING8	pattern
p		unused, p=pad(n)

Reply Encoding (except for last in series)

# of Bytes	Value	Description
1	1	reply
1	n	length of name in bytes
2	CARD16	sequence number
4	7+2m+(n+p)/4	reply length
12	CHARINFO	min-bounds
4		unused
12	CHARINFO	max-bounds
4		unused
2	CARD16	min-char-or-byte2
2	CARD16	max-char-or-byte2
2	CARD16	default-char
2	m	number of FONTPROPs in properties
1		draw-direction:
	0	**LeftToRight**
	1	**RightToLeft**
1	CARD8	min-byte1
1	CARD8	max-byte1
1	BOOL	all-chars-exist
2	INT16	font-ascent
2	INT16	font-descent
4	CARD32	replies-hint
8m	LISTofFONTPROP	properties
n	STRING8	name
p		unused, p=pad(n)

LISTofFONTPROP is *n* repetitions of the encoding for FONTPROP shown in the table below:

# of Bytes	Value	Description
4	ATOM	name
4		value

The encoding for CHARINFO is shown in the table below:

# of Bytes	Value	Description
2	INT16	left-side-bearing
2	INT16	right-side-bearing
2	INT16	character-width
2	INT16	ascent
2	INT16	descent
2	CARD16	attributes

Reply Encoding (last in series)

# of Bytes	Value	Description
1	1	reply
1	0	last-reply indicator
2	CARD16	sequence number
4	7	reply length
52		unused

ListHosts

Name

ListHosts

Request Contents

Opcode and request length only.

Reply Contents

mode: { **Enabled**, **Disabled** }
hosts: LISTofHOST

Errors

This request has no errors.

Description

This request returns the hosts on the access control list and states whether use of the list at connection setup is currently enabled or disabled.

Each HOST is padded to a multiple of four bytes.

Request Encoding

# of Bytes	Value	Description
1	110	opcode
1		unused
2	1	request length

Reply Encoding

# of Bytes	Value	Description
1	1	reply
1		mode:
	0	**Disabled**
	1	**Enabled**
2	CARD16	sequence number
4	n/4	reply length
2	CARD16	number of HOSTs in hosts
22		unused
n	LISTofHOST	hosts
		(n always a multiple of 4)

ListInstalledColormaps

Name

ListInstalledColormaps

Request Contents

window : WINDOW

Reply Contents

cmaps: LISTofCOLORMAP

Errors

Window

Description

This request returns a list of the currently installed colormaps for the screen of the specified window. The order of colormaps is not significant, and there is no explicit indication of the required list (see **InstallColormap** request).

Request Encoding

# of Bytes	Value	Description
1	83	opcode
1		unused
2	2	request length
4	WINDOW	window

Reply Encoding

# of Bytes	Value	Description
1	1	reply
1		unused
2	CARD16	sequence number
4	n	reply length
2	n	number of COLORMAPs in cmaps
22		unused
4n	LISTofCOLORMAP	cmaps

ListProperties

Name
ListProperties

Request Contents
window: WINDOW

Reply Contents
atoms: LISTofATOM

Errors
Window

Description
This request returns the atoms of properties currently defined on the window.

Request Encoding

# of Bytes	Value	Description
1	21	opcode
1		unused
2	2	request length
4	WINDOW	window

Reply Encoding

# of Bytes	Value	Description
1	1	reply
1		unused
2	CARD16	sequence number
4	n	reply length
2	n	number of ATOMs in atoms
22		unused
4n	LISTofATOM	atoms

LookupColor

Name

LookupColor

Request Contents

cmap: COLORMAP
name: STRING8

Reply Contents

exact-red, exact-green, exact-blue: CARD16
visual-red, visual-green, visual-blue: CARD16

Errors

Colormap , Name

Description

This request looks up the string name of a color with respect to the screen associated with cmap
and returns both the exact color values and the closest values provided by the hardware with
respect to the visual type of cmap. The name should use the ISO Latin-1 encoding, and upper
case and lower case do not matter.

Request Encoding

# of Bytes	Value	Description
1	92	opcode
1		unused
2	3+(n+p)/4	request length
4	COLORMAP	cmap
2	n	length of name
2		unused
n	STRING8	name
p		unused, p=pad(n)

Reply Encoding

# of Bytes	Value	Description
1	1	reply
1		unused
2	CARD16	sequence number
4	0	reply length
2	CARD16	exact-red
2	CARD16	exact-green
2	CARD16	exact-blue

# of Bytes	Value	Description
2	CARD16	visual-red
2	CARD16	visual-green
2	CARD16	visual-blue
12		unused

MapNotify

Name

MapNotify

Event Contents

event, *window*: WINDOW
override-redirect: BOOL

Description

This event is reported to clients selecting **StructureNotify** on the window and to clients selecting **SubstructureNotify** on the parent. It is generated when the window changes state from unmapped to mapped. The event is the window on which the event was generated, and the window is the window that is mapped. The override-redirect flag is from the window's attribute.

Request Encoding

# of Bytes	Value	Description
1	19	code
1		unused
2	CARD16	sequence number
4	WINDOW	event
4	WINDOW	window
1	BOOL	override-redirect
19		unused

MappingNotify

Name

MappingNotify

Event Contents

request: {**Modifier**, **Keyboard**, **Pointer**}
first-keycode, *count*: CARD8

Description

This event is sent to all clients. There is no mechanism to express disinterest in this event. The detail indicates the kind of change that occurred: **Modifiers** for a successful **SetModifier-Mapping**, **Keyboard** for a successful **ChangeKeyboardMapping**, and **Pointer** for a successful **SetPointerMapping**. If the detail is **Keyboard**, then first-keycode and count indicate the range of altered keycodes.

Request Encoding

# of Bytes	Value	Description
1	34	code
1		unused
2	CARD16	sequence number
1		request:
	0	**Modifier**
	1	**Keyboard**
	2	**Pointer**
1	KEYCODE	first-keycode
1	CARD8	count
25		unused

Name

MapRequest

Event Contents

parent, *window*: WINDOW

Description

This event is reported to the client selecting **SubstructureRedirect** on the parent and is generated when a **MapWindow** request is issued on an unmapped window with an override-redirect attribute of **False**.

Request Encoding

# of Bytes	Value	Description
1	20	code
1		unused
2	CARD16	sequence number
4	WINDOW	parent
4	WINDOW	window
20		unused

Name
MapSubwindows

Request Contents
window: WINDOW

Errors
Window

Description
This request performs a **MapWindow** request on all unmapped children of the window, in top-to-bottom stacking order.

Request Encoding

# of Bytes	Value	Description
1	9	opcode
1		unused
2	2	request length
4	WINDOW	window

MapWindow

Name
MapWindow

Request Contents
window: WINDOW

Errors
Window

Description
If the window is already mapped, this request has no effect.

If the override-redirect attribute of the window is **False** and some other client has selected **SubstructureRedirect** on the parent, then a **MapRequest** event is generated, but the window remains unmapped. Otherwise, the window is mapped, and a **MapNotify** event is generated.

If the window is now viewable and its contents have been discarded, the window is tiled with its background (if no background is defined, the existing screen contents are not altered), and zero or more exposure events are generated. If a backing-store has been maintained while the window was unmapped, no exposure events are generated. If a backing-store will now be maintained, a full-window exposure is always generated. Otherwise, only visible regions may be reported. Similar tiling and exposure take place for any newly viewable inferiors.

Request Encoding

# of Bytes	Value	Description
1	8	opcode
1		unused
2	2	request length
4	WINDOW	window

Name
MotionNotify

Event Contents
root, event: WINDOW
child: WINDOW or **None**
same-screen: BOOL
root-x, root-y, event-x, event-y: INT16
detail: (See Description.)
state: SETofKEYBUTMASK
time: TIMESTAMP

Description
ButtonPress, **ButtonRelease**, **KeyPress**, **KeyRelease**, and **MotionNotify** are generated either when a key or button logically changes state or when the pointer logically moves. The generation of these logical changes may lag the physical changes if device event processing is frozen. Note that **KeyPress** and **KeyRelease** are generated for all keys, even those mapped to modifier bits. The source of the event is the window the pointer is in. The window the event is reported with respect to is called the event window. The event window is found by starting with the source window and looking up the hierarchy for the first window on which any client has selected interest in the event (provided no intervening window prohibits event generation by including the event type in its do-not-propagate-mask). The actual window used for reporting can be modified by active grabs and, in the case of keyboard events, can be modified by the focus window.

The root is the root window of the source window, and root-x and root-y are the pointer coordinates relative to root's origin at the time of the event. Event is the event window. If the event window is on the same screen as root, then event-x and event-y are the pointer coordinates relative to the event window's origin. Otherwise, event-x and event-y are zero. If the source window is an inferior of the event window, then child is set to the child of the event window that is an ancestor of (or is) the source window. Otherwise, it is set to **None**. The state component gives the logical state of the buttons and modifier keys just before the event. The detail component type varies with the event type:

Event	Component
KeyPress, **KeyRelease**	KEYCODE
ButtonPress, **ButtonRelease**	BUTTON
MotionNotify	{**Normal**, **Hint**}

MotionNotify events are only generated when the motion begins and ends in the window. The granularity of motion events is not guaranteed, but a client selecting for motion events is guaranteed to get at least one event when the pointer moves and comes to rest. Selecting **PointerMotion** receives events independent of the state of the pointer buttons. By selecting some subset of **Button[1-5]Motion** instead, **MotionNotify** events will only be received when one or more of the specified buttons are pressed. By selecting **ButtonMotion**, **MotionNotify** events will be received only when at least one button is pressed. The events are always of type **MotionNotify**, independent of the selection. If **PointerMotionHint** is selected, the server is free to send only one **MotionNotify** event (with detail **Hint**) to the client for the event window until either the key or the button state changes, the pointer leaves the event window, or the client issues a **QueryPointer** or **GetMotionEvents** request.

Request Encoding

# of Bytes	Value	Description
1	6	code
1		detail:
	0	**Normal**
	1	**Hint**
2	CARD16	sequence number
4	TIMESTAMP	time
4	WINDOW	root
4	WINDOW	event
4	WINDOW	child:
	0	**None**
2	INT16	root-x
2	INT16	root-y
2	INT16	event-x
2	INT16	event-y
2	SETofKEYBUTMASK	state
1	BOOL	same-screen
1		unused

NoExpose

Name
NoExpose

Event Contents
drawable: DRAWABLE
major-opcode: CARD8
minor-opcode: CARD16

Description
This event is reported to clients selecting graphics-exposures in a graphics context and is generated when a graphics request that might produce **GraphicsExpose** events does not produce any. The drawable specifies the destination used for the graphics request.

The major and minor opcodes identify the graphics request used. For the core protocol, major-opcode is always **CopyArea** or **CopyPlane**, and the minor-opcode is always zero.

Request Encoding

# of Bytes	Value	Description
1	14	code
1		unused
2	CARD16	sequence number
4	DRAWABLE	drawable
2	CARD16	minor-opcode
1	CARD8	major-opcode
21		unused

Name

NoOperation

Request Contents

Opcode and request length only.

Errors

This request has no errors.

Description

This request has no arguments and no results, but the request length field can be nonzero, which allows the request to be any multiple of four bytes in length. The bytes contained in the request are uninterpreted by the server.

This request can be used in its minimum four-byte form as padding where necessary by client libraries that find it convenient to force requests to begin on 64-bit boundaries.

Request Encoding

# of Bytes	Value	Description
1	127	opcode
1		unused
2	1	request length

OpenFont

Name
  OpenFont

Request Contents
  fid: FONT
  name: STRING8

Errors
  IDChoice, **Name**, **Alloc**

Description
This request loads the specified font, if necessary, and associates identifier fid with it. The font name should use the ISO Latin-1 encoding, and upper case and lower case do not matter.

Fonts are not associated with a particular screen and can be stored as a component of any graphics context.

Request Encoding

# of Bytes	Value	Description
1	45	opcode
1		unused
2	3+(n+p)/4	request length
4	FONT	fid
2	n	length of name
2		unused
n	STRING8	name
p		unused, p=pad(n)

Name

PolyArc

Request Contents

drawable: DRAWABLE
gc: GCONTEXT
arcs: LISTofARC

Errors

Drawable, **GContext**, **Match**

Description

This request draws circular or elliptical arcs. Each arc is specified by a rectangle and two angles. The angles are signed integers in degrees scaled by 64, with positive indicating counterclockwise motion and negative indicating clockwise motion. The start of the arc is specified by angle1 relative to the three-o'clock position from the center of the rectangle, and the path and extent of the arc is specified by angle2 relative to the start of the arc. If the magnitude of angle2 is greater than 360 degrees, it is truncated to 360 degrees. The x and y coordinates of the rectangle are relative to the origin of the drawable. For an arc specified as [x,y,w,h,a1,a2], the origin of the major and minor axes is at [x+(w/2),y+(h/2)], and the infinitely thin path describing the entire circle/ellipse intersects the horizontal axis at [x,y+(h/2)] and [x+w,y+(h/2)] and intersects the vertical axis at [x+(w/2),y] and [x+(w/2),y+h]. These coordinates can be fractional; that is, they are not truncated to discrete coordinates. The path should be defined by the ideal mathematical path. For a wide line with line-width lw, the bounding outlines for filling are given by the two infinitely thin paths consisting of all points whose perpendicular distance from the path of the circle/ellipse is equal to lw/2 (which may be a fractional value). The cap-style and join-style are applied the same as for a line corresponding to the tangent of the circle/ellipse at the endpoint.

For an arc specified as [x,y,w,h,a1,a2], the angles must be specified in the effectively skewed coordinate system of the ellipse (for a circle, the angles and coordinate systems are identical). The relationship between these angles and angles expressed in the normal coordinate system of the screen (as measured with a protractor) is as follows:

```
skewed-angle = atan (tan (normal-angle) * w / h) + adjust
```

The skewed-angle and normal-angle are expressed in radians (rather than in degrees scaled by 64) in the range [0,2*PI]. The atan returns a value in the range [–PI/2,PI/2]. The adjust is:

0	for normal-angle in the range [0,PI/2]
PI	for normal-angle in the range [PI/2,(3*PI)/2]
2*PI	for normal-angle in the range [(3*PI)/2,2*PI]

The arcs are drawn in the order listed. If the last point in one arc coincides with the first point in the following arc, the two arcs will join correctly. If the first point in the first arc coincides with the last point in the last arc, the two arcs will join correctly. For any given arc, no pixel is drawn more than once. If two arcs join correctly and the line-width is greater than zero and the arcs intersect, no pixel is drawn more than once. Otherwise, the intersecting pixels of intersecting arcs are drawn multiple times. Specifying an arc with one endpoint and a clockwise extent draws the same pixels as specifying the other endpoint and an equivalent counterclockwise extent, except as it affects joins.

By specifying one axis to be zero, a horizontal or vertical line can be drawn.

Angles are computed based solely on the coordinate system, ignoring the aspect ratio.

GC components: function, plane-mask, line-width, line-style, cap-style, join-style, fill-style, subwindow-mode, clip-x-origin, clip-y-origin, clip-mask

GC mode-dependent components: foreground, background, tile, stipple, tile-stipple-x-origin, tile-stipple-y-origin, dash-offset, dashes

Request Encoding

# of Bytes	Value	Description
1	68	opcode
1		unused
2	3+3n	request length
4	DRAWABLE	drawable
4	GCONTEXT	gc
12n	LISTofARC	arcs

PolyFillArc

Name
PolyFillArc

Request Contents
drawable : DRAWABLE
gc : GCONTEXT
arcs : LISTofARC

Errors
Drawable , **GContext** , **Match**

Description
For each arc, this request fills the region closed by the infinitely thin path described by the specified arc and one or two line segments, depending on the arc-mode. For **Chord** , the single line segment joining the endpoints of the arc is used. For **PieSlice** , the two line segments joining the endpoints of the arc with the center point are used. The arcs are as specified in the **PolyArc** request.

The arcs are filled in the order listed. For any given arc, no pixel is drawn more than once. If regions intersect, the intersecting pixels are drawn multiple times.

GC components: function, plane-mask, fill-style, arc-mode, subwindow-mode, clip-x-origin, clip-y-origin, clip-mask

GC mode-dependent components: foreground, background, tile, stipple, tile-stipple-x-origin, tile-stipple-y-origin

Request Encoding

# of Bytes	Value	Description
1	71	opcode
1		unused
2	3+3n	request length
4	DRAWABLE	drawable
4	GCONTEXT	gc
12n	LISTofARC	arcs

PolyFillRectangle

Name

PolyFillRectangle

Request Contents

drawable: DRAWABLE
gc: GCONTEXT
rectangles: LISTofRECTANGLE

Errors

Drawable, **GContext**, **Match**

Description

This request fills the specified rectangles, as if a four-point **FillPoly** were specified for each rectangle:

```
[x,y] [x+width,y] [x+width,y+height] [x,y+height]
```

The x and y coordinates of each rectangle are relative to the drawable's origin and define the upper-left corner of the rectangle.

The rectangles are drawn in the order listed. For any given rectangle, no pixel is drawn more than once. If rectangles intersect, the intersecting pixels are drawn multiple times.

GC components: function, plane-mask, fill-style, subwindow-mode, clip-x-origin, clip-y-origin, clip-mask

GC mode-dependent components: foreground, background, tile, stipple, tile-stipple-x-origin, tile-stipple-y-origin

Request Encoding

# of Bytes	Value	Description
1	70	opcode
1		unused
2	3+2n	request length
4	DRAWABLE	drawable
4	GCONTEXT	gc
8n	LISTofRECTANGLE	rectangles

PolyLine

Name
PolyLine

Request Contents
drawable: DRAWABLE
gc: GCONTEXT
coordinate-mode: { **Origin**, **Previous** }
points: LISTofPOINT

Errors
Drawable, **GContext**, **Value**, **Match**

Description
This request draws lines between each pair of points (point[i],point[i+1]). The lines are drawn in the order listed. The lines join correctly at all intermediate points, and if the first and last points coincide, the first and last lines also join correctly.

For any given line, no pixel is drawn more than once. If thin (zero line-width) lines intersect, the intersecting pixels are drawn multiple times. If wide lines intersect, the intersecting pixels are drawn only once, as though the entire **PolyLine** were a single filled shape.

The first point is always relative to the drawable's origin. The rest are relative either to that origin or to the previous point, depending on the coordinate-mode.

GC components: function, plane-mask, line-width, line-style, cap-style, join-style, fill-style, subwindow-mode, clip-x-origin, clip-y-origin, clip-mask

GC mode-dependent components: foreground, background, tile, stipple, tile-stipple-x-origin, tile-stipple-y-origin, dash-offset, dashes

Request Encoding

# of Bytes	Value	Description
1	65	opcode
1		coordinate-mode:
	0	**Origin**
	1	**Previous**
2	3+n	request length
4	DRAWABLE	drawable
4	GCONTEXT	gc
4n	LISTofPOINT	points

PolyPoint

Name
PolyPoint

Request Contents
drawable: DRAWABLE
gc: GCONTEXT
coordinate-mode: { **Origin**, **Previous** }
points: LISTofPOINT

Errors
Drawable, **GContext**, **Value**, **Match**

Description
This request combines the foreground pixel in gc with the pixel at each point in the drawable. The points are drawn in the order listed.

The first point is always relative to the drawable's origin. The rest are relative either to that origin or to the previous point, depending on the coordinate-mode.

GC components: function, plane-mask, foreground, subwindow-mode, clip-x-origin, clip-y-origin, clip-mask

Request Encoding

# of Bytes	Value	Description
1	64	opcode
1		coordinate-mode:
	0	**Origin**
	1	**Previous**
2	3+n	request length
4	DRAWABLE	drawable
4	GCONTEXT	gc
4n	LISTofPOINT	points

PolyRectangle

Name

PolyRectangle

Request Contents

drawable: DRAWABLE
gc: GCONTEXT
rectangles: LISTofRECTANGLE

Errors

Drawable, **GContext**, **Match**

Description

This request draws the outlines of the specified rectangles, as if a five-point **PolyLine** were specified for each rectangle:

```
[x,y] [x+width,y] [x+width,y+height] [x,y+height] [x,y]
```

The x and y coordinates of each rectangle are relative to the drawable's origin and define the upper-left corner of the rectangle.

The rectangles are drawn in the order listed. For any given rectangle, no pixel is drawn more than once. If rectangles intersect, the intersecting pixels are drawn multiple times.

GC components: function, plane-mask, line-width, line-style, join-style, fill-style, subwindow-mode, clip-x-origin, clip-y-origin, clip-mask

GC mode-dependent components: foreground, background, tile, stipple, tile-stipple-x-origin, tile-stipple-y-origin, dash-offset, dashes

Request Encoding

# of Bytes	Value	Description
1	67	opcode
1		unused
2	3+2n	request length
4	DRAWABLE	drawable
4	GCONTEXT	gc
8n	LISTofRECTANGLE	rectangles

PolySegment

Name
PolySegment

Request Contents
drawable: DRAWABLE
gc: GCONTEXT
segments: LISTofSEGMENT

where:

SEGMENT: [x1, y1, x2, y2: INT16]

Errors
Drawable, **GContext**, **Match**

Description
For each segment, this request draws a line between [x1,y1] and [x2,y2]. The lines are drawn in the order listed. No joining is performed at coincident endpoints. For any given line, no pixel is drawn more than once. If lines intersect, the intersecting pixels are drawn multiple times.

GC components: function, plane-mask, line-width, line-style, cap-style, fill-style, subwindow-mode, clip-x-origin, clip-y-origin, clip-mask

GC mode-dependent components: foreground, background, tile, stipple, tile-stipple-x-origin, tile-stipple-y-origin, dash-offset, dashes

Request Encoding

# of Bytes	Value	Description
1	66	opcode
1		unused
2	3+2n	request length
4	DRAWABLE	drawable
4	GCONTEXT	gc
8n	LISTofSEGMENT	segments

LISTofSEGMENT is *n* repetitions of the encoding for SEGMENT shown in the table below:

# of Bytes	Value	Description
2	INT16	x1
2	INT16	y1
2	INT16	x2
2	INT16	y2

Name
PolyText8

Request Contents
drawable: DRAWABLE
gc: GCONTEXT
x, y: INT16
items: LISTofTEXTITEM8

where:

TEXTITEM8:	TEXTELT8 or FONT
TEXTELT8:	[delta: INT8
	string: STRING8]

Errors
Drawable, GContext, Match, Font

Description
The x and y coordinates are relative to the drawable's origin and specify the baseline starting position (the initial character origin). Each text item is processed in turn. A font item causes the font to be stored in gc and to be used for subsequent text. Switching among fonts does not affect the next character origin. A text element delta specifies an additional change in the position along the x axis before the string is drawn; the delta is always added to the character origin. Each character image, as defined by the font in gc, is treated as an additional mask for a fill operation on the drawable.

All contained FONTs are always transmitted most-significant byte first.

If a **Font** error is generated for an item, the previous items may have been drawn.

For fonts defined with 2-byte matrix indexing, each STRING8 byte is interpreted as a byte2 value of a CHAR2B with a byte1 value of zero.

GC components: function, plane-mask, fill-style, font, subwindow-mode, clip-x-origin, clip-y-origin, clip-mask

GC mode-dependent components: foreground, background, tile, stipple, tile-stipple-x-origin, tile-stipple-y-origin

Request Encoding

# of Bytes	Value	Description
1	74	opcode
1		unused
2	4+(n+p)/4	request length
4	DRAWABLE	drawable
4	GCONTEXT	gc

# of Bytes	Value	Description
2	INT16	x
2	INT16	y
n	LISTofTEXTITEM8	items
p		unused, p=pad(n)
		(p is always 0 or 1)

LISTofTEXTITEM8 is *n* repetitions of the encoding for TEXTITEM8 shown in the tables below:

# of Bytes	Value	Description
1	n	length of string (cannot be 255)
1	INT8	delta
n	STRING8	string

or:

# of Bytes	Value	Description
1	255	font-shift indicator
1		font byte 3 (most-significant)
1		font byte 2
1		font byte 1
1		font byte 0 (least-significant)

PolyText16

Name
PolyText16

Request Contents
drawable: DRAWABLE
gc: GCONTEXT
x, y: INT16
items: LISTofTEXTITEM16

where:

TEXTITEM16:	TEXTELT16 or FONT
TEXTELT16:	[delta: INT8
	string: STRING16]

Errors
Drawable, GContext, Match, Font

Description
This request is similar to **PolyText8**, except 2-byte (or 16-bit) characters are used. For fonts defined with linear indexing rather than 2-byte matrix indexing, the server will interpret each CHAR2B as a 16-bit number that has been transmitted most-significant byte first (that is, byte1 of the CHAR2B is taken as the most-significant byte).

Request Encoding

# of Bytes	Value	Description
1	75	opcode
1		unused
2	4+(n+p)/4	request length
4	DRAWABLE	drawable
4	GCONTEXT	gc
2	INT16	x
2	INT16	y
n	LISTofTEXTITEM16	items
p		unused, p=pad(n) (p is always 0 or 1)

LISTofTEXTITEM16 is *n* repetitions of the encoding for TEXTITEM16 shown in the tables below:

# of Bytes	Value	Description
1	n	number of CHAR2Bs in string (cannot be 255)

# of Bytes	Value	Description
1	INT8	delta
n	STRING16	string

or:

# of Bytes	Value	Description
1	255	font-shift indicator
1		font byte 3 (most-significant)
1		font byte 2
1		font byte 1
1		font byte 0 (least-significant)

Name
PropertyNotify

Event Contents
window: WINDOW
atom: ATOM
state: { **NewValue**, **Deleted** }
time: TIMESTAMP

Description
This event is reported to clients selecting **PropertyChange** on the window and is generated with state **NewValue** when a property of the window is changed using **ChangeProperty** or **RotateProperties**, even when adding zero-length data using **ChangeProperty** and when replacing all or part of a property with identical data using **ChangeProperty** or **Rotate-Properties**. It is generated with state **Deleted** when a property of the window is deleted using request **DeleteProperty** or **GetProperty**. The timestamp indicates the server time when the property was changed.

Request Encoding

# of Bytes	Value	Description
1	28	code
1		unused
2	CARD16	sequence number
4	WINDOW	window
4	ATOM	atom
4	TIMESTAMP	time
1		state:
	0	**NewValue**
	1	**Deleted**
15		unused

PutImage

Name
PutImage

Request Contents
drawable: DRAWABLE
gc: GCONTEXT
depth: CARD8
width, *height*: CARD16
dst-x, *dst-y*: INT16
left-pad: CARD8
format: {**Bitmap**, **XYPixmap**, **ZPixmap**}
data: LISTofBYTE

Errors
Drawable, **GContext**, **Match**, **Value**

Description
This request combines an image with a rectangle of the drawable. The dst-x and dst-y coordinates are relative to the drawable's origin.

If **Bitmap** format is used, then depth must be one (or a **Match** error results), and the image must be in XY format. The foreground pixel in gc defines the source for bits set to 1 in the image, and the background pixel defines the source for the bits set to 0.

For **XYPixmap** and **ZPixmap**, the depth must match the depth of the drawable (or a **Match** error results). For **XYPixmap**, the image must be sent in XY format. For **ZPixmap**, the image must be sent in the Z format defined for the given depth.

The left-pad must be zero for **ZPixmap** format (or a **Match** error results). For **Bitmap** and **XYPixmap** format, left-pad must be less than bitmap-scanline-pad as given in the server connection setup information (or a **Match** error results). The first left-pad bits in every scanline are to be ignored by the server. The actual image begins that many bits into the data. The width argument defines the width of the actual image and does not include left-pad.

GC components: function, plane-mask, subwindow-mode, clip-x-origin, clip-y-origin, clip-mask

GC mode-dependent components: foreground, background

Request Encoding

# of Bytes	Value	Description
1	72	opcode
1		format:
	0	**Bitmap**
	1	**XYPixmap**
	2	**ZPixmap**

# of Bytes	Value	Description
2	6+(n+p)/4	request length
4	DRAWABLE	drawable
4	GCONTEXT	gc
2	CARD16	width
2	CARD16	height
2	INT16	dst-x
2	INT16	dst-y
1	CARD8	left-pad
1	CARD8	depth
2		unused
n	LISTofBYTE	data
p		unused, p=pad(n)

QueryBestSize

Name

QueryBestSize

Request Contents

class: { **Cursor** , **Tile** , **Stipple** }
drawable : DRAWABLE
width , *height* : CARD16

Reply Contents

width, height: CARD16

Errors

Drawable , **Value** , **Match**

Description

This request returns the best size that is closest to the argument size. For **Cursor** , this is the largest size that can be fully displayed. For **Tile** , this is the size that can be tiled fastest. For **Stipple** , this is the size that can be stippled fastest.

For **Cursor** , the drawable indicates the desired screen. For **Tile** and **Stipple** , the drawable indicates the screen and also possibly the window class and depth. An **InputOnly** window cannot be used as the drawable for **Tile** or **Stipple** (or a **Match** error results).

Request Encoding

# of Bytes	Value	Description
1	97	opcode
1		class:
	0	**Cursor**
	1	**Tile**
	2	**Stipple**
2	3	request length
4	DRAWABLE	drawable
2	CARD16	width
2	CARD16	height

Reply Encoding

# of Bytes	Value	Description
1	1	reply
1		unused
2	CARD16	sequence number
4	0	reply length

# of Bytes	Value	Description
2	CARD16	width
2	CARD16	height
20		unused

QueryColors

Name
QueryColors

Request Contents
cmap: COLORMAP
pixels: LISTofCARD32

Reply Contents
colors: LISTofRGB

where:

RGB: [red, green, blue: CARD16]

Errors
Colormap, **Value**

Description
This request returns the color values stored in cmap for the specified pixels. The values returned for an unallocated entry are undefined. A **Value** error is generated if a pixel is not a valid index into cmap. If more than one pixel is in error, it is arbitrary as to which pixel is reported.

Request Encoding

# of Bytes	Value	Description
1	91	opcode
1		unused
2	2+n	request length
4	COLORMAP	cmap
4n	LISTofCARD32	pixels

Reply Encoding

# of Bytes	Value	Description
1	1	reply
1		unused
2	CARD16	sequence number
4	2n	reply length
2	n	number of RGBs in colors
22		unused
8n	LISTofRGB	colors

LISTofRGB is *n* repetitions of the encoding for RGB shown in the table below:

# of Bytes	Value	Description
2	CARD16	red
2	CARD16	green
2	CARD16	blue
2		unused

Name
QueryExtension

Request Contents
name: STRING8

Reply Contents
present: BOOL
major-opcode: CARD8
first-event: CARD8
first-error: CARD8

Errors
This request has no errors.

Description
This request determines if the named extension is present. If so, the major opcode for the extension is returned, if it has one. Otherwise, zero is returned. Any minor opcode and the request formats are specific to the extension. If the extension involves additional event types, the base event type code is returned. Otherwise, zero is returned. The format of the events is specific to the extension. If the extension involves additional error codes, the base error code is returned. Otherwise, zero is returned. The format of additional data in the errors is specific to the extension.

The extension name should use the ISO Latin-1 encoding, and upper case and lower case matter.

Request Encoding

# of Bytes	Value	Description
1	98	opcode
1		unused
2	2+(n+p)/4	request length
2	n	length of name
2		unused
n	STRING8	name
p		unused, p=pad(n)

Reply Encoding

# of Bytes	Value	Description
1	1	reply
1		unused
2	CARD16	sequence number

# of Bytes	Value	Description
4	0	reply length
1	BOOL	present
1	CARD8	major-opcode
1	CARD8	first-event
1	CARD8	first-error
20		unused

QueryFont

Name

   QueryFont

Request Contents

   font: FONTABLE

Reply Contents

   font-info: FONTINFO
   char-infos: LISTofCHARINFO

   where:

FONTINFO:	[draw-direction: {**LeftToRight**, **RightToLeft**}
	min-char-or-byte2, max-char-or-byte2: CARD16
	min-byte1, max-byte1: CARD8
	all-chars-exist: BOOL
	default-char: CARD16
	min-bounds: CHARINFO
	max-bounds: CHARINFO
	font-ascent: INT16
	font-descent: INT16
	properties: LISTofFONTPROP]
FONTPROP:	[name: ATOM
	value: 32-bit value]
CHARINFO:	[left-side-bearing: INT16
	right-side-bearing: INT16
	character-width: INT16
	ascent: INT16
	descent: INT16
	attributes: CARD16]

Errors

   Font

Description

   This request returns logical information about a font. If a gcontext is given for font, the currently contained font is used.

   The draw-direction is just a hint and indicates whether most char-infos have a positive, **Left-ToRight**, or a negative, **RightToLeft**, character-width metric. The core protocol defines no support for vertical text.

   If min-byte1 and max-byte1 are both zero, then min-char-or-byte2 specifies the linear character index corresponding to the first element of char-infos, and max-char-or-byte2 specifies the linear character index of the last element. If either min-byte1 or max-byte1 are nonzero, then both min-char-or-byte2 and max-char-or-byte2 will be less than 256 and the 2-byte character index values corresponding to char-infos element N (counting from 0) are:

```
byte1 = N/D + min-byte1
byte2 = N\D + min-char-or-byte2
```

where:

D	=	max-char-or-byte2 − min-char-or-byte2 + 1
/	=	integer division
\	=	integer modulus

If char-infos has length zero, then min-bounds and max-bounds will be identical, and the effective char-infos is one filled with this char-info, of length:

```
L = D * (max-byte1 − min-byte1 + 1)
```

That is, all glyphs in the specified linear or matrix range have the same information, as given by min-bounds (and max-bounds). If all-chars-exist is **True**, then all characters in char-infos have nonzero bounding boxes.

The default-char specifies the character that will be used when an undefined or nonexistent character is used. Note that default-char is a CARD16, not CHAR2B. For a font using 2-byte matrix format, the default-char has byte1 in the most-significant byte and byte2 in the least-significant byte. If the default-char itself specifies an undefined or nonexistent character, then no printing is performed for an undefined or nonexistent character.

The min-bounds and max-bounds contain the minimum and maximum values of each individual CHARINFO component over all char-infos (ignoring nonexistent characters). The bounding box of the font (that is, the smallest rectangle enclosing the shape obtained by superimposing all characters at the same origin [x,y]) has its upper-left coordinate at:

```
[x+min-bounds.left-side-bearing,y-max-bounds.ascent]
```

with a width of:

```
max-bounds.right-side-bearing − min-bounds.left-side-bearing
```

and a height of:

```
max-bounds.ascent + max-bounds.descent
```

The font-ascent is the logical extent of the font above the baseline and is used for determining line spacing. Specific characters may extend beyond this. The font-descent is the logical extent of the font at or below the baseline and is used for determining line spacing. Specific characters may extend beyond this. If the baseline is at Y-coordinate y, then the logical extent of the font is inclusive between the Y-coordinate values (y-font-ascent) and (y+font-descent-1).

A font is not guaranteed to have any properties. The interpretation of the property value (for example, INT32, CARD32) must be derived from a prior knowledge of the property. When possible, fonts should have at least the following properties (note that upper case and lower case matter).

Property	Type	Description
MIN_SPACE	CARD32	The minimum interword spacing, in pixels.
NORM_SPACE	CARD32	The normal interword spacing, in pixels.
MAX_SPACE	CARD32	The maximum interword spacing, in pixels.
END_SPACE	CARD32	The additional spacing at the end of sentences, in pixels.
SUPERSCRIPT_X SUPERSCRIPT_Y	INT32	Offsets from the character origin where superscripts should begin, in pixels. If the origin is at [x,y], then superscripts should begin at: [x + SUPERSCRIPT_X, y − SUPERSCRIPT_Y]
SUBSCRIPT_X SUBSCRIPT_Y	INT32	Offsets from the character origin where subscripts should begin, in pixels. If the origin is at [x,y], then subscripts should begin at: [x + SUBSCRIPT_X, y + SUBSCRIPT_Y]
UNDERLINE_POSITION	INT32	Y offset from the baseline to the top of an underline, in pixels. If the baseline is Y-coordinate y, then the top of the underline is at: (y + UNDERLINE_POSITION)
UNDERLINE_THICKNESS	CARD32	Thickness of the underline, in pixels.
STRIKEOUT_ASCENT STRIKEOUT_DESCENT	INT32	Vertical extents for boxing or voiding characters, in pixels. If the baseline is at Y-coordinate y, then the top of the strikeout box is at: (y − STRIKEOUT_ASCENT) and the height of the box is: (STRIKEOUT_ASCENT + STRIKEOUT_DESCENT)
ITALIC_ANGLE	INT32	The angle of the dominant staffs of characters in the font, in degrees scaled by 64, relative to the three-o'clock position from the character origin, with positive indicating counterclockwise motion (as in Arc requests).
X_HEIGHT	INT32	1 ex as in TeX, but expressed in units of pixels. Often the height of lower case x.
QUAD_WIDTH	INT32	1 em as in TeX, but expressed in units of pixels. Often the width of the digits 0-9.
CAP_HEIGHT	INT32	Y offset from the baseline to the top of the capital letters, ignoring accents, in pixels. If the baseline is at Y-coordinate y, then the top of the capitals is at: (y − CAP_HEIGHT)

Property	Type	Description
WEIGHT	CARD32	The weight or boldness of the font, expressed as a value between 0 and 1000.
POINT_SIZE	CARD32	The point size, expressed in 1/10, of this font at the ideal resolution.
RESOLUTION	CARD32	The number of pixels per point, expressed in 1/100, at which this font was created.

For a character origin at [x,y], the bounding box of a character (that is, the smallest rectangle enclosing the character's shape), described in terms of CHARINFO components, is a rectangle with its upper-left corner at:

```
[x+left-side-bearing,y-ascent]
```

with a width of:

```
right-side-bearing - left-side-bearing
```

and a height of:

```
ascent + descent
```

and the origin for the next character is defined to be:

```
[x+character-width,y]
```

Note that the baseline is logically viewed as being just below nondescending characters (when descent is zero, only pixels with Y-coordinates less than y are drawn) and that the origin is logically viewed as being coincident with the left edge of a nonkerned character (when left-side-bearing is zero, no pixels with X-coordinate less than x are drawn).

Note that CHARINFO metric values can be negative.

A nonexistent character is represented with all CHARINFO components zero.

The interpretation of the per-character attributes field is server-dependent.

Request Encoding

# of Bytes	Value	Description
1	47	opcode
1		unused
2	2	request length
4	FONTABLE	font

Reply Encoding

# of Bytes	Value	Description
1	1	reply
1		unused
2	CARD16	sequence number
4	7+2n+3m	reply length
12	CHARINFO	min-bounds
4		unused
12	CHARINFO	max-bounds
4		unused
2	CARD16	min-char-or-byte2
2	CARD16	max-char-or-byte2
2	CARD16	default-char
2	n	number of FONTPROPs in properties
1		draw-direction:
	0	**LeftToRight**
	1	**RightToLeft**
1	CARD8	min-byte1
1	CARD8	max-byte1
1	BOOL	all-chars-exist
2	INT16	font-ascent
2	INT16	font-descent
4	m	number of CHARINFOs in char-infos
8n	LISTofFONTPROP	properties
12m	LISTofCHARINFO	char-infos

LISTofFONTPROP is *n* repetitions of the encoding for FONTPROP shown in the table below:

# of Bytes	Value	Description
4	ATOM	name
4		value

LISTofCHARINFO is *n* repetitions of the encoding for CHARINFO shown in the table below:

# of Bytes	Value	Description
2	INT16	left-side-bearing
2	INT16	right-side-bearing
2	INT16	character-width
2	INT16	ascent
2	INT16	descent
2	CARD16	attributes

QueryKeymap

Name
QueryKeymap

Request Contents
Opcode and request length only.

Reply Contents
keys: LISTofCARD8

Errors
This request has no errors.

Description
This request returns a bit vector for the logical state of the keyboard. Each bit set to 1 indicates that the corresponding key is currently pressed. The vector is represented as 32 bytes. Byte N (from 0) contains the bits for keys 8N to 8N+7 with the least-significant bit in the byte representing key 8N. Note that the logical state of a device (as seen by means of the protocol) may lag the physical state if device event processing is frozen.

Request Encoding

# of Bytes	Value	Description
1	44	opcode
1		unused
2	1	request length

Reply Encoding

# of Bytes	Value	Description
1	1	reply
1		unused
2	CARD16	sequence number
4	2	reply length
32	LISTofCARD8	keys

QueryPointer

Name
QueryPointer

Request Contents
window: WINDOW

Reply Contents
root: WINDOW
child: WINDOW or **None**
same-screen: BOOL
root-x, root-y, win-x, win-y: INT16
mask: SETofKEYBUTMASK

Errors
Window

Description
The root window the pointer is logically on and the pointer coordinates relative to the root's origin are returned. If same-screen is **False**, then the pointer is not on the same screen as the argument window, child is **None**, and win-x and win-y are zero. If same-screen is **True**, then win-x and win-y are the pointer coordinates relative to the argument window's origin, and child is the child containing the pointer, if any. The current logical state of the modifier keys and the buttons are also returned. Note that the logical state of a device (as seen by means of the protocol) may lag the physical state if device event processing is frozen.

Request Encoding

# of Bytes	Value	Description
1	38	opcode
1		unused
2	2	request length
4	WINDOW	window

Reply Encoding

# of Bytes	Value	Description
1	1	reply
1	BOOL	same-screen
2	CARD16	sequence number
4	0	reply length
4	WINDOW	root
4	WINDOW	child:
	0	**None**

# of Bytes	Value	Description
2	INT16	root-x
2	INT16	root-y
2	INT16	win-x
2	INT16	win-y
2	SETofKEYBUTMASK	mask
6		unused

Name

QueryTextExtents

Request Contents

font: FONTABLE
string: STRING16

Reply Contents

draw-direction: { **LeftToRight**, **RightToLeft** }
font-ascent: INT16
font-descent: INT16
overall-ascent: INT16
overall-descent: INT16
overall-width: INT32
overall-left: INT32
overall-right: INT32

Errors

Font

Description

This request returns the logical extents of the specified string of characters in the specified font. If a gcontext is given for font, the currently contained font is used. The draw-direction, font-ascent, and font-descent are the same as described in **QueryFont**. The overall-ascent is the maximum of the ascent metrics of all characters in the string, and the overall-descent is the maximum of the descent metrics. The overall-width is the sum of the character-width metrics of all characters in the string. For each character in the string, let W be the sum of the character-width metrics of all characters preceding it in the string, let L be the left-side-bearing metric of the character plus W, and let R be the right-side-bearing metric of the character plus W. The overall-left is the minimum L of all characters in the string, and the overall-right is the maximum R.

For fonts defined with linear indexing rather than 2-byte matrix indexing, the server will interpret each CHAR2B as a 16-bit number that has been transmitted most-significant byte first (that is, byte1 of the CHAR2B is taken as the most-significant byte).

If the font has no defined default-char, then undefined characters in the string are taken to have all zero metrics.

Request Encoding

# of Bytes	Value	Description
1	48	opcode
1	BOOL	odd length, True if p=2
2	2+(2n+p)/4	request length

# of Bytes	Value	Description
4	FONTABLE	font
2n	STRING16	string
p		unused, p=pad(2n)

Reply Encoding

# of Bytes	Value	Description
1	1	reply
1		draw-direction:
	0	**LeftToRight**
	1	**RightToLeft**
2	CARD16	sequence number
4	0	reply length
2	INT16	font-ascent
2	INT16	font-descent
2	INT16	overall-ascent
2	INT16	overall-descent
4	INT32	overall-width
4	INT32	overall-left
4	INT32	overall-right
4		unused

Name
QueryTree

Request Contents
window: WINDOW

Reply Contents
root: WINDOW
parent: WINDOW or **None**
children: LISTofWINDOW

Errors
Window

Description
This request returns the root, the parent, and the children of the window. The children are listed in bottom-to-top stacking order.

Request Encoding

# of Bytes	Value	Description
1	15	opcode
1		unused
2	2	request length
4	WINDOW	window

Reply Encoding

# of Bytes	Value	Description
1	1	reply
1		unused
2	CARD16	sequence number
4	n	reply length
4	WINDOW	root
4	WINDOW	parent:
	0	**None**
2	n	number of WINDOWs in children
14		unused
4n	LISTofWINDOW	children

RecolorCursor

Name

RecolorCursor

Request Contents

cursor: CURSOR
fore-red, fore-green, fore-blue: CARD16
back-red, back-green, back-blue: CARD16

Errors

Cursor

Description

This request changes the color of a cursor. If the cursor is being displayed on a screen, the change is visible immediately.

Request Encoding

# of Bytes	Value	Description
1	96	opcode
1		unused
2	5	request length
4	CURSOR	cursor
2	CARD16	fore-red
2	CARD16	fore-green
2	CARD16	fore-blue
2	CARD16	back-red
2	CARD16	back-green
2	CARD16	back-blue

ReparentNotify

Name

ReparentNotify

Event Contents

event, *window*, *parent*: WINDOW
x, *y*: INT16
override-redirect: BOOL

Description

This event is reported to clients selecting **SubstructureNotify** on either the old or the new parent and to clients selecting **StructureNotify** on the window. It is generated when the window is reparented. The event is the window on which the event was generated. The window is the window that has been rerooted. The parent specifies the new parent. The x and y coordinates are relative to the new parent's origin and specify the position of the upper-left outer corner of the window. The override-redirect flag is from the window's attribute.

Request Encoding

# of Bytes	Value	Description
1	21	code
1		unused
2	CARD16	sequence number
4	WINDOW	event
4	WINDOW	window
4	WINDOW	parent
2	INT16	x
2	INT16	y
1	BOOL	override-redirect
11		unused

ReparentWindow

Name
ReparentWindow

Request Contents
window, *parent*: WINDOW
x, *y*: INT16

Errors
Window, **Match**

Description
If the window is mapped, an **UnmapWindow** request is performed automatically first. The window is then removed from its current position in the hierarchy and is inserted as a child of the specified parent. The x and y coordinates are relative to the parent's origin and specify the new position of the upper-left outer corner of the window. The window is placed on top in the stacking order with respect to siblings. A **ReparentNotify** event is then generated. The override-redirect attribute of the window is passed on in this event; a value of **True** indicates that a window manager should not tamper with this window. Finally, if the window was originally mapped, a **MapWindow** request is performed automatically.

Normal exposure processing on formerly obscured windows is performed. The server might not generate exposure events for regions from the initial unmap that are immediately obscured by the final map.

A **Match** error is generated if:

- The new parent is not on the same screen as the old parent.

- The new parent is the window itself or an inferior of the window.

- The window has a **ParentRelative** background, and the new parent is not the same depth as the window.

Request Encoding

# of Bytes	Value	Description
1	7	opcode
1		unused
2	4	request length
4	WINDOW	window
4	WINDOW	parent
2	INT16	x
2	INT16	y

ResizeRequest

Name

ResizeRequest

Event Contents

window: WINDOW
width, *height*: CARD16

Description

This event is reported to the client selecting **ResizeRedirect** on the window and is generated when a **ConfigureWindow** request by some other client on the window attempts to change the size of the window. The width and height are the inside size, not including the border.

Request Encoding

# of Bytes	Value	Description
1	25	code
1		unused
2	CARD16	sequence number
4	WINDOW	window
2	CARD16	width
2	CARD16	height
20		unused

RotstateProperties

Name
RotateProperties

Request Contents
window: WINDOW
delta: INT16
properties: LISTofATOM

Errors
Window, **Atom**, **Match**

Description
If the property names in the list are viewed as being numbered starting from zero, and there are N property names in the list, then the value associated with property name I becomes the value associated with property name (I+delta)mod N, for all I from zero to N−1. The effect is to rotate the states by delta places around the virtual ring of property names (right for positive delta, left for negative delta).

If delta mod N is nonzero, a **PropertyNotify** event is generated for each property in the order listed.

If an atom occurs more than once in the list or no property with that name is defined for the window, a **Match** error is generated. If an **Atom** or a **Match** error is generated, no properties are changed.

Request Encoding

# of Bytes	Value	Description
1	114	opcode
1		unused
2	3+n	request length
4	WINDOW	window
2	n	number of properties
2	INT16	delta
4n	LISTofATOM	properties

Name
SelectionClear

Event Contents
owner: WINDOW
selection: ATOM
time: TIMESTAMP

Description
This event is reported to the current owner of a selection and is generated when a new owner is being defined by means of **SetSelectionOwner**. The timestamp is the last-change time recorded for the selection. The owner argument is the window that was specified by the current owner in its **SetSelectionOwner** request.

Request Encoding

# of Bytes	Value	Description
1	29	code
1		unused
2	CARD16	sequence number
4	TIMESTAMP	time
4	WINDOW	owner
4	ATOM	selection
16		unused

SelectionNotify

Name
SelectionNotify

Event Contents
requestor: WINDOW
selection, *target*: ATOM
property: ATOM or **None**
time: TIMESTAMP or **CurrentTime**

Description
This event is generated by the server in response to a **ConvertSelection** request when there is no owner for the selection. When there is an owner, it should be generated by the owner using **SendEvent**. The owner of a selection should send this event to a requestor either when a selection has been converted and stored as a property or when a selection conversion could not be performed (indicated with property **None**).

Request Encoding

# of Bytes	Value	Description
1	31	code
1		unused
2	CARD16	sequence number
4	TIMESTAMP 0	time: **CurrentTime**
4	WINDOW	requestor
4	ATOM	selection
4	ATOM	target
4	ATOM 0	property: **None**
8		unused

Name

SelectionRequest

Event Contents

owner: WINDOW
selection: ATOM
target: ATOM
property: ATOM or **None**
requestor: WINDOW
time: TIMESTAMP or **CurrentTime**

Description

This event is reported to the owner of a selection and is generated when a client issues a **ConvertSelection** request. The owner argument is the window that was specified in the **Set-SelectionOwner** request. The remaining arguments are as in the **ConvertSelection** request.

The owner should convert the selection based on the specified target type. If a property is specified, the owner should store the result as that property on the requestor window and then send a **SelectionNotify** event to the requestor using **SendEvent** with an empty event-mask (that is, the event should be sent to the creator of the requestor window). If **None** is specified as the property, the owner should choose a property name, store the result as that property on the requestor window, and then send a **SelectionNotify** giving that actual property name. If the selection cannot be converted as requested, the owner should send a **SelectionNotify** with the property set to **None**.

Request Encoding

# of Bytes	Value	Description
1	30	code
1		unused
2	CARD16	sequence number
4	TIMESTAMP	time:
	0	**CurrentTime**
4	WINDOW	owner
4	WINDOW	requestor
4	ATOM	selection
4	ATOM	target
4	ATOM	property:
	0	**None**
4		unused

SendEvent

Name

SendEvent

Request Contents

destination: WINDOW or **PointerWindow** or **InputFocus**
propagate: BOOL
event-mask: SETofEVENT
event: any event

Errors

Window, **Value**

Description

If **PointerWindow** is specified, destination is replaced with the window that the pointer is in. If **InputFocus** is specified and the focus window contains the pointer, destination is replaced with the window that the pointer is in. Otherwise, destination is replaced with the focus window.

If the event-mask is the empty set, then the event is sent to the client that created the destination window. If that client no longer exists, no event is sent.

If propagate is **False**, then the event is sent to every client selecting on destination any of the event types in event-mask.

If propagate is **True** and no clients have selected on destination any of the event types in event-mask, then destination is replaced with the closest ancestor of destination for which some client has selected a type in event-mask and no intervening window has that type in its do-not-propagate-mask. If no such window exists or if the window is an ancestor of the focus window and **InputFocus** was originally specified as the destination, then the event is not sent to any clients. Otherwise, the event is reported to every client selecting on the final destination any of the types specified in event-mask.

The event code must be one of the core events or one of the events defined by an extension (or a **Value** error results) so that the server can correctly byte-swap the contents as necessary. The contents of the event are otherwise unaltered and unchecked by the server except to force on the most-significant bit of the event code and to set the sequence number in the event correctly.

Active grabs are ignored for this request.

Request Encoding

# of Bytes	Value	Description
1	25	opcode
1	BOOL	propagate
2	11	request length
4	WINDOW	destination:
	0	**PointerWindow**
	1	**InputFocus**

# of Bytes	Value	Description
4	SETofEVENT	event-mask
32		standard event format

SetAccessControl

Name

SetAccessControl

Request Contents

mode: { **Enable** , **Disable** }

Errors

Value , **Access**

Description

This request enables or disables the use of the access control list at connection setups.

The client must reside on the same host as the server and/or have been granted permission by a server-dependent method to execute this request (or an **Access** error results).

Request Encoding

# of Bytes	Value	Description
1	111	opcode
1		mode:
	0	**Disable**
	1	**Enable**
2	1	request length

Name

SetClipRectangles

Request Contents

gc: GCONTEXT
clip-x-origin, *clip-y-origin*: INT16
rectangles: LISTofRECTANGLE
ordering: {**UnSorted**, **YSorted**, **YXSorted**, **YXBanded**}

Errors

GContext, **Value**, **Alloc**, **Match**

Description

This request changes clip-mask in gc to the specified list of rectangles and sets the clip origin. Output will be clipped to remain contained within the rectangles. The clip origin is interpreted relative to the origin of whatever destination drawable is specified in a graphics request. The rectangle coordinates are interpreted relative to the clip origin. The rectangles should be nonintersecting or graphics results will be undefined. Note that the list of rectangles can be empty, which effectively disables output. This is the opposite of passing **None** as the clip-mask in **CreateGC** and **ChangeGC**.

If known by the client, ordering relations on the rectangles can be specified with the ordering argument. This may provide faster operation by the server. If an incorrect ordering is specified, the server may generate a **Match** error, but it is not required to do so. If no error is generated, the graphics results are undefined. **UnSorted** means that the rectangles are in arbitrary order. **YSorted** means that the rectangles are nondecreasing in their Y origin. **YXSorted** additionally constrains **YSorted** order in that all rectangles with an equal Y origin are nondecreasing in their X origin. **YXBanded** additionally constrains **YXSorted** by requiring that, for every possible Y scanline, all rectangles that include that scanline have identical Y origins and Y extents.

Request Encoding

# of Bytes	Value	Description
1	59	opcode
1		ordering:
	0	**UnSorted**
	1	**YSorted**
	2	**YXSorted**
	3	**YXBanded**
2	3+2n	request length
4	GCONTEXT	gc

# of Bytes	Value	Description
2	INT16	clip-x-origin
2	INT16	clip-y-origin
8n	LISTofRECTANGLE	rectangles

SetCloseDownMode

Name

SetCloseDownMode

Request Contents

mode: { **Destroy**, **RetainPermanent**, **RetainTemporary** }

Errors

Value

Description

This request defines what will happen to the client's resources at connection close. A connection starts in **Destroy** mode. The meaning of the close-down mode is described in Appendix A, *Connection Close*.

Request Encoding

# of Bytes	Value	Description
1	112	opcode
1		mode:
	0	**Destroy**
	1	**RetainPermanent**
	2	**RetainTemporary**
2	1	request length

SetDashes

Name
SetDashes

Request Contents
gc: GCONTEXT
dash-offset: CARD16
dashes: LISTofCARD8

Errors
GContext, Value, Alloc

Description
This request sets dash-offset and dashes in gc for dashed line styles. Dashes cannot be empty (or a **Value** error results). Specifying an odd-length list is equivalent to specifying the same list concatenated with itself to produce an even-length list. The initial and alternating elements of dashes are the even dashes; the others are the odd dashes. Each element specifies a dash length in pixels. All of the elements must be nonzero (or a **Value** error results). The dash-offset defines the phase of the pattern, specifying how many pixels into dashes the pattern should actually begin in any single graphics request. Dashing is continuous through path elements combined with a join-style, but it is reset to the dash-offset each time a cap-style is applied at a line endpoint.

The unit of measure for dashes is the same as in the ordinary coordinate system. Ideally, a dash length is measured along the slope of the line, but implementations are only required to match this ideal for horizontal and vertical lines. Failing the ideal semantics, it is suggested that the length be measured along the major axis of the line. The major axis is defined as the x axis for lines drawn at an angle of between –45 and +45 degrees or between 315 and 225 degrees from the x axis. For all other lines, the major axis is the y axis.

Request Encoding

# of Bytes	Value	Description
1	58	opcode
1		unused
2	3+(n+p)/4	request length
4	GCONTEXT	gc
2	CARD16	dash-offset
2	n	length of dashes
n	LISTofCARD8	dashes
p		unused, p=pad(n)

SetFontPath

Name

SetFontPath

Request Contents

path: LISTofSTRING8

Errors

Value

Description

This request defines the search path for font lookup. There is only one search path per server, not one per client. The interpretation of the strings is operating-system-dependent, but the strings are intended to specify directories to be searched in the order listed.

Setting the path to the empty list restores the default path defined for the server.

As a side effect of executing this request, the server is guaranteed to flush all cached information about fonts for which there currently are no explicit resource IDs allocated.

The meaning of an error from this request is system specific.

Request Encoding

# of Bytes	Value	Description
1	51	opcode
1		unused
2	2+(n+p)/4	request length
2	CARD16	number of STRs in path
2		unused
n	LISTofSTR	path
p		unused, p=pad(n)

Name

SetInputFocus

Request Contents

focus: WINDOW or **PointerRoot** or **None**
revert-to: {**Parent**, **PointerRoot**, **None**}
time: TIMESTAMP or **CurrentTime**

Errors

Window, **Value**, **Match**

Description

This request changes the input focus and the last-focus-change time. The request has no effect if the specified time is earlier than the current last-focus-change time or is later than the current server time. Otherwise, the last-focus-change time is set to the specified time with **Current-Time** replaced by the current server time.

If **None** is specified as the focus, all keyboard events are discarded until a new focus window is set. In this case, the revert-to argument is ignored.

If a window is specified as the focus, it becomes the keyboard's focus window. If a generated keyboard event would normally be reported to this window or one of its inferiors, the event is reported normally. Otherwise, the event is reported with respect to the focus window.

If **PointerRoot** is specified as the focus, the focus window is dynamically taken to be the root window of whatever screen the pointer is on at each keyboard event. In this case, the revert-to argument is ignored.

This request generates **FocusIn** and **FocusOut** events.

The specified focus window must be viewable at the time of the request (or a **Match** error results). If the focus window later becomes not viewable, the new focus window depends on the revert-to argument. If revert-to is **Parent**, the focus reverts to the parent (or the closest viewable ancestor) and the new revert-to value is taken to be **None**. If revert-to is **Pointer-Root** or **None**, the focus reverts to that value. When the focus reverts, **FocusIn** and **Focus-Out** events are generated, but the last-focus-change time is not affected.

Request Encoding

# of Bytes	Value	Description
1	42	opcode
1		revert-to:
	0	**None**
	1	**PointerRoot**
	2	**Parent**
2	3	request length

# of Bytes	Value	Description
4	WINDOW 0 1	focus: **None** **PointerRoot**
4	TIMESTAMP 0	time: **CurrentTime**

SetModifierMapping

Name

SetModifierMapping

Request Contents

keycodes-per-modifier : CARD8
keycodes : LISTofKEYCODE

Reply Contents

status: {**Success**, **Busy**, **Failed**}

Errors

Value, **Alloc**

Description

This request specifies the keycodes (if any) of the keys to be used as modifiers. The number of keycodes in the list must be 8*keycodes-per-modifier (or a **Length** error results). The keycodes are divided into eight sets, with each set containing keycodes-per-modifier elements. The sets are assigned to the modifiers **Shift**, **Lock**, **Control**, **Mod1**, **Mod2**, **Mod3**, **Mod4**, and **Mod5**, in order. Only nonzero keycode values are used within each set; zero values are ignored. All of the nonzero keycodes must be in the range specified by min-keycode and max-keycode in the connection setup (or a **Value** error results). The order of keycodes within a set does not matter. If no nonzero values are specified in a set, the use of the corresponding modifier is disabled, and the modifier bit will always be zero. Otherwise, the modifier bit will be one whenever at least one of the keys in the corresponding set is in the down position.

A server can impose restrictions on how modifiers can be changed (for example, if certain keys do not generate up transitions in hardware, if auto-repeat cannot be disabled on certain keys, or if multiple keys per modifier are not supported). The status reply is **Failed** if some such restriction is violated, and none of the modifiers are changed.

If the new nonzero keycodes specified for a modifier differ from those currently defined and any (current or new) keys for that modifier are logically in the down state, then the status reply is **Busy**, and none of the modifiers are changed.

This request generates a **MappingNotify** event on a **Success** status.

Request Encoding

# of Bytes	Value	Description
1	118	opcode
1	n	keycodes-per-modifier
2	1+2n	request length
8n	LISTofKEYCODE	keycodes

Reply Encoding

# of Bytes	Value	Description
1	1	reply
1		status:
	0	**Success**
	1	**Busy**
	2	**Failed**
2	CARD16	sequence number
4	0	reply length
24		unused

SetPointerMapping

Name

SetPointerMapping

Request Contents

map: LISTofCARD8

Reply Contents

status: {**Success**, **Busy**}

Errors

Value

Description

This request sets the mapping of the pointer. Elements of the list are indexed starting from one. The length of the list must be the same as **GetPointerMapping** would return (or a **Value** error results). The index is a core button number, and the element of the list defines the effective number.

A zero element disables a button. Elements are not restricted in value by the number of physical buttons, but no two elements can have the same nonzero value (or a **Value** error results).

If any of the buttons to be altered are logically in the down state, the status reply is **Busy**, and the mapping is not changed.

This request generates a **MappingNotify** event on a **Success** status.

Request Encoding

# of Bytes	Value	Description
1	116	opcode
1	n	length of map
2	1+(n+p)/4	request length
n	LISTofCARD8	map
p		unused, p=pad(n)

Reply Encoding

# of Bytes	Value	Description
1	1	reply
1		status:
	0	**Success**
	1	**Busy**

# of Bytes	Value	Description
2	CARD16	sequence number
4	0	reply length
24		unused

Name

SetScreenSaver

Request Contents

timeout, *interval*: INT16
prefer-blanking: {**Yes**, **No**, **Default**}
allow-exposures: {**Yes**, **No**, **Default**}

Errors

Value

Description

The timeout and interval are specified in seconds; setting a value to −1 restores the default. Other negative values generate a **Value** error. If the timeout value is zero, screen-saver is disabled. If the timeout value is nonzero, screen-saver is enabled. Once screen-saver is enabled, if no input from the keyboard or pointer is generated for timeout seconds, screen-saver is activated. For each screen, if blanking is preferred and the hardware supports video blanking, the screen will simply go blank. Otherwise, if either exposures are allowed or the screen can be regenerated without sending exposure events to clients, the screen is changed in a server-dependent fashion to avoid phosphor burn. Otherwise, the state of the screens does not change, and screen-saver is not activated. At the next keyboard or pointer input or at the next **ForceScreenSaver** with mode **Reset**, screen-saver is deactivated, and all screen states are restored.

If the server-dependent screen-saver method is amenable to periodic change, interval serves as a hint about how long the change period should be, with zero hinting that no periodic change should be made. Examples of ways to change the screen include scrambling the color map periodically, moving an icon image about the screen periodically, or tiling the screen with the root window background tile, randomly reorigined periodically.

Request Encoding

# of Bytes	Value	Description
1	107	opcode
1		unused
2	3	request length
2	INT16	timeout
2	INT16	interval
1		prefer-blanking:
	0	**No**
	1	**Yes**
	2	**Default**

# of Bytes	Value	Description
1		allow-exposures:
	0	**No**
	1	**Yes**
	2	**Default**
2		unused

SetSelectionOwner

Name

SetSelectionOwner

Request Contents

selection : ATOM
owner : WINDOW or **None**
time : TIMESTAMP or **CurrentTime**

Errors

Atom , **Window**

Description

This request changes the owner, owner window, and last-change time of the specified selection. This request has no effect if the specified time is earlier than the current last-change time of the specified selection or is later than the current server time. Otherwise, the last-change time is set to the specified time with **CurrentTime** replaced by the current server time. If the owner window is specified as **None**, then the owner of the selection becomes **None** (that is, no owner). Otherwise, the owner of the selection becomes the client executing the request. If the new owner (whether a client or **None**) is not the same as the current owner and the current owner is not **None**, then the current owner is sent a **SelectionClear** event.

If the client that is the owner of a selection is later terminated (that is, its connection is closed) or if the owner window it has specified in the request is later destroyed, then the owner of the selection automatically reverts to **None**, but the last-change time is not affected.

The selection atom is uninterpreted by the server. The owner window is returned by the **GetSelectionOwner** request and is reported in **SelectionRequest** and **SelectionClear** events.

Selections are global to the server.

Request Encoding

# of Bytes	Value	Description
1	22	opcode
1		unused
2	4	request length
4	WINDOW	owner:
	0	**None**
4	ATOM	selection
4	TIMESTAMP	time:
	0	**CurrentTime**

Name
StoreColors

Request Contents
cmap: COLORMAP
items: LISTofCOLORITEM

where:

COLORITEM: [pixel: CARD32
                    do-red, do-green, do-blue: BOOL
                    red, green, blue: CARD16]

Errors
Colormap, **Access**, **Value**

Description
This request changes the colormap entries of the specified pixels. The do-red, do-green, and do-blue fields indicate which components should actually be changed. If the colormap is an installed map for its screen, the changes are visible immediately.

All specified pixels that are allocated writable in cmap (by any client) are changed, even if one or more pixels produce an error. A **Value** error is generated if a specified pixel is not a valid index into cmap, and an **Access** error is generated if a specified pixel is unallocated or is allocated read-only. If more than one pixel is in error, it is arbitrary as to which pixel is reported.

Request Encoding

# of Bytes	Value	Description
1	89	opcode
1		unused
2	2+3n	request length
4	COLORMAP	cmap
12n	LISTofCOLORITEM	items

LISTofCOLORITEM is *n* repetitions of the encoding for COLORITEM shown in the table below:

# of Bytes	Value	Description
4	CARD32	pixel
2	CARD16	red
2	CARD16	green
2	CARD16	blue

# of Bytes	Value	Description
1		do-red, do-green, do-blue:
	#x01	do-red (1 is True, 0 is False)
	#x02	do-green (1 is True, 0 is False)
	#x04	do-blue (1 is True, 0 is False)
	#xf8	unused
1		unused

StoreNamedColor

Name
StoreNamedColor

Request Contents
cmap: COLORMAP
pixel: CARD32
name: STRING8
do-red, *do-green*, *do-blue*: BOOL

Errors
Colormap, Name, Access, Value

Description
This request looks up the named color with respect to the screen associated with cmap and then does a **StoreColors** in cmap. The name should use the ISO Latin-1 encoding, and upper case and lower case do not matter. The **Access** and **Value** errors are the same as in **StoreColors**.

Request Encoding

# of Bytes	Value	Description
1	90	opcode
1		do-red, do-green, do-blue:
	#x01	do-red (1 is True, 0 is False)
	#x02	do-green (1 is True, 0 is False)
	#x04	do-blue (1 is True, 0 is False)
	#xf8	unused
2	4+(n+p)/4	request length
4	COLORMAP	cmap
4	CARD32	pixel
2	n	length of name
2		unused
n	STRING8	name
p		unused, p=pad(n)

TranslateCoordinates

Name

TranslateCoordinates

Request Contents

src-window, *dst-window*: WINDOW
src-x, *src-y*: INT16

Reply Contents

same-screen: BOOL
child: WINDOW or **None**
dst-x, dst-y: INT16

Errors

Window

Description

The src-x and src-y coordinates are taken relative to src-window's origin and are returned as
dst-x and dst-y coordinates relative to dst-window's origin. If same-screen is **False**, then src-
window and dst-window are on different screens, and dst-x and dst-y are zero. If the coordinates are contained in a mapped child of dst-window, then that child is returned.

Request Encoding

# of Bytes	Value	Description
1	40	opcode
1		unused
2	4	request length
4	WINDOW	src-window
4	WINDOW	dst-window
2	INT16	src-x
2	INT16	src-y

Reply Encoding

# of Bytes	Value	Description
1	1	reply
1	BOOL	same-screen
2	CARD16	sequence number
4	0	reply length
4	WINDOW	child:
	0	**None**

# of Bytes	Value	Description
2	INT16	dst-x
2	INT16	dst-y
16		unused

UngrabButton

Name
UngrabButton

Request Contents
modifiers: SETofKEYMASK or **AnyModifier**
button: BUTTON or **AnyButton**
grab-window: WINDOW

Errors
Window, Value

Description
This request releases the passive button/key combination on the specified window if it was grabbed by this client. A modifiers argument of **AnyModifier** is equivalent to issuing the request for all possible modifier combinations (including the combination of no modifiers). A button of **AnyButton** is equivalent to issuing the request for all possible buttons. The request has no effect on an active grab.

Request Encoding

# of Bytes	Value	Description
1	29	opcode
1	BUTTON	button:
	0	**AnyButton**
2	3	request length
4	WINDOW	grab-window
2	SETofKEYMASK	modifiers:
	#x8000	**AnyModifier**
2		unused

UngrabKey

Name
UngrabKey

Request Contents
key: KEYCODE or **AnyKey**
modifiers: SETofKEYMASK or **AnyModifier**
grab-window: WINDOW

Errors
Window, **Value**

Description
This request releases the key combination on the specified window if it was grabbed by this client. A modifiers argument of **AnyModifier** is equivalent to issuing the request for all possible modifier combinations (including the combination of no modifiers). A key of **AnyKey** is equivalent to issuing the request for all possible keycodes. This request has no effect on an active grab.

Request Encoding

# of Bytes	Value	Description
1	34	opcode
1	KEYCODE	key:
	0	**AnyKey**
2	3	request length
4	WINDOW	grab-window
2	SETofKEYMASK	modifiers:
	#x8000	**AnyModifier**
2		unused

UngrabKeyboard

Name
UngrabKeyboard

Request Contents
time : TIMESTAMP or **CurrentTime**

Errors
This request has no errors.

Description
This request releases the keyboard if this client has it actively grabbed (as a result of either **GrabKeyboard** or **GrabKey**) and releases any queued events. The request has no effect if the specified time is earlier than the last-keyboard-grab time or is later than the current server time.

This request generates **FocusIn** and **FocusOut** events.

An **UngrabKeyboard** is performed automatically if the event window for an active keyboard grab becomes not viewable.

Request Encoding

# of Bytes	Value	Description
1	32	opcode
1		unused
2	2	request length
4	TIMESTAMP	time:
	0	**CurrentTime**

UngrabPointer

Name
UngrabPointer

Request Contents
time : TIMESTAMP or **CurrentTime**

Errors
This request has no errors.

Description
This request releases the pointer if this client has it actively grabbed (from either **GrabPointer** or **GrabButton** or from a normal button press) and releases any queued events. The request has no effect if the specified time is earlier than the last-pointer-grab time or is later than the current server time.

This request generates **EnterNotify** and **LeaveNotify** events.

An **UngrabPointer** request is performed automatically if the event window or confine-to window for an active pointer grab becomes not viewable or if window reconfiguration causes the confine-to window to lie completely outside the boundaries of the root window.

Request Encoding

# of Bytes	Value	Description
1	27	opcode
1		unused
2	2	request length
4	TIMESTAMP	time:
	0	**CurrentTime**

UngrabServer

Name

UngrabServer

Request Contents

Opcode and request length only.

Errors

This request has no errors.

Description

This request restarts processing of requests and close-downs on other connections.

Request Encoding

# of Bytes	Value	Description
1	37	opcode
1		unused
2	1	request length

UninstallColormap

Name

UninstallColormap

Request Contents

cmap: COLORMAP

Errors

Colormap

Description

If cmap is on the required list for its screen (see **InstallColormap** request), it is removed from the list. As a side effect, cmap might be uninstalled, and additional colormaps might be implicitly installed or uninstalled. Which colormaps get installed or uninstalled is server-dependent except that the required list must remain installed.

If cmap becomes uninstalled, a **ColormapNotify** event is generated on every window having cmap as an attribute. In addition, for every other colormap that is installed or uninstalled as a result of the request, a **ColormapNotify** event is generated on every window having that colormap as an attribute.

Request Encoding

# of Bytes	Value	Description
1	82	opcode
1		unused
2	2	request length
4	COLORMAP	cmap

UnmapNotify

Name
UnmapNotify

Event Contents
event, *window*: WINDOW
from-configure: BOOL

Description
This event is reported to clients selecting **StructureNotify** on the window and to clients selecting **SubstructureNotify** on the parent. It is generated when the window changes state from mapped to unmapped. The event is the window on which the event was generated, and the window is the window that is unmapped. The from-configure flag is **True** if the event was generated as a result of the window's parent being resized when the window itself had a win-gravity of **Unmap**.

Request Encoding

# of Bytes	Value	Description
1	18	code
1		unused
2	CARD16	sequence number
4	WINDOW	event
4	WINDOW	window
1	BOOL	from-configure
19		unused

UnmapSubwindows

Name

UnmapSubwindows

Request Contents

window: WINDOW

Errors

Window

Description

This request performs an **UnmapWindow** request on all mapped children of the window, in bottom-to-top stacking order.

Request Encoding

# of Bytes	Value	Description
1	11	opcode
1		unused
2	2	request length
4	WINDOW	window

UnmapWindow

Name
UnmapWindow

Request Contents
window: WINDOW

Errors
Window

Description
If the window is already unmapped, this request has no effect. Otherwise, the window is unmapped, and an **UnmapNotify** event is generated. Normal exposure processing on formerly obscured windows is performed.

Request Encoding

# of Bytes	Value	Description
1	10	opcode
1		unused
2	2	request length
4	WINDOW	window

Name

VisibilityNotify

Event Contents

window: WINDOW
state: {**Unobscured**, **PartiallyObscured**, **FullyObscured**}

Description

This event is reported to clients selecting **VisibilityChange** on the window. In the following, the state of the window is calculated ignoring all of the window's subwindows. When a window changes state from partially or fully obscured or not viewable to viewable and completely unobscured, an event with **Unobscured** is generated. When a window changes state from viewable and completely unobscured or not viewable to viewable and partially obscured, an event with **PartiallyObscured** is generated. When a window changes state from viewable and completely unobscured, from viewable and partially obscured, or from not viewable to viewable and fully obscured, an event with **FullyObscured** is generated.

VisibilityNotify events are never generated on **InputOnly** windows.

All **VisibilityNotify** events caused by a hierarchy change are generated after any hierarchy event caused by that change (for example, **UnmapNotify**, **MapNotify**, **ConfigureNotify**, **GravityNotify**, **CirculateNotify**). Any **VisibilityNotify** event on a given window is generated before any **Expose** events on that window, but it is not required that all **VisibilityNotify** events on all windows be generated before all **Expose** events on all windows. The ordering of **VisibilityNotify** events with respect to **FocusOut**, **EnterNotify**, and **LeaveNotify** events is not constrained.

Request Encoding

# of Bytes	Value	Description
1	15	code
1		unused
2	CARD16	sequence number
4	WINDOW	window
1		state:
	0	**Unobscured**
	1	**PartiallyObscured**
	2	**FullyObscured**
23		unused

WarpPointer

Name
WarpPointer

Request Contents
src-window: WINDOW or **None**
dst-window: WINDOW or **None**
src-x, src-y: INT16
src-width, src-height: CARD16
dst-x, dst-y: INT16

Errors
Window

Description
If dst-window is **None**, this request moves the pointer by offsets [dst-x,dst-y] relative to the current position of the pointer. If dst-window is a window, this request moves the pointer to [dst-x,dst-y] relative to dst-window's origin. However, if src-window is not **None**, the move only takes place if src-window contains the pointer and the pointer is contained in the specified rectangle of src-window.

The src-x and src-y coordinates are relative to src-window's origin. If src-height is zero, it is replaced with the current height of src-window minus src-y. If src-width is zero, it is replaced with the current width of src-window minus src-x.

This request cannot be used to move the pointer outside the confine-to window of an active pointer grab. An attempt will only move the pointer as far as the closest edge of the confine-to window.

This request will generate events just as if the user had instantaneously moved the pointer.

Request Encoding

# of Bytes	Value	Description
1	41	opcode
1		unused
2	6	request length
4	WINDOW	src-window:
	0	**None**
4	WINDOW	dst-window:
	0	**None**
2	INT16	src-x
2	INT16	src-y

# of Bytes	Value	Description
2	CARD16	src-width
2	CARD16	src-height
2	INT16	dst-x
2	INT16	dst-y

Part Three:

Appendices

Part Three consists of background material from the X protocol specification (Appendices A through F), and reference aids (Appendices G through K).

Connection Close

Keysyms

Errors

Predefined Atoms

Keyboards and Pointers

Flow Control and Concurrency

Request Group Summary

Alphabetical Listing of Requests

Xlib Functions to Protocol Requests

Protocol Requests to Xlib Functions

Events Briefly Described

A
Connection Close

At connection close, all event selections made by the client are discarded. If the client has the pointer actively grabbed, an **UngrabPointer** is performed. If the client has the keyboard actively grabbed, an **UngrabKeyboard** is performed. All passive grabs by the client are released. If the client has the server grabbed, an **UngrabServer** is performed. All selections (see **SetSelectionOwner** request) owned by the client are disowned. If close-down mode (see **SetCloseDownMode** request) is **RetainPermanent** or **RetainTemporary**, then all resources (including colormap entries) allocated by the client are marked as permanent or temporary, respectively (but this does not prevent other clients from explicitly destroying them). If the mode is **Destroy**, all of the client's resources are destroyed.

When a client's resources are destroyed, for each window in the client's save-set, if the window is an inferior of a window created by the client, the save-set window is reparented to the closest ancestor such that the save-set window is not an inferior of a window created by the client. If the save-set window is unmapped, a **MapWindow** request is performed on it (even if it was not an inferior of a window created by the client). The reparenting leaves unchanged the absolute coordinates (with respect to the root window) of the upper-left outer corner of the save-set window. After save-set processing, all windows created by the client are destroyed. For each nonwindow resource created by the client, the appropriate **Free** request is performed. All colors and colormap entries allocated by the client are freed.

A server goes through a cycle of having no connections and having some connections. At every transition to the state of having no connections as a result of a connection closing with a **Destroy** close-down mode, the server resets its state as if it had just been started. This starts by destroying all lingering resources from clients that have terminated in **Retain-Permanent** or **RetainTemporary** mode. It additionally includes deleting all but the predefined atom identifiers, deleting all properties on all root windows, resetting all device maps and attributes (key click, bell volume, acceleration), resetting the access control list, restoring the standard root tiles and cursors, restoring the default font path, and restoring the input focus to state **PointerRoot**.

Note that closing a connection with a close-down mode of **RetainPermanent** or **Retain-Temporary** will not cause the server to reset.

B
Keysyms

X Protocol X11, Release 3

For convenience, keysym values are viewed as split into four bytes:

- Byte 1 (for the purposes of this encoding) is the most-significant 5 bits (because of the 29-bit effective values).
- Byte 2 is the next most-significant 8 bits.
- Byte 3 is the next most-significant 8 bits.
- Byte 4 is the least-significant 8 bits.

The standard keysym values all have the zero values for bytes 1 and 2. Byte 3 indicates a character code set, and byte 4 indicates a particular character within that set.

Byte 3	Byte 4
0	Latin-1
1	Latin-2
2	Latin-3
3	Latin-4
4	Kana
5	Arabic
6	Cyrillic
7	Greek
8	Technical
9	Special
10	Publishing
11	Apl
12	Hebrew
255	Keyboard

Each character set contains gaps where codes have been removed that were duplicates with codes in previous character sets (that is, character sets with lesser byte 3 value).

The 94 and 96 character code sets have been moved to occupy the righthand quadrant (decimal 129 through 256), so the ASCII subset has a unique encoding across byte 4, which corresponds to the ASCII character code. However, this cannot be guaranteed with future registrations and does not apply to all of the Keyboard set.

To the best of our knowledge, the Latin, Kana, Arabic, Cyrillic, Greek, Apl, and Hebrew sets are from the appropriate ISO and/or ECMA international standards. There are no Technical, Special, or Publishing international standards, so these sets are based on Digital Equipment Corporation standards.

The ordering between the sets (byte 3) is essentially arbitrary. Although the national and international standards bodies are commencing deliberations regarding international 2-byte and 4-byte character sets, we do not know of any proposed layouts.

The order may be arbitrary, but it is important in dealing with duplicate coding. As far as possible, keysym values are the same as the character code. In the Latin-1 to Latin-4 sets, all duplicate glyphs occupy the same code position. However, duplicates between Greek and Technical do not occupy the same code position. Thus, applications wishing to use the technical character set must transform the keysym by means of an array.

There is a difference between European and US usage of the names Pilcrow, Paragraph, and Section, as follows:

US Name	European Name	Code Position in Latin-1
Section sign	Paragraph sign	10/07
Paragraph sign	Pilcrow sign	11/06

We have adopted the names used by both the ISO and ECMA standards. Thus, 11/06 is the Pilcrow sign, and 10/07 is the Paragraph sign (Section sign). This favors the European usage.

The Keyboard set is a miscellaneous collection of commonly occurring keys on keyboards. Within this set, the keypad symbols are generally duplicates of symbols found on keys on the main part of the keyboard, but they are distinguished here because they often have a distinguishable semantics associated with them.

Keyboards tend to be comparatively standard with respect to the alphanumeric keys, but they differ radically on the miscellaneous function keys. Many function keys are left over from early timesharing days or are designed for a specific application. Keyboard layouts from large manufacturers tend to have lots of keys for every conceivable purpose, whereas small workstation manufacturers often add keys that are solely for support of some of their unique functionality. There are two ways of thinking about how to define keysyms for such a world:

• The Engraving approach

• The Common approach

The Engraving approach is to create a keysym for every unique key engraving. This is effectively taking the union of all key engravings on all keyboards. For example, some keyboards label function keys across the top as F1 through Fn, and others label them as PF1 through PFn. These would be different keys under the Engraving approach. Likewise, Lock would differ from Shift Lock, which is different from the up-arrow symbol that has the effect of changing lower case to upper case. There are lots of other aliases such as Del, DEL, Delete, Remove, and so forth. The Engraving approach makes it easy to decide if a new entry should be added to the keysym set: if it does not exactly match an existing one, then a new one is created. One estimate is that there would be on the order of 300–500 Keyboard keysyms using this approach, without counting foreign translations and variations.

The Common approach tries to capture all of the keys present on an interesting number of keyboards, folding likely aliases into the same keysym. For example, Del, DEL, and Delete are all merged into a single keysym. Vendors would be expected to augment the keysym set (using the vendor-specific encoding space) to include all of their unique keys that were not included in the standard set. Each vendor decides which of its keys map into the standard keysyms, which presumably can be overridden by a user. It is more difficult to implement this approach, because judgment is required about when a sufficient set of keyboards implements an engraving to justify making it a keysym in the standard set and about which engravings should be merged into a single keysym. Under this scheme, there are an estimated 100–150 keysyms.

Although neither scheme is perfect or elegant, the Common approach has been selected because it makes it easier to write a portable application. Having the Delete functionality merged into a single keysym allows an application to implement a deletion function and expect reasonable bindings on a wide set of workstations. Under the Common approach, application writers are still free to look for and interpret vendor-specific keysyms, but because they are in the extended set, the application developer is more conscious that they are writing the application in a nonportable fashion.

In the listings below, Code Pos is a representation of byte 4 of the keysym value, expressed as most-significant/least-significant 4-bit values. The Code Pos numbers are for reference only and do not affect the keysym value. In all cases, the keysym value is:

```
byte3 * 256 + byte4
```

Byte	Byte	Code	Name	Set
000	032	02/00	Space	Latin-1
000	033	02/01	Exclamation Point	Latin-1
000	034	02/02	Quotation Mark	Latin-1
000	035	02/03	Number Sign	Latin-1
000	036	02/04	Dollar Sign	Latin-1
000	037	02/05	Percent Sign	Latin-1
000	038	02/06	Ampersand	Latin-1
000	039	02/07	Apostrophe	Latin-1
000	040	02/08	Left Parenthesis	Latin-1
000	041	02/09	Right Parenthesis	Latin-1
000	042	02/10	Asterisk	Latin-1
000	043	02/11	Plus Sign	Latin-1
000	044	02/12	Comma	Latin-1
000	045	02/13	Hyphen, Minus Sign	Latin-1

Byte	Byte	Code	Name	Set
000	046	02/14	Full Stop	Latin-1
000	047	02/15	Solidus	Latin-1
000	048	03/00	Digit Zero	Latin-1
000	049	03/01	Digit One	Latin-1
000	050	03/02	Digit Two	Latin-1
000	051	03/03	Digit Three	Latin-1
000	052	03/04	Digit Four	Latin-1
000	053	03/05	Digit Five	Latin-1
000	054	03/06	Digit Six	Latin-1
000	055	03/07	Digit Seven	Latin-1
000	056	03/08	Digit Eight	Latin-1
000	057	03/09	Digit Nine	Latin-1
000	058	03/10	Colon	Latin-1
000	059	03/11	SemiColon	Latin-1
000	060	03/12	Less Than Sign	Latin-1
000	061	03/13	Equals Sign	Latin-1
000	062	03/14	Greater Than Sign	Latin-1
000	063	03/15	Question Mark	Latin-1
000	064	04/00	Commercial At	Latin-1
000	065	04/01	Latin Capital Letter A	Latin-1
000	066	04/02	Latin Capital Letter B	Latin-1
000	067	04/03	Latin Capital Letter C	Latin-1
000	068	04/04	Latin Capital Letter D	Latin-1
000	069	04/05	Latin Capital Letter E	Latin-1
000	070	04/06	Latin Capital Letter F	Latin-1
000	071	04/07	Latin Capital Letter G	Latin-1
000	072	04/08	Latin Capital Letter H	Latin-1
000	073	04/09	Latin Capital Letter I	Latin-1
000	074	04/10	Latin Capital Letter J	Latin-1
000	075	04/11	Latin Capital Letter K	Latin-1
000	076	04/12	Latin Capital Letter L	Latin-1
000	077	04/13	Latin Capital Letter M	Latin-1
000	078	04/14	Latin Capital Letter N	Latin-1
000	079	04/15	Latin Capital Letter O	Latin-1
000	080	05/00	Latin Capital Letter P	Latin-1
000	081	05/01	Latin Capital Letter Q	Latin-1
000	082	05/02	Latin Capital Letter R	Latin-1
000	083	05/03	Latin Capital Letter S	Latin-1
000	084	05/04	Latin Capital Letter T	Latin-1
000	085	05/05	Latin Capital Letter U	Latin-1
000	086	05/06	Latin Capital Letter V	Latin-1
000	087	05/07	Latin Capital Letter W	Latin-1
000	088	05/08	Latin Capital Letter X	Latin-1
000	089	05/09	Latin Capital Letter Y	Latin-1
000	090	05/10	Latin Capital Letter Z	Latin-1
000	091	05/11	Left Square Bracket	Latin-1

Byte	Byte	Code	Name	Set
000	092	05/12	Reverse Solidus	Latin-1
000	093	05/13	Right Square Bracket	Latin-1
000	094	05/14	Circumflex Accent	Latin-1
000	095	05/15	Low Line	Latin-1
000	096	06/00	Grave Accent	Latin-1
000	097	06/01	Latin Small Letter a	Latin-1
000	098	06/02	Latin Small Letter b	Latin-1
000	099	06/03	Latin Small Letter c	Latin-1
000	100	06/04	Latin Small Letter d	Latin-1
000	101	06/05	Latin Small Letter e	Latin-1
000	102	06/06	Latin Small Letter f	Latin-1
000	103	06/07	Latin Small Letter g	Latin-1
000	104	06/08	Latin Small Letter h	Latin-1
000	105	06/09	Latin Small Letter i	Latin-1
000	106	06/10	Latin Small Letter j	Latin-1
000	107	06/11	Latin Small Letter k	Latin-1
000	108	06/12	Latin Small Letter l	Latin-1
000	109	06/13	Latin Small Letter m	Latin-1
000	110	06/14	Latin Small Letter n	Latin-1
000	111	06/15	Latin Small Letter o	Latin-1
000	112	07/00	Latin Small Letter p	Latin-1
000	113	07/01	Latin Small Letter q	Latin-1
000	114	07/02	Latin Small Letter r	Latin-1
000	115	07/03	Latin Small Letter s	Latin-1
000	116	07/04	Latin Small Letter t	Latin-1
000	117	07/05	Latin Small Letter u	Latin-1
000	118	07/06	Latin Small Letter v	Latin-1
000	119	07/07	Latin Small Letter w	Latin-1
000	120	07/08	Latin Small Letter x	Latin-1
000	121	07/09	Latin Small Letter y	Latin-1
000	122	07/10	Latin Small Letter z	Latin-1
000	123	07/11	Left Curly Bracket	Latin-1
000	124	07/12	Vertical Line	Latin-1
000	125	07/13	Right Curly Bracket	Latin-1
000	126	07/14	Tilde	Latin-1
000	160	10/00	No-Break Space	Latin-1
000	161	10/01	Inverted Exclamation Mark	Latin-1
000	162	10/02	Cent Sign	Latin-1
000	163	10/03	Pound Sign	Latin-1
000	164	10/04	Currency Sign	Latin-1
000	165	10/05	Yen Sign	Latin-1
000	166	10/06	Broken Vertical Bar	Latin-1
000	167	10/07	Paragraph Sign, Section Sign	Latin-1
000	168	10/08	DiaeresiS	Latin-1
000	169	10/09	Copyright Sign	Latin-1
000	170	10/10	Feminine Ordinal Indicator	Latin-1

Byte	Byte	Code	Name	Set
000	171	10/11	Left Angle Quotation Mark	Latin-1
000	172	10/12	Not Sign	Latin-1
000	174	10/14	Registered Trademark Sign	Latin-1
000	175	10/15	Macron	Latin-1
000	176	11/00	Degree Sign, Ring Above	Latin-1
000	177	11/01	Plus-Minus Sign	Latin-1
000	178	11/02	SuperScript Two	Latin-1
000	179	11/03	SuperScript Three	Latin-1
000	180	11/04	Acute Accent	Latin-1
000	181	11/05	Micro Sign	Latin-1
000	182	11/06	Pilcrow Sign	Latin-1
000	183	11/07	Middle Dot	Latin-1
000	184	11/08	Cedilla	Latin-1
000	185	11/09	SuperScript One	Latin-1
000	186	11/10	Masculine Ordinal Indicator	Latin-1
000	187	11/11	Right Angle Quotation Mark	Latin-1
000	188	11/12	Vulgar Fraction One Quarter	Latin-1
000	189	11/13	Vulgar Fraction One Half	Latin-1
000	190	11/14	Vulgar Fraction Three Quarters	Latin-1
000	191	11/15	Inverted Question Mark	Latin-1
000	192	12/00	Latin Capital Letter A with Grave Accent	Latin-1
000	193	12/01	Latin Capital Letter A with Acute Accent	Latin-1
000	194	12/02	Latin Capital Letter A with Circumflex Accent	Latin-1
000	195	12/03	Latin Capital Letter A with Tilde	Latin-1
000	196	12/04	Latin Capital Letter A with Diaeresis	Latin-1
000	197	12/05	Latin Capital Letter A with Ring above	Latin-1
000	198	12/06	Latin Capital Diphthong Ae	Latin-1
000	199	12/07	Latin Capital Letter C witH Cedilla	Latin-1
000	200	12/08	Latin Capital Letter E with Grave Accent	Latin-1
000	201	12/09	Latin Capital Letter E with Acute Accent	Latin-1
000	202	12/10	Latin Capital Letter E with Circumflex Accent	Latin-1
000	203	12/11	Latin Capital Letter E with Diaeresis	Latin-1
000	204	12/12	Latin Capital Letter I with Grave Accent	Latin-1
000	205	12/13	Latin Capital Letter I with Acute Accent	Latin-1
000	206	12/14	Latin Capital Letter I with Circumflex Accent	Latin-1
000	207	12/15	Latin Capital Letter I with Diaeresis	Latin-1
000	208	13/00	Icelandic Capital Letter Eth	Latin-1
000	209	13/01	Latin Capital Letter N with Tilde	Latin-1
000	210	13/02	Latin Capital Letter O with Grave Accent	Latin-1
000	211	13/03	Latin Capital Letter O with Acute Accent	Latin-1
000	212	13/04	Latin Capital Letter O with Circumflex Accent	Latin-1
000	213	13/05	Latin Capital Letter O with Tilde	Latin-1
000	214	13/06	Latin Capital Letter O with Diaeresis	Latin-1
000	215	13/07	Multiplication Sign	Latin-1
000	216	13/08	Latin Capital Letter O with Obilque Stroke	Latin-1
000	217	13/09	Latin Capital Letter U with Grave Accent	Latin-1

Byte	Byte	Code	Name	Set
000	218	13/10	Latin Capital Letter U with Acute Accent	Latin-1
000	219	13/11	Latin Capital Letter U with Circumflex Accent	Latin-1
000	220	13/12	Latin Capital Letter U with Diaeresis	Latin-1
000	221	13/13	Latin Capital Letter Y with Acute Accent	Latin-1
000	222	13/14	Icelandic Capital Letter Thorn	Latin-1
000	223	13/15	German Small Letter Sharp s	Latin-1
000	224	14/00	Latin Small Letter a with Grave Accent	Latin-1
000	225	14/01	Latin Small Letter a with Acute Accent	Latin-1
000	226	14/02	Latin Small Letter a with Circumflex Accent	Latin-1
000	227	14/03	Latin Small Letter a with Tilde	Latin-1
000	228	14/04	Latin Small Letter a with Diaeresis	Latin-1
000	229	14/05	Latin Small Letter a with Ring Above	Latin-1
000	230	14/06	Latin Small Diphthong ae	Latin-1
000	231	14/07	Latin Small Letter c with Cedilla	Latin-1
000	232	14/08	Latin Small Letter e with Grave Accent	Latin-1
000	233	14/09	Latin Small Letter e with Acute Accent	Latin-1
000	234	14/10	Latin Small Letter e with Circumflex Accent	Latin-1
000	235	14/11	Latin Small Letter e with Diaeresis	Latin-1
000	236	14/12	Latin Small Letter i with Grave Accent	Latin-1
000	237	14/13	Latin Small Letter i with Acute Accent	Latin-1
000	238	14/14	Latin Small Letter i with Circumflex Accent	Latin-1
000	239	14/15	Latin Small Letter i with Diaeresis	Latin-1
000	240	15/00	Icelandic Small Letter Eth	Latin-1
000	241	15/01	Latin Small Letter n with Tilde	Latin-1
000	242	15/02	Latin Small Letter o with Grave Accent	Latin-1
000	243	15/03	Latin Small Letter o with Acute Accent	Latin-1
000	244	15/04	Latin Small Letter o with Circumflex Accent	Latin-1
000	245	15/05	Latin Small Letter o with Tilde	Latin-1
000	246	15/06	Latin Small Letter o with Diaeresis	Latin-1
000	247	15/07	Division Sign	Latin-1
000	248	15/08	Latin Small Letter o with Obilque Stroke	Latin-1
000	249	15/09	Latin Small Letter u with Grave Accent	Latin-1
000	250	15/10	Latin Small Letter u with Acute Accent	Latin-1
000	251	15/11	Latin Small Letter u with Circumflex Accent	Latin-1
000	252	15/12	Latin Small Letter u with Diaeresis	Latin-1
000	253	15/13	Latin Small Letter y with Acute Accent	Latin-1
000	254	15/14	Icelandic Small Letter Thorn	Latin-1
000	255	15/15	Latin Small Letter y with Diaeresis	Latin-1
001	161	10/01	Latin Capital Letter A with Ogonek	Latin-2
001	162	10/02	Breve	Latin-2
001	163	10/03	Latin Capital Letter L with Stroke	Latin-2
001	165	10/05	Latin Capital Letter L with Caron	Latin-2
001	166	10/06	Latin Capital Letter S with Acute Accent	Latin-2
001	169	10/09	Latin Capital Letter S with Caron	Latin-2

Byte	Byte	Code	Name	Set
001	170	10/10	Latin Capital Letter S with Cedilla	Latin-2
001	171	10/11	Latin Capital Letter T with Caron	Latin-2
001	172	10/12	Latin Capital Letter Z with Acute Accent	Latin-2
001	174	10/14	Latin Capital Letter Z with Caron	Latin-2
001	175	10/15	Latin Capital Letter Z with Dot Above	Latin-2
001	177	11/01	Latin Small Letter a with Ogonek	Latin-2
001	178	11/02	Ogonek	Latin-2
001	179	11/03	Latin Small Letter l with Stroke	Latin-2
001	181	11/05	Latin Small Letter l with Caron	Latin-2
001	182	11/06	Latin Small Letter s with Acute Accent	Latin-2
001	183	11/07	Caron	Latin-2
001	185	11/09	Latin Small Letter s with Caron	Latin-2
001	186	11/10	Latin Small Letter s with Cedilla	Latin-2
001	187	11/11	Latin Small Letter t with Caron	Latin-2
001	188	11/12	Latin Small Letter z with Acute Accent	Latin-2
001	189	11/13	Double Acute Accent	Latin-2
001	190	11/14	Latin Small Letter z with Caron	Latin-2
001	191	11/15	Latin Small Letter z with Dot Above	Latin-2
001	192	12/00	Latin Capital Letter R with Acute Accent	Latin-2
001	195	12/03	Latin Capital Letter A with Breve	Latin-2
001	197	12/05	Latin Capital Letter L with Acute Accent	Latin-2
001	198	12/06	Latin Capital Letter C with Acute Accent	Latin-2
001	200	12/08	Latin Capital Letter C with Caron	Latin-2
001	202	12/10	Latin Capital Letter E with Ogonek	Latin-2
001	204	12/12	Latin Capital Letter E with Caron	Latin-2
001	207	12/15	Latin Capital Letter D with Caron	Latin-2
001	208	13/00	Latin Capital Letter D with Stroke	Latin-2
001	209	13/01	Latin Capital Letter N with Acute Accent	Latin-2
001	210	13/02	Latin Capital Letter N with Caron	Latin-2
001	213	13/05	Latin Capital Letter O with Double Acute Accent	Latin-2
001	216	13/08	Latin Capital Letter R with Caron	Latin-2
001	217	13/09	Latin Capital Letter U with Ring Above	Latin-2
001	219	13/11	Latin Capital Letter U with Double Acute Accent	Latin-2
001	222	13/14	Latin Capital Letter T with Cedilla	Latin-2
001	224	14/00	Latin Small Letter r with Acute Accent	Latin-2
001	227	14/03	Latin Small Letter a with Breve	Latin-2
001	229	14/05	Latin Small Letter l with Acute Accent	Latin-2
001	230	14/06	Latin Small Letter c with Acute Accent	Latin-2
001	232	14/08	Latin Small Letter c with Caron	Latin-2
001	234	14/10	Latin Small Letter e with Ogonek	Latin-2
001	236	14/12	Latin Small Letter e with Caron	Latin-2
001	239	14/15	Latin Small Letter d with Caron	Latin-2
001	240	15/00	Latin Small Letter d with Stroke	Latin-2
001	241	15/01	Latin Small Letter n with Acute Accent	Latin-2
001	242	15/02	Latin Small Letter n with Caron	Latin-2
001	245	15/05	Latin Small Letter o with Double Acute Accent	Latin-2

Byte	Byte	Code	Name	Set
001	248	15/08	Latin Small Letter r with Caron	Latin-2
001	249	15/09	Latin Small Letter u with RING Above	Latin-2
001	251	15/11	Latin Small Letter u with Double Acute Accent	Latin-2
001	254	15/14	Latin Small Letter t with Cedilla	Latin-2
001	255	15/15	Dot Above	Latin-2
002	161	10/01	Latin Capital Letter H with Stroke	Latin-3
002	166	10/06	Latin Capital Letter H with Circumflex Accent	Latin-3
002	169	10/09	Latin Capital Letter I with Dot Above	Latin-3
002	171	10/11	Latin Capital Letter G with Breve	Latin-3
002	172	10/12	Latin Capital Letter J with Circumflex Accent	Latin-3
002	177	11/01	Latin Small Letter h with Stroke	Latin-3
002	182	11/06	Latin Small Letter h with Circumflex Accent	Latin-3
002	185	11/09	Small Dotless Letter i	Latin-3
002	187	11/11	Latin Small Letter g with Breve	Latin-3
002	188	11/12	Latin Small Letter j with Circumflex Accent	Latin-3
002	197	12/05	Latin Capital Letter C with Dot Above	Latin-3
002	198	12/06	Latin Capital Letter C with Circumflex Accent	Latin-3
002	213	13/05	Latin Capital Letter G with Dot Above	Latin-3
002	216	13/08	Latin Capital Letter G with Circumflex Accent	Latin-3
002	221	13/13	Latin Capital Letter U with Breve	Latin-3
002	222	13/14	Latin Capital Letter S with Circumflex Accent	Latin-3
002	229	14/05	Latin Small Letter c with Dot Above	Latin-3
002	230	14/06	Latin Small Letter c with Circumflex Accent	Latin-3
002	245	15/05	Latin Small Letter g with Dot Above	Latin-3
002	248	15/08	Latin Small Letter g with Circumflex Accent	Latin-3
002	253	15/13	Latin Small Letter u with Breve	Latin-3
002	254	15/14	Latin Small Letter s with Circumflex Accent	Latin-3
003	162	10/02	Latin Small Letter Kappa	Latin-4
003	163	10/03	Latin Capital Letter R with Cedilla	Latin-4
003	165	10/05	Latin Capital Letter I with Tilde	Latin-4
003	166	10/06	Latin Capital Letter L with Cedilla	Latin-4
003	170	10/10	Latin Capital Letter E with Macron	Latin-4
003	171	10/11	Latin Capital Letter G with Cedilla	Latin-4
003	172	10/12	Latin Capital Letter T with Obilque Stroke	Latin-4
003	179	11/03	Latin Small Letter r with Cedilla	Latin-4
003	181	11/05	Latin Small Letter i with Tilde	Latin-4
003	182	11/06	Latin Small Letter l with Cedilla	Latin-4
003	186	11/10	Latin Small Letter e with Macron	Latin-4
003	187	11/11	Latin Small Letter g with Acute Accent	Latin-4
003	188	11/12	Latin Small Letter t with Oblique Stroke	Latin-4
003	189	11/13	Lappish Capital Letter Eng	Latin-4
003	191	11/15	Lappish Small Letter Eng	Latin-4

Keysyms

Byte	Byte	Code	Name	Set
003	192	12/00	Latin Capital Letter A with Macron	Latin-4
003	199	12/07	Latin Capital Letter I with Ogonek	Latin-4
003	204	12/12	Latin Capital Letter E with Dot Above	Latin-4
003	207	12/15	Latin Capital Letter I with Macron	Latin-4
003	209	13/01	Latin Capital Letter N with Cedilla	Latin-4
003	210	13/02	Latin Capital Letter O with Macron	Latin-4
003	211	13/03	Latin Capital Letter K with Cedilla	Latin-4
003	217	13/09	Latin Capital Letter U with Ogonek	Latin-4
003	221	13/13	Latin Capital Letter U with Tilde	Latin-4
003	222	13/14	Latin Capital Letter U with Macron	Latin-4
003	224	14/00	Latin Small Letter a with Macron	Latin-4
003	231	14/07	Latin Small Letter i with Ogonek	Latin-4
003	236	14/12	Latin Small Letter e with Dot Above	Latin-4
003	239	14/15	Latin Small Letter i with Macron	Latin-4
003	241	15/01	Latin Small Letter n with Cedilla	Latin-4
003	242	15/02	Latin Small Letter o with Macron	Latin-4
003	243	15/03	Latin Small Letter k with Cedilla	Latin-4
003	249	15/09	Latin Small Letter u with Ogonek	Latin-4
003	253	15/13	Latin Small Letter u with Tilde	Latin-4
003	254	15/14	Latin Small Letter u with Macron	Latin-4
004	126	07/14	Overline	Kana
004	161	10/01	Kana Full STop	Kana
004	162	10/02	Kana Opening Bracket	Kana
004	163	10/03	Kana Closing Bracket	Kana
004	164	10/04	Kana Comma	Kana
004	165	10/05	Kana Middle Dot	Kana
004	166	10/06	Kana Letter Wo	Kana
004	167	10/07	Kana Letter Small A	Kana
004	168	10/08	Kana Letter Small I	Kana
004	169	10/09	Kana Letter Small U	Kana
004	170	10/10	Kana Letter Small E	Kana
004	171	10/11	Kana Letter Small O	Kana
004	172	10/12	Kana Letter Small Ya	Kana
004	173	10/13	Kana Letter Small Yu	Kana
004	174	10/14	Kana Letter Small Yo	Kana
004	175	10/15	Kana Letter Small Tu	Kana
004	176	11/00	Prolonged Sound Symbol	Kana
004	177	11/01	Kana Letter A	Kana
004	178	11/02	Kana Letter I	Kana
004	179	11/03	Kana Letter U	Kana
004	180	11/04	Kana Letter E	Kana
004	181	11/05	Kana Letter O	Kana
004	182	11/06	Kana Letter Ka	Kana
004	183	11/07	Kana Letter Ki	Kana

Byte	Byte	Code	Name	Set
004	184	11/08	Kana Letter Ku	Kana
004	185	11/09	Kana Letter Ke	Kana
004	186	11/10	Kana Letter Ko	Kana
004	187	11/11	Kana Letter Sa	Kana
004	188	11/12	Kana Letter Shi	Kana
004	189	11/13	Kana Letter Su	Kana
004	190	11/14	Kana Letter Se	Kana
004	191	11/15	Kana Letter So	Kana
004	192	12/00	Kana Letter Ta	Kana
004	193	12/01	Kana Letter Ti	Kana
004	194	12/02	Kana Letter Tu	Kana
004	195	12/03	Kana Letter Te	Kana
004	196	12/04	Kana Letter To	Kana
004	197	12/05	Kana Letter Na	Kana
004	198	12/06	Kana Letter Ni	Kana
004	199	12/07	Kana Letter Nu	Kana
004	200	12/08	Kana Letter Ne	Kana
004	201	12/09	Kana Letter No	Kana
004	202	12/10	Kana Letter Ha	Kana
004	203	12/11	Kana Letter Hi	Kana
004	204	12/12	Kana Letter Hu	Kana
004	205	12/13	Kana Letter He	Kana
004	206	12/14	Kana Letter Ho	Kana
004	207	12/15	Kana Letter Ma	Kana
004	208	13/00	Kana Letter Mi	Kana
004	209	13/01	Kana Letter Mu	Kana
004	210	13/02	Kana Letter Me	Kana
004	211	13/03	Kana Letter Mo	Kana
004	212	13/04	Kana Letter Ya	Kana
004	213	13/05	Kana Letter Yu	Kana
004	214	13/06	Kana Letter Yo	Kana
004	215	13/07	Kana Letter Ra	Kana
004	216	13/08	Kana Letter Ri	Kana
004	217	13/09	Kana Letter Ru	Kana
004	218	13/10	Kana Letter Re	Kana
004	219	13/11	Kana Letter Ro	Kana
004	220	13/12	Kana Letter Wa	Kana
004	221	13/13	Kana Letter N	Kana
004	222	13/14	Voiced Sound Symbol	Kana
004	223	13/15	Semivoiced Sound Symbol	Kana
005	172	10/12	Arabic Comma	Arabic
005	187	11/11	Arabic Semicolon	Arabic
005	191	11/15	Arabic Question Mark	Arabic
005	193	12/01	Arabic Letter Hamza	Arabic

Byte	Byte	Code	Name	Set
005	194	12/02	Arabic Letter Madda On Alef	Arabic
005	195	12/03	Arabic Letter Hamza On Alef	Arabic
005	196	12/04	Arabic Letter Hamza On Waw	Arabic
005	197	12/05	Arabic Letter Hamza Under Alef	Arabic
005	198	12/06	Arabic Letter Hamza On Yeh	Arabic
005	199	12/07	Arabic Letter Alef	Arabic
005	200	12/08	Arabic Letter Beh	Arabic
005	201	12/09	Arabic Letter Teh Marbuta	Arabic
005	202	12/10	Arabic Letter Teh	Arabic
005	203	12/11	Arabic Letter Theh	Arabic
005	204	12/12	Arabic Letter Jeem	Arabic
005	205	12/13	Arabic Letter Hah	Arabic
005	206	12/14	Arabic Letter Khah	Arabic
005	207	12/15	Arabic Letter Dal	Arabic
005	208	13/00	Arabic Letter Thal	Arabic
005	209	13/01	Arabic Letter Ra	Arabic
005	210	13/02	Arabic Letter Zain	Arabic
005	211	13/03	Arabic Letter Seen	Arabic
005	212	13/04	Arabic Letter Sheen	Arabic
005	213	13/05	Arabic Letter Sad	Arabic
005	214	13/06	Arabic Letter Dad	Arabic
005	215	13/07	Arabic Letter Tah	Arabic
005	216	13/08	Arabic Letter Zah	Arabic
005	217	13/09	Arabic Letter Ain	Arabic
005	218	13/10	Arabic Letter Ghain	Arabic
005	224	14/00	Arabic Letter Tatweel	Arabic
005	225	14/01	Arabic Letter Feh	Arabic
005	226	14/02	Arabic Letter Qaf	Arabic
005	227	14/03	Arabic Letter Kaf	Arabic
005	228	14/04	Arabic Letter Lam	Arabic
005	229	14/05	Arabic Letter Meem	Arabic
005	230	14/06	Arabic Letter Noon	Arabic
005	231	14/07	Arabic Letter Heh	Arabic
005	232	14/08	Arabic Letter Waw	Arabic
005	233	14/09	Arabic Letter Alef Maksura	Arabic
005	234	14/10	Arabic Letter Yeh	Arabic
005	235	14/11	Arabic Letter Fathatan	Arabic
005	236	14/12	Arabic Letter Dammatan	Arabic
005	237	14/13	Arabic Letter Kasratan	Arabic
005	238	14/14	Arabic Letter Fatha	Arabic
005	239	14/15	Arabic Letter Damma	Arabic
005	240	15/00	Arabic Letter Kasra	Arabic
005	241	15/01	Arabic Letter Shadda	Arabic
005	242	15/02	Arabic Letter Sukun	Arabic

Byte	Byte	Code	Name	Set
006	161	10/01	Serbian Small Letter Dje	Cyrillic
006	162	10/02	Macedonia Small Letter Gje	Cyrillic
006	163	10/03	Cyrillic Small Letter Io	Cyrillic
006	164	10/04	Ukrainian Small Letter Je	Cyrillic
006	165	10/05	Macedonia Small Letter Dse	Cyrillic
006	166	10/06	Ukrainian Small Letter I	Cyrillic
006	167	10/07	Ukrainian Small Letter Yi	Cyrillic
006	168	10/08	Serbian Small Letter Je	Cyrillic
006	169	10/09	Serbian Small Letter Lje	Cyrillic
006	170	10/10	Serbian Small Letter Nje	Cyrillic
006	171	10/11	Serbian Small Letter Tshe	Cyrillic
006	172	10/12	Macedonia Small Letter Kje	Cyrillic
006	174	10/14	Byelorussian Small Letter Short U	Cyrillic
006	175	10/15	Serbian Small Letter Dze	Cyrillic
006	176	11/00	Numero Sign	Cyrillic
006	177	11/01	Serbian Capital Letter Dje	Cyrillic
006	178	11/02	Macedonia Capital Letter Gje	Cyrillic
006	179	11/03	Cyrillic Capital Letter Io	Cyrillic
006	180	11/04	Ukrainian Capital Letter Je	Cyrillic
006	181	11/05	Macedonia Capital Letter Dse	Cyrillic
006	182	11/06	Ukrainian Capital Letter I	Cyrillic
006	183	11/07	Ukrainian Capital Letter Yi	Cyrillic
006	184	11/08	Serbian Capital Letter Je	Cyrillic
006	185	11/09	Serbian Capital Letter Lje	Cyrillic
006	186	11/10	Serbian Capital Letter Nje	Cyrillic
006	187	11/11	Serbian Capital Letter Tshe	Cyrillic
006	188	11/12	Macedonia Capital Letter Kje	Cyrillic
006	190	11/14	Byelorussian Capital Letter Short U	Cyrillic
006	191	11/15	Serbian Capital Letter Dze	Cyrillic
006	192	12/00	Cyrillic Small Letter Yu	Cyrillic
006	193	12/01	Cyrillic Small Letter A	Cyrillic
006	194	12/02	Cyrillic Small Letter Be	Cyrillic
006	195	12/03	Cyrillic Small Letter Tse	Cyrillic
006	196	12/04	Cyrillic Small Letter De	Cyrillic
006	197	12/05	Cyrillic Small Letter Ie	Cyrillic
006	198	12/06	Cyrillic Small Letter Ef	Cyrillic
006	199	12/07	Cyrillic Small Letter Ghe	Cyrillic
006	200	12/08	Cyrillic Small Letter Ha	Cyrillic
006	201	12/09	Cyrillic Small Letter I	Cyrillic
006	202	12/10	Cyrillic Small Letter Short I	Cyrillic
006	203	12/11	Cyrillic Small Letter Ka	Cyrillic
006	204	12/12	Cyrillic Small Letter El	Cyrillic
006	205	12/13	Cyrillic Small Letter Em	Cyrillic
006	206	12/14	Cyrillic Small Letter En	Cyrillic
006	207	12/15	Cyrillic Small Letter O	Cyrillic
006	208	13/00	Cyrillic Small Letter Pe	Cyrillic

Byte	Byte	Code	Name	Set
006	209	13/01	Cyrillic Small Letter Ya	Cyrillic
006	210	13/02	Cyrillic Small Letter Er	Cyrillic
006	211	13/03	Cyrillic Small Letter Es	Cyrillic
006	212	13/04	Cyrillic Small Letter Te	Cyrillic
006	213	13/05	Cyrillic Small Letter U	Cyrillic
006	214	13/06	Cyrillic Small Letter Zhe	Cyrillic
006	215	13/07	Cyrillic Small Letter Ve	Cyrillic
006	216	13/08	Cyrillic Small Soft Sign	Cyrillic
006	217	13/09	Cyrillic Small Letter Yeru	Cyrillic
006	218	13/10	Cyrillic Small Letter Ze	Cyrillic
006	219	13/11	Cyrillic Small Letter Sha	Cyrillic
006	220	13/12	Cyrillic Small Letter E	Cyrillic
006	221	13/13	Cyrillic Small Letter Shcha	Cyrillic
006	222	13/14	Cyrillic Small Letter Che	Cyrillic
006	223	13/15	Cyrillic Small Hard Sign	Cyrillic
006	224	14/00	Cyrillic Capital Letter Yu	Cyrillic
006	225	14/01	Cyrillic Capital Letter A	Cyrillic
006	226	14/02	Cyrillic Capital Letter Be	Cyrillic
006	227	14/03	Cyrillic Capital Letter Tse	Cyrillic
006	228	14/04	Cyrillic Capital Letter De	Cyrillic
006	229	14/05	Cyrillic Capital Letter Ie	Cyrillic
006	230	14/06	Cyrillic Capital Letter Ef	Cyrillic
006	231	14/07	Cyrillic Capital Letter Ghe	Cyrillic
006	232	14/08	Cyrillic Capital Letter Ha	Cyrillic
006	233	14/09	Cyrillic Capital Letter I	Cyrillic
006	234	14/10	Cyrillic Capital Letter Short I	Cyrillic
006	235	14/11	Cyrillic Capital Letter Ka	Cyrillic
006	236	14/12	Cyrillic Capital Letter El	Cyrillic
006	237	14/13	Cyrillic Capital Letter Em	Cyrillic
006	238	14/14	Cyrillic Capital Letter En	Cyrillic
006	239	14/15	Cyrillic Capital Letter O	Cyrillic
006	240	15/00	Cyrillic Capital Letter Pe	Cyrillic
006	241	15/01	Cyrillic Capital Letter Ya	Cyrillic
006	242	15/02	Cyrillic Capital Letter Er	Cyrillic
006	243	15/03	Cyrillic Capital Letter Es	Cyrillic
006	244	15/04	Cyrillic Capital Letter Te	Cyrillic
006	245	15/05	Cyrillic Capital Letter U	Cyrillic
006	246	15/06	Cyrillic Capital Letter Zhe	Cyrillic
006	247	15/07	Cyrillic Capital Letter Ve	Cyrillic
006	248	15/08	Cyrillic Capital Soft Sign	Cyrillic
006	249	15/09	Cyrillic Capital Letter Yeru	Cyrillic
006	250	15/10	Cyrillic Capital Letter Ze	Cyrillic
006	251	15/11	Cyrillic Capital Letter Sha	Cyrillic
006	252	15/12	Cyrillic Capital Letter E	Cyrillic
006	253	15/13	Cyrillic Capital Letter Shcha	Cyrillic
006	254	15/14	Cyrillic Capital Letter Che	Cyrillic

Byte	Byte	Code	Name	Set
006	255	15/15	Cyrillic Capital Hard Sign	Cyrillic
007	161	10/01	Greek Capital Letter Alpha with Accent	Greek
007	162	10/02	Greek Capital Letter Epsilon with Accent	Greek
007	163	10/03	Greek Capital Letter Eta with Accent	Greek
007	164	10/04	Greek Capital Letter Iota with Accent	Greek
007	165	10/05	Greek Capital Letter Iota with Diaeresis	Greek
007	166	10/06	Greek Capital Letter Iota with Accent+Diaeresis	Greek
007	167	10/07	Greek Capital Letter Omicron with Accent	Greek
007	168	10/08	Greek Capital Letter Upsilon with Accent	Greek
007	169	10/09	Greek Capital Letter Upsilon with Diaeresis	Greek
007	170	10/10	Greek Capital Letter Upsilon with Accent+Diaeresis	Greek
007	171	10/11	Greek Capital Letter Omega with Accent	Greek
007	177	11/01	Greek Small Letter Alpha with Accent	Greek
007	178	11/02	Greek Small Letter Epsilon with Accent	Greek
007	179	11/03	Greek Small Letter ETA with Accent	Greek
007	180	11/04	Greek Small Letter Iota with Accent	Greek
007	181	11/05	Greek Small Letter Iota with Diaeresis	Greek
007	182	11/06	Greek Small Letter Iota with Accent+Diaeresis	Greek
007	183	11/07	Greek Small Letter Omicron with Accent	Greek
007	184	11/08	Greek Small Letter Upsilon with Accent	Greek
007	185	11/09	Greek Small Letter Upsilon with Diaeresis	Greek
007	186	11/10	Greek Small Letter Upsilon with Accent+Diaeresis	Greek
007	187	11/11	Greek Small Letter Omega with Accent	Greek
007	193	12/01	Greek Capital Letter Alpha	Greek
007	194	12/02	Greek Capital Letter Beta	Greek
007	195	12/03	Greek Capital Letter Gamma	Greek
007	196	12/04	Greek Capital Letter Delta	Greek
007	197	12/05	Greek Capital Letter Epsilon	Greek
007	198	12/06	Greek Capital Letter Zeta	Greek
007	199	12/07	Greek Capital Letter Eta	Greek
007	200	12/08	Greek Capital Letter Theta	Greek
007	201	12/09	Greek Capital Letter Iota	Greek
007	202	12/10	Greek Capital Letter Kappa	Greek
007	203	12/11	Greek Capital Letter Lambda	Greek
007	204	12/12	Greek Capital Letter Mu	Greek
007	205	12/13	Greek Capital Letter Nu	Greek
007	206	12/14	Greek Capital Letter Xi	Greek
007	207	12/15	Greek Capital Letter Omicron	Greek
007	208	13/00	Greek Capital Letter Pi	Greek
007	209	13/01	Greek Capital Letter Rho	Greek
007	210	13/02	Greek Capital Letter Sigma	Greek
007	212	13/04	Greek Capital Letter Tau	Greek
007	213	13/05	Greek Capital Letter Upsilon	Greek
007	214	13/06	Greek Capital Letter Phi	Greek

Byte	Byte	Code	Name	Set
007	215	13/07	Greek Capital Letter Chi	Greek
007	216	13/08	Greek Capital Letter Psi	Greek
007	217	13/09	Greek Capital Letter Omega	Greek
007	225	14/01	Greek Small Letter Alpha	Greek
007	226	14/02	Greek Small Letter Beta	Greek
007	227	14/03	Greek Small Letter Gamma	Greek
007	228	14/04	Greek Small Letter Delta	Greek
007	229	14/05	Greek Small Letter Epsilon	Greek
007	230	14/06	Greek Small Letter Zeta	Greek
007	231	14/07	Greek Small Letter Eta	Greek
007	232	14/08	Greek Small Letter Theta	Greek
007	233	14/09	Greek Small Letter Iota	Greek
007	234	14/10	Greek Small Letter Kappa	Greek
007	235	14/11	Greek Small Letter Lambda	Greek
007	236	14/12	Greek Small Letter Mu	Greek
007	237	14/13	Greek Small Letter Nu	Greek
007	238	14/14	Greek Small Letter Xi	Greek
007	239	14/15	Greek Small Letter Omicron	Greek
007	240	15/00	Greek Small Letter Pi	Greek
007	241	15/01	Greek Small Letter Rho	Greek
007	242	15/02	Greek Small Letter Sigma	Greek
007	243	15/03	Greek Small Letter Final Small Sigma	Greek
007	244	15/04	Greek Small Letter Tau	Greek
007	245	15/05	Greek Small Letter Upsilon	Greek
007	246	15/06	Greek Small Letter Phi	Greek
007	247	15/07	Greek Small Letter Chi	Greek
007	248	15/08	Greek Small Letter Psi	Greek
007	249	15/09	Greek Small Letter Omega	Greek
008	161	10/01	Left Radical	Technical
008	162	10/02	Top Left Radical	Technical
008	163	10/03	Horizontal Connector	Technical
008	164	10/04	Top Integral	Technical
008	165	10/05	Bottom Integral	Technical
008	166	10/06	Vertical Connector	Technical
008	167	10/07	Top Left Square Bracket	Technical
008	168	10/08	Bottom Left Square Bracket	Technical
008	169	10/09	Top Right Square Bracket	Technical
008	170	10/10	Bottom Right Square Bracket	Technical
008	171	10/11	Top Left Parenthesis	Technical
008	172	10/12	Bottom Left Parenthesis	Technical
008	173	10/13	Top Right Parenthesis	Technical
008	174	10/14	Bottom Right Parenthesis	Technical
008	175	10/15	Left Middle Curly Brace	Technical
008	176	11/00	Right Middle Curly Brace	Technical

Byte	Byte	Code	Name	Set
008	177	11/01	Top Left Summation	Technical
008	178	11/02	Bottom Left Summation	Technical
008	179	11/03	Top Vertical Summation Connector	Technical
008	180	11/04	Bottom Vertical Summation Connector	Technical
008	181	11/05	Top Right Summation	Technical
008	182	11/06	Bottom Right Summation	Technical
008	183	11/07	Right Middle Summation	Technical
008	188	11/12	Less Than Or Equal Sign	Technical
008	189	11/13	Not Equal Sign	Technical
008	190	11/14	Greater Than Or Equal Sign	Technical
008	191	11/15	Integral	Technical
008	192	12/00	Therefore	Technical
008	193	12/01	Variation, Proportional To	Technical
008	194	12/02	Infinity	Technical
008	197	12/05	Nabla, Del	Technical
008	200	12/08	Is Approximate To	Technical
008	201	12/09	Similar Or Equal To	Technical
008	205	12/13	If And Only If	Technical
008	206	12/14	Implies	Technical
008	207	12/15	Identical To	Technical
008	214	13/06	Radical	Technical
008	218	13/10	IS Included In	Technical
008	219	13/11	Includes	Technical
008	220	13/12	Intersection	Technical
008	221	13/13	Union	Technical
008	222	13/14	Logical And	Technical
008	223	13/15	Logical Or	Technical
008	239	14/15	Partial Derivative	Technical
008	246	15/06	Function	Technical
008	251	15/11	Left Arrow	Technical
008	252	15/12	Upward Arrow	Technical
008	253	15/13	Right Arrow	Technical
008	254	15/14	Downward Arrow	Technical
009	223	13/15	Blank	Special
009	224	14/00	Solid Diamond	Special
009	225	14/01	Checkerboard	Special
009	226	14/02	"Ht"	Special
009	227	14/03	"Ff"	Special
009	228	14/04	"Cr"	Special
009	229	14/05	"Lf"	Special
009	232	14/08	"Nl"	Special
009	233	14/09	"Vt"	Special
009	234	14/10	Lower-Right Corner	Special
009	235	14/11	Upper-Right Corner	Special

Byte	Byte	Code	Name	Set
009	236	14/12	Upper-Left Corner	Special
009	237	14/13	Lower-Left Corner	Special
009	238	14/14	Crossing-Lines	Special
009	239	14/15	Horizontal Line, Scan 1	Special
009	240	15/00	Horizontal Line, Scan 3	Special
009	241	15/01	Horizontal Line, Scan 5	Special
009	242	15/02	Horizontal Line, Scan 7	Special
009	243	15/03	Horizontal Line, Scan 9	Special
009	244	15/04	Left "T"	Special
009	245	15/05	Right "T"	Special
009	246	15/06	Bottom "T"	Special
009	247	15/07	Top "T"	Special
009	248	15/08	Vertical Bar	Special
010	161	10/01	Em Space	Publish
010	162	10/02	En Space	Publish
010	163	10/03	3/Em Space	Publish
010	164	10/04	4/Em Space	Publish
010	165	10/05	Digit Space	Publish
010	166	10/06	Punctuation Space	Publish
010	167	10/07	Thin Space	Publish
010	168	10/08	Hair Space	Publish
010	169	10/09	Em Dash	Publish
010	170	10/10	En Dash	Publish
010	172	10/12	Significant Blank Symbol	Publish
010	174	10/14	Ellipsis	Publish
010	175	10/15	Double Baseline Dot	Publish
010	176	11/00	Vulgar Fraction One Third	Publish
010	177	11/01	Vulgar Fraction Two Thirds	Publish
010	178	11/02	Vulgar Fraction One Fifth	Publish
010	179	11/03	Vulgar Fraction Two Fifths	Publish
010	180	11/04	Vulgar Fraction Three Fifths	Publish
010	181	11/05	Vulgar Fraction Four Fifths	Publish
010	182	11/06	Vulgar Fraction One Sixth	Publish
010	183	11/07	Vulgar Fraction Five Sixths	Publish
010	184	11/08	Care Of	Publish
010	187	11/11	Figure Dash	Publish
010	188	11/12	Left Angle Bracket	Publish
010	189	11/13	Decimal Point	Publish
010	190	11/14	Right Angle Bracket	Publish
010	191	11/15	Marker	Publish
010	195	12/03	Vulgar Fraction One Eighth	Publish
010	196	12/04	Vulgar Fraction Three Eighths	Publish
010	197	12/05	Vulgar Fraction Five Eighths	Publish
010	198	12/06	Vulgar Fraction Seven Eighths	Publish

Byte	Byte	Code	Name	Set
010	201	12/09	Trademark Sign	Publish
010	202	12/10	Signature Mark	Publish
010	203	12/11	Trademark Sign In Circle	Publish
010	204	12/12	Left Open Triangle	Publish
010	205	12/13	Right Open Triangle	Publish
010	206	12/14	Em Open Circle	Publish
010	207	12/15	Em Open Rectangle	Publish
010	208	13/00	Left Single Quotation Mark	Publish
010	209	13/01	Right Single Quotation Mark	Publish
010	210	13/02	Left Double Quotation Mark	Publish
010	211	13/03	Right Double Quotation Mark	Publish
010	212	13/04	Prescription, Take, Recipe	Publish
010	214	13/06	Minutes	Publish
010	215	13/07	Seconds	Publish
010	217	13/09	Latin Cross	Publish
010	218	13/10	Hexagram	Publish
010	219	13/11	Filled Rectangle Bullet	Publish
010	220	13/12	Filled Left Triangle Bullet	Publish
010	221	13/13	Filled Right Triangle Bullet	Publish
010	222	13/14	Em Filled Circle	Publish
010	223	13/15	Em Filled Rectangle	Publish
010	224	14/00	En Open Circle Bullet	Publish
010	225	14/01	En Open Square Bullet	Publish
010	226	14/02	Open Rectangular Bullet	Publish
010	227	14/03	Open Triangular Bullet Up	Publish
010	228	14/04	Open Triangular Bullet Down	Publish
010	229	14/05	Open Star	Publish
010	230	14/06	En Filled Circle Bullet	Publish
010	231	14/07	En Filled Square Bullet	Publish
010	232	14/08	Filled Triangular Bullet Up	Publish
010	233	14/09	Filled Triangular Bullet Down	Publish
010	234	14/10	Left Pointer	Publish
010	235	14/11	Right Pointer	Publish
010	236	14/12	Club	Publish
010	237	14/13	Diamond	Publish
010	238	14/14	Heart	Publish
010	240	15/00	Maltese Cross	Publish
010	241	15/01	Dagger	Publish
010	242	15/02	Double Dagger	Publish
010	243	15/03	Check Mark, Tick	Publish
010	244	15/04	Ballot Cross	Publish
010	245	15/05	Musical Sharp	Publish
010	246	15/06	Musical Flat	Publish
010	247	15/07	Male Symbol	Publish
010	248	15/08	Female Symbol	Publish
010	249	15/09	Telephone Symbol	Publish

Keysyms

Byte	Byte	Code	Name	Set
010	250	15/10	Telephone Recorder Symbol	Publish
010	251	15/11	Phonograph CopyRight Sign	Publish
010	252	15/12	Caret	Publish
010	253	15/13	Single Low Quotation Mark	Publish
010	254	15/14	Double Low Quotation Mark	Publish
010	255	15/15	Cursor	Publish
011	163	10/03	Left Caret	Apl
011	166	10/06	Right Caret	Apl
011	168	10/08	Down Caret	Apl
011	169	10/09	Up Caret	Apl
011	192	12/00	Overbar	Apl
011	194	12/02	Down Tack	Apl
011	195	12/03	UP Shoe (Cap)	Apl
011	196	12/04	Down Stile	Apl
011	198	12/06	Underbar	Apl
011	202	12/10	Jot	Apl
011	204	12/12	Quad	Apl
011	206	12/14	UP Tack	Apl
011	207	12/15	Circle	Apl
011	211	13/03	UP Stile	Apl
011	214	13/06	Down Shoe (Cup)	Apl
011	216	13/08	Right Shoe	Apl
011	218	13/10	Left Shoe	Apl
011	220	13/12	Left Tack	Apl
011	252	15/12	Right Tack	Apl
012	224	14/00	Hebrew Letter Aleph	Hebrew
012	225	14/01	Hebrew Letter Beth	Hebrew
012	226	14/02	Hebrew Letter Gimmel	Hebrew
012	227	14/03	Hebrew Letter Daleth	Hebrew
012	228	14/04	Hebrew Letter He	Hebrew
012	229	14/05	Hebrew Letter Waw	Hebrew
012	230	14/06	Hebrew Letter Zayin	Hebrew
012	231	14/07	Hebrew Letter Het	Hebrew
012	232	14/08	Hebrew Letter Teth	Hebrew
012	233	14/09	Hebrew Letter Yod	Hebrew
012	234	14/10	Hebrew Letter Final Kaph	Hebrew
012	235	14/11	Hebrew Letter Kaph	Hebrew
012	236	14/12	Hebrew Letter Lamed	Hebrew
012	237	14/13	Hebrew Letter Final Mem	Hebrew
012	238	14/14	Hebrew Letter Mem	Hebrew
012	239	14/15	Hebrew Letter Final Nun	Hebrew
012	240	15/00	Hebrew Letter Nun	Hebrew

Byte	Byte	Code	Name	Set
012	241	15/01	Hebrew Letter Samekh	Hebrew
012	242	15/02	Hebrew Letter A'yin	Hebrew
012	243	15/03	Hebrew Letter Final Pe	Hebrew
012	244	15/04	Hebrew Letter PE	Hebrew
012	245	15/05	Hebrew Letter Final Zadi	Hebrew
012	246	15/06	Hebrew Letter Zadi	Hebrew
012	247	15/07	Hebrew Kuf	Hebrew
012	248	15/08	Hebrew Resh	Hebrew
012	249	15/09	Hebrew Shin	Hebrew
012	250	15/10	Hebrew Taf	Hebrew
255	008	00/08	BackSpace, Back Space, Back Char	Keyboard
255	009	00/09	Tab	Keyboard
255	010	00/10	Linefeed, Lf	Keyboard
255	011	00/11	Clear	Keyboard
255	013	00/13	Return, Enter	Keyboard
255	019	01/03	Pause, Hold, Scroll Lock	Keyboard
255	027	01/11	Escape	Keyboard
255	032	02/00	Multi-Key Character Preface	Keyboard
255	033	02/01	Kanji, Kanji Convert	Keyboard
255	080	05/00	HOME	Keyboard
255	081	05/01	Left, Move Left, Left Arrow	Keyboard
255	082	05/02	UP, Move UP, UP Arrow	Keyboard
255	083	05/03	Right, Move Right, Right Arrow	Keyboard
255	084	05/04	Down, Move Down, Down Arrow	Keyboard
255	085	05/05	Prior, Previous	Keyboard
255	086	05/06	Next	Keyboard
255	087	05/07	End, Eol	Keyboard
255	088	05/08	Begin, Bol	Keyboard
255	096	06/00	Select, Mark	Keyboard
255	097	06/01	Print	Keyboard
255	098	06/02	Execute, Rdn, Do	Keyboard
255	099	06/03	Insert, Insert Here	Keyboard
255	101	06/05	Undo, Oops	Keyboard
255	102	06/06	Redo, Again	Keyboard
255	103	06/07	Menu	Keyboard
255	104	06/08	Find, Search	Keyboard
255	105	06/09	Cancel, Stop, Abort, Exit	Keyboard
255	106	06/10	Help, Question Mark	Keyboard
255	107	06/11	Break	Keyboard
255	126	07/14	Mode Switch, Script Switch, Character Set Switch	Keyboard
255	127	07/15	Num Lock	Keyboard
255	128	08/00	Keypad Space	Keyboard
255	137	08/09	Keypad Tab	Keyboard
255	141	08/13	Keypad Enter	Keyboard

Keysyms

Byte	Byte	Code	Name	Set
255	145	09/01	Keypad F1, PF1, A	Keyboard
255	146	09/02	Keypad F2, PF2, B	Keyboard
255	147	09/03	Keypad F3, PF3, C	Keyboard
255	148	09/04	Keypad F4, PF4, D	Keyboard
255	170	10/10	Keypad Multiplication Sign, Asterisk	Keyboard
255	171	10/11	Keypad Plus Sign	Keyboard
255	172	10/12	Keypad Separator, Comma	Keyboard
255	173	10/13	Keypad Minus Sign, Hyphen	Keyboard
255	174	10/14	Keypad Decimal Point, Full Stop	Keyboard
255	175	10/15	Keypad Division Sign, Solidus	Keyboard
255	176	11/00	Keypad Digit Zero	Keyboard
255	177	11/01	Keypad Digit One	Keyboard
255	178	11/02	Keypad Digit Two	Keyboard
255	179	11/03	Keypad Digit Three	Keyboard
255	180	11/04	Keypad Digit Four	Keyboard
255	181	11/05	Keypad Digit Five	Keyboard
255	182	11/06	Keypad Digit Six	Keyboard
255	183	11/07	Keypad Digit Seven	Keyboard
255	184	11/08	Keypad Digit Eight	Keyboard
255	185	11/09	Keypad Digit Nine	Keyboard
255	189	11/13	Keypad Equals Sign	Keyboard
255	190	11/14	F1	Keyboard
255	191	11/15	F2	Keyboard
255	192	12/00	F3	Keyboard
255	193	12/01	F4	Keyboard
255	194	12/02	F5	Keyboard
255	195	12/03	F6	Keyboard
255	196	12/04	F7	Keyboard
255	197	12/05	F8	Keyboard
255	198	12/06	F9	Keyboard
255	199	12/07	F10	Keyboard
255	200	12/08	F11, L1	Keyboard
255	201	12/09	F12, L2	Keyboard
255	202	12/10	F13, L3	Keyboard
255	203	12/11	F14, L4	Keyboard
255	204	12/12	F15, L5	Keyboard
255	205	12/13	F16, L6	Keyboard
255	206	12/14	F17, L7	Keyboard
255	207	12/15	F18, L8	Keyboard
255	208	13/00	F19, L9	Keyboard
255	209	13/01	F20, L10	Keyboard
255	210	13/02	F21, R1	Keyboard
255	211	13/03	F22, R2	Keyboard
255	212	13/04	F23, R3	Keyboard
255	213	13/05	F24, R4	Keyboard
255	214	13/06	F25, R5	Keyboard

Byte	Byte	Code	Name		Set
255	215	13/07	F26, R6		Keyboard
255	216	13/08	F27, R7		Keyboard
255	217	13/09	F28, R8		Keyboard
255	218	13/10	F29, R9		Keyboard
255	219	13/11	F30, R10		Keyboard
255	220	13/12	F31, R11		Keyboard
255	221	13/13	F32, R12		Keyboard
255	222	13/14	F33, R13		Keyboard
255	223	13/15	F34, R14		Keyboard
255	224	14/00	F35, R15		Keyboard
255	225	14/01	Left Shift		Keyboard
255	226	14/02	Right Shift		Keyboard
255	227	14/03	Left Control		Keyboard
255	228	14/04	Right Control		Keyboard
255	229	14/05	Caps Lock		Keyboard
255	230	14/06	Shift Lock		Keyboard
255	231	14/07	Left Meta		Keyboard
255	232	14/08	Right Meta		Keyboard
255	233	14/09	Left ALT		Keyboard
255	234	14/10	Right ALT		Keyboard
255	235	14/11	Left Super		Keyboard
255	236	14/12	Right Super		Keyboard
255	237	14/13	Left Hyper		Keyboard
255	238	14/14	Right Hyper		Keyboard
255	255	15/15	Delete, Rubout		Keyboard

Keysyms

C
Errors

This section lists and describes the various types of errors. In general, when a request terminates with an error, the request has no side effects (that is, there is no partial execution). The only requests for which this is not true are **ChangeWindowAttributes**, **ChangeGC**, **PolyText8**, **PolyText16**, **FreeColors**, **StoreColors**, and **ChangeKeyboardControl**. All these requests perform an operation multiple times or set multiple values, and all the operations or values up to the one containing the error will be performed.

The following error codes can be returned by the various requests.

Access
An attempt is made to grab a key/button combination already grabbed by another client.

An attempt is made to free a colormap entry not allocated by the client.

An attempt is made to store into a read-only or an unallocated colormap entry.

An attempt is made to modify the access control list from other than the local host (or otherwise authorized client).

An attempt is made to select an event type that only one client can select at a time when another client has already selected it.

Alloc
The server failed to allocate the requested resource. Note that the explicit listing of **Alloc** errors in request only covers allocation errors at a very coarse level and is not intended to cover all cases of a server running out of allocation space in the middle of service. The semantics when a server runs out of allocation space are left unspecified, but a server may generate an **Alloc** error on any request for this reason, and clients should be prepared to receive such errors and handle or discard them.

Atom
A value for an ATOM argument does not name a defined ATOM.

BadAccess
An attempt to grab a key/button combination already grabbed by another client.

An attempt to free a colormap entry not allocated by the client.

An attempt to store into a read-only or an unallocated colormap entry.

An attempt to modify the access control list from other than the local host (or otherwise authorized client).

An attempt to select an event type, that at most one client can select at a time, when another client has already selected it.

BadAlloc　　The server failed to allocate the requested abstraction.

Note that the explicit listing of Alloc errors in requests only covers allocation errors at a very coarse level and is not intended to cover all cases of a server running out of allocation space in the middle of service. The semantics when a server runs out of allocation space are left unspecified, but a server may generate an Alloc error on any request for this reason, and clients should be prepared to receive such errors and handle or discard them.

BadAtom　　A value for an ATOM argument does not name a defined ATOM.

BadColormap　　A value for a COLORMAP argument does not name a defined COLORMAP.

BadCursor　　A value for a CURSOR argument does not name a defined CURSOR.

BadDrawable　　A value for a DRAWABLE argument does not name a defined WINDOW or PIXMAP.

BadFont　　A value for a FONT argument does not name a defined FONT.

A value for a FONTABLE argument does not name a defined FONT or a defined GCONTEXT.

BadGContext　　A value for a GCONTEXT argument does not name a defined GCONTEXT.

BadIDChoice　　The value chosen for an abstraction identifier either is not included in the range assigned to the client or is already in use.

BadImplementation　　The server does not implement some aspect of the request. A server that generates this error for a core request is deficient. As such, this error is not listed for any of the requests, but clients should be prepared to receive such errors and handle or discard them.

BadLength　　The length of a request is shorter or longer than that required to minimally contain the arguments.

The length of a request exceeds the maximum length accepted by the server.

BadMatch	An **InputOnly** window is used as a DRAWABLE.
	In a graphics request, the GCONTEXT argument does not have the same root and depth as the destination DRAWABLE argument.
	Some argument (or pair of arguments) has the correct type and range, but it fails to "match" in some other way required by the request.
BadName	A font or color of the specified name does not exist.
BadPixmap	A value for a PIXMAP argument does not name a defined PIXMAP.
BadRequest	The major or minor opcode does not specify a valid request.
BadValue	Some numeric value falls outside the range of values accepted by the request. Unless a specific range is specified for an argument, the full range defined by the argument's type is accepted. Any argument defined as a set of alternatives typically can generate this error (due to the encoding).
BadWindow	A value for a WINDOW argument does not name a defined WINDOW.
	NOTE: The **BadAtom, BadColormap, BadCursor, BadDrawable, BadFont, BadGContext, BadPixmap,** and **BadWindow** errors are also used when the argument type is extended by union with a set of fixed alternatives; for example, <WINDOW or **PointerRoot** or None>.
Colormap	A value for a COLORMAP argument does not name a defined COLORMAP.
Cursor	A value for a CURSOR argument does not name a defined CURSOR.
Drawable	A value for a DRAWABLE argument does not name a defined WINDOW or PIXMAP.
Font	A value for a FONT argument does not name a defined FONT.
	A value for a FONTABLE argument does not name a defined FONT or a defined GCONTEXT.
GContext	A value for a GCONTEXT argument does not name a defined GCONTEXT.
IDChoice	The value chosen for a resource identifier either is not included in the range assigned to the client or is already in use.
Implementation	The server does not implement some aspect of the request. A server that generates this error for a core request is deficient. As such, this error is not listed for any of the requests, but clients

Errors

should be prepared to receive such errors and handle or discard them.

Length
The length of a request is shorter or longer than that required to minimally contain the arguments.

The length of a request exceeds the maximum length accepted by the server.

Match
An **InputOnly** window is used as a DRAWABLE.

In a graphics request, the GCONTEXT argument does not have the same root and depth as the destination DRAWABLE argument.

Some argument (or pair of arguments) has the correct type and range, but it fails to match in some other way required by the request.

Name
A font or color of the specified name does not exist.

Pixmap
A value for a PIXMAP argument does not name a defined PIXMAP.

Request
The major or minor opcode does not specify a valid request.

Value
Some numeric value falls outside the range of values accepted by the request. Unless a specific range is specified for an argument, the full range defined by the argument's type is accepted. Any argument defined as a set of alternatives typically can generate this error (due to the encoding).

Window
A value for a WINDOW argument does not name a defined WINDOW.

Encoding

The encoding of each error follows:

Access

# Bytes	Value	Description
1	0	Error
1	10	code
2	CARD16	sequence number
4		unused
2	CARD16	minor opcode
1	CARD8	major opcode
21		unused

Alloc

# Bytes	Value	Description
1	0	Error
1	11	code
2	CARD16	sequence number
4		unused
2	CARD16	minor opcode
1	CARD8	major opcode
21		unused

Atom

# Bytes	Value	Description
1	0	Error
1	5	code
2	CARD16	sequence number
4	CARD32	bad atom id
2	CARD16	minor opcode
1	CARD8	major opcode
21		unused

Colormap

# Bytes	Value	Description
1	0	Error
1	12	code
2	CARD16	sequence number
4	CARD32	bad resource id
2	CARD16	minor opcode
1	CARD8	major opcode
21		unused

Cursor

# Bytes	Value	Description
1	0	Error
1	6	code
2	CARD16	sequence number
4	CARD32	bad resource id
2	CARD16	minor opcode
1	CARD8	major opcode
21		unused

Drawable

# Bytes	Value	Description
1	0	Error
1	9	code
2	CARD16	sequence number
4	CARD32	bad resource id
2	CARD16	minor opcode
1	CARD8	major opcode
21		unused

Font

# Bytes	Value	Description
1	0	Error
1	7	code
2	CARD16	sequence number
4	CARD32	bad resource id
2	CARD16	minor opcode
1	CARD8	major opcode
21		unused

GContext

# Bytes	Value	Description
1	0	Error
1	13	code
2	CARD16	sequence number
4	CARD32	bad resource id
2	CARD16	minor opcode
1	CARD8	major opcode
21		unused

IDChoice

# Bytes	Value	Description
1	0	Error
1	14	code
2	CARD16	sequence number
4	CARD32	bad resource id
2	CARD16	minor opcode
1	CARD8	major opcode
21		unused

Implementation

# Bytes	Value	Description
1	0	Error
1	17	code
2	CARD16	sequence number
4		unused
2	CARD16	minor opcode
1	CARD8	major opcode
21		unused

Length

# Bytes	Value	Description
1	0	Error
1	16	code
2	CARD16	sequence number
4		unused
2	CARD16	minor opcode
1	CARD8	major opcode
21		unused

Match

# Bytes	Value	Description
1	0	Error
1	8	code
2	CARD16	sequence number
4		unused
2	CARD16	minor opcode
1	CARD8	major opcode
21		unused

Name

# Bytes	Value	Description
1	0	Error
1	15	code
2	CARD16	sequence number
4		unused
2	CARD16	minor opcode
1	CARD8	major opcode
21		unused

Pixmap

# Bytes	Value	Description
1	0	Error
1	4	code
2	CARD16	sequence number
4	CARD32	bad resource id
2	CARD16	minor opcode
1	CARD8	major opcode
21		unused

Request

# Bytes	Value	Description
1	0	Error
1	1	code
2	CARD16	sequence number
4		unused
2	CARD16	minor opcode
1	CARD8	major opcode
21		unused

Value

# Bytes	Value	Description
1	0	Error
1	2	code
2	CARD16	sequence number
4	<32-bits>	bad value
2	CARD16	minor opcode
1	CARD8	major opcode
21		unused

Window

# Bytes	Value	Description
1	0	Error
1	3	code
2	CARD16	sequence number
4	CARD32	bad resource id
2	CARD16	minor opcode
1	CARD8	major opcode
21		unused

D
Predefined Atoms

A property is a named piece of data attached to a window, stored by the server. Clients use them primarily to pass information between clients through the server. For this to work, both clients need to know the name of the property where the data will be stored. Property names are strings, so instead of passing arbitrary length strings over the network, the server chooses an ID to represent each property name. This ID is called an Atom. When a client wants to use a particular property, it knows the name but not the Atom, so it calls **Intern-Atom** *to get the Atom for the property name. This is a round-trip because the server maintains the mapping between strings and atoms. Since there are a number of standard properties that are used by many clients, the X protocol defines the Atoms of these properties ahead of time, so that clients need not call* **InternAtom**. *This speeds the startup of applications. Client libraries such as Xlib provide symbolic constants that contain the predefined values for these atoms, which clients can use in their code. -Ed.*

Predefined atoms are not strictly necessary and may not be useful in all environments, but they will eliminate many **InternAtom** requests in most applications. Note that they are predefined only in the sense of having numeric values, not in the sense of having required semantics. The core protocol imposes no semantics on these names, except as they are used in FONTPROP structures (see **QueryFont** request).

To avoid conflicts with possible future names for which semantics might be imposed (either at the protocol level or in terms of higher level user interface models), names beginning with an underscore should be used for atoms that are private to a particular vendor or organization. To guarantee no conflicts between vendors and organizations, additional prefixes need to be used. However, the protocol does not define the mechanism for choosing such prefixes. For names private to a single application or end user but stored in globally accessible locations, it is suggested that two leading underscores be used to avoid conflicts with other names.

The following names have predefined atom values. Note that upper case and lower case matter.

Arc	End_Space	Resolution	Underline_Position
Atom	Family_Name	Resource_Manager	Underline_Thickness
Bitmap	Font	Rgb_Best_Map	Visualid
Cap_Height	Font_Name	Rgb_Blue_Map	Weight
Cardinal	Full_Name	Rgb_Color_Map	Window
Colormap	Integer	Rgb_Default_Map	Wm_Class
Copyright	Italic_Angle	Rgb_Gray_Map	Wm_Client_Machine
Cursor	Max_Space	Rgb_Green_Map	Wm_Command
Cut_Buffer0	Min_Space	Rgb_Red_Map	Wm_Hints
Cut_Buffer1	Norm_Space	Secondary	Wm_Icon_Name
Cut_Buffer2	Notice	Strikeout_Ascent	Wm_Icon_Size
Cut_Buffer3	Pixmap	Strikeout_Descent	Wm_Name
Cut_Buffer4	Point	String	Wm_Normal_Hints
Cut_Buffer5	Point_Size	Subsc.Lpt_X	Wm_Size_Hints
Cut_Buffer6	Primary	Subsc.Lpt_Y	Wm_Transient_For
Cut_Buffer7	Quad_Width	Supersc.Lpt_X	Wm_Zoom_Hints
Drawable	Rectangle	Supersc.Lpt_Y	X_Height

Encoding

Primary	1	Rgb_Color_Map	24	Supersc.Lpt_X	47
Secondary	2	Rgb_Best_Map	25	Supersc.Lpt_Y	48
Arc	3	Rgb_Blue_Map	26	Subsc.Lpt_X	49
Atom	4	Rgb_Default_Map	27	Subsc.Lpt_Y	50
Bitmap	5	Rgb_Gray_Map	28	Underline_Position	51
Cardinal	6	Rgb_Green_Map	29	Underline_Thickness	52
Colormap	7	Rgb_Red_Map	30	Strikeout_Ascent	53
Cursor	8	String	31	Strikeout_Descent	54
Cut_Buffer0	9	VisualId	32	Italic_Angle	55
Cut_Buffer1	10	Window	33	X_Height	56
Cut_Buffer2	11	Wm_Command	34	Quad_Width	57
Cut_Buffer3	12	Wm_Hints	35	Weight	58
Cut_Buffer4	13	Wm_Client_Machine	36	Point_Size	59
Cut_Buffer5	14	Wm_Icon_Name	37	Resolution	60
Cut_Buffer6	15	Wm_Icon_Size	38	Copyright	61
Cut_Buffer7	16	Wm_Name	39	Notice	62
Drawable	17	Wm_Normal_Hints	40	Font_Name	63
Font	18	Wm_Size_Hints	41	Family_Name	64
Integer	19	Wm_Zoom_Hints	42	Full_Name	65
Pixmap	20	Min_Space	43	Cap_Height	66
Point	21	Norm_Space	44	Wm_Class	67
Rectangle	22	Max_Space	45	Wm_Transient_For	68
Resource_Manager	23	End_Space	46		

E
Keyboards and Pointers

Keyboards

A keycode represents a physical (or logical) key. Keycodes lie in the inclusive range [8,255]. A keycode value carries no intrinsic information, although server implementors may attempt to encode geometry information (for example, matrix) to be interpreted in a server-dependent fashion. The mapping between keys and keycodes cannot be changed using the protocol.

A keysym is an encoding of a symbol on the cap of a key. The set of defined keysyms include the character sets Latin-1, Latin-2, Latin-3, Latin-4, Kana, Arabic, Cryllic, Greek, Technical, Special, Publish, Apl, and Hebrew as well as a set of symbols common on keyboards (Return, Help, Tab, and so on). Keysyms with the most-significant bit (of the 29 bits) set are reserved as vendor-specific.

A list of keysyms is associated with each keycode, and the length of the list can vary with each keycode. The list is intended to convey the set of symbols on the corresponding key. By convention, if the list contains a single keysym and that keysym is alphabetic and case distinction is relevant for it, then it should be treated as equivalent to a two-element list of the lower case and upper case keysyms. For example, if the list contains the single keysym for upper case *A*, then the client should treat it as if it were instead a pair with lower case *a* as the first keysym and upper case *A* as the second keysym.

For any keycode, the first keysym in the list normally should be chosen as the interpretation of a **KeyPress** when no modifier keys are down. The second keysym in the list normally should be chosen when the **Shift** modifier is on or when the Lock modifier is on and **Lock** is interpreted as ShiftLock. When the **Lock** modifier is on and is interpreted as CapsLock, it is suggested that the **Shift** modifier first be applied to choose a keysym. However, if that keysym is lower case alphabetic, the corresponding upper case keysym should be used instead. Other interpretations of CapsLock are possible. For example, it may be viewed as equivalent to ShiftLock, applying only when the first keysym is lower case alphabetic and the second keysym is the corresponding upper case alphabetic. No interpretation of keysyms beyond the first two in a list is suggested here. No spatial geometry of the symbols on the key is defined by their order in the keysym list, although a geometry might be defined on a vendor-specific basis.

The mapping between keycodes and keysyms is not used directly by the server; it is merely stored for reading and writing by clients.

The keymask modifier named **Lock** is intended to be mapped to either a CapsLock or a Shift-Lock key, but which one is left as application-specific and/or user-specific. However, it is suggested that the determination be made according to the associated keysym(s) of the corresponding keycode.

Pointers

When a button press is processed with the pointer in some window W and no active pointer grab is in progress, the ancestors of W are searched from the root down, looking for a passive grab to activate. If no matching passive grab on the button exists, then an active grab is started automatically for the client receiving the event, and the last-pointer-grab time is set to the current server time. The effect is essentially equivalent to a **GrabButton** with arguments:

Argument	Value
event-mask	Client's selected pointer events on the event window
pointer-mode and keyboard-mode	**Asynchronous**
owner-events	**True**, if the client has **OwnerGrabButton** selected on the event window; otherwise, **False**
confine-to	**None**
cursor	**None**

The grab is terminated automatically when the logical state of the pointer has all buttons released. **UngrabPointer** and **ChangeActivePointerGrab** can both be used to modify the active grab.

Buttons are always numbered starting with one.

Encoding

Keyboards

Keycode values are always greater than 7 (and less than 256).

Keysym values with the bit #x10000000 set are reserved as vendor-specific.

The names and encodings of the standard keysym values are contained in Appendix B, *Keysyms*.

Pointers

Button values are numbered starting with one.

F
Flow Control and Concurrency

Whenever the server is writing to a given connection, it is permissible for the server to stop reading from that connection (but if the writing would block, it must continue to service other connections). The server is not required to buffer more than a single request per connection at one time. For a given connection to the server, a client can block while reading from the connection but should undertake to read (events and errors) when writing would block. Failure on the part of a client to obey this rule could result in a deadlocked connection, although deadlock is probably unlikely unless either the transport layer has very little buffering or the client attempts to send large numbers of requests without ever reading replies or checking for errors and events.

If a server is implemented with internal concurrency, the overall effect must be as if individual requests are executed to completion in some serial order, and requests from a given connection must be executed in delivery order (that is, the total execution order is a shuffle of the individual streams). The execution of a request includes validating all arguments, collecting all data for any reply, and generating and queueing all required events. However, it does not include the actual transmission of the reply and the events. In addition, the effect of any other cause that can generate multiple events (for example, activation of a grab or pointer motion) must effectively generate and queue all required events indivisibly with respect to all other causes and requests. For a request from a given client, any events destined for that client that are caused by executing the request must be sent to the client before any reply or error is sent.

G
Request Group Summary

Group Listing with Brief Description

This quick reference will help you find and use the correct protocol request for a particular application. It supplies two lists:

- Group Listing with Brief Descriptions
- Alphabetical Listing of Requests

Colors and Colormaps

AllocColor	Allocate a read-only colorcell specifying the color with RGB values.
AllocColorCells	Allocate read/write colorcells. This request does not set the colors of the allocated cells.
AllocColorPlanes	Allocate read/write colorcells for overlays. This request does not set the colors of the allocated cells.
AllocNamedColor	Allocate a read-only colorcell specifying the color with a color name.
CopyColormapAndFree	Copy into a new virtual colormap the colorcells that one client has allocated, and free these colorcells in the old colormap.
CreateColormap	Create a virtual colormap.
FreeColormap	Free a virtual colormap.
FreeColors	Deallocate colorcells.
InstallColormap	Copy a virtual colormap into the display hardware, so that it will actually be used to translate pixel values.

ListInstalledColormaps	List the IDs of the colormaps installed in the hardware.
LookupColor	Return the RGB values associated with a color name, and return the closest RGB values available on the display hardware.
QueryColors	Return the colors in the specified cells of a colormap.
StoreColors	Store colors into cells allocated by **AllocColorCells** or **AllocColorPlanes**.
StoreNamedColor	Store colors into cells allocated by **AllocColorCells** or **AllocColorPlanes**.
UninstallColormap	Remove a virtual colormap from the display hardware, so it will not be used to translate pixel values.

Cursors

CreateCursor	Create a cursor resource from characters in a special cursor font.
CreateGlyphCursor	Create a cursor resource from characters in any font.
FreeCursor	Destroy a cursor resource.
RecolorCursor	Change the foreground and background colors of a cursor.

Drawing Graphics

ClearArea	Clear an area of a window.
CopyArea	Copy an area of a window to another area in the same or a different window. If the source area is obscured, this request will generate a **GraphicsExpose** event to identify the area of the destination for which the source is not available.
CopyPlane	Copy a single plane of one drawable into any number of planes of another, applying two pixel values to translate the depth of the single plane.
FillPoly	Fill a polygon, without drawing the complete outline.
PolyArc	Draw one or more arcs, each of which is a partial ellipse aligned with the x and y axis.
PolyFillArc	Fill one or more arcs, without drawing the arc itself.
PolyFillRectangle	Fill one or more rectangles, without drawing the entire outline.
PolyLine	Draw one or more connected lines.

PolyPoint	Draw one or more points.
PolyRectangle	Draw one or more rectangles.
PolySegment	Draw one or more disconnected lines.

Events

GetInputFocus	Return the current keyboard focus window.
GetMotionEvents	Some servers are equipped with a buffer that records the position history of the pointer. This request will return segments of this history for selected time periods.
SetInputFocus	Set a window and its descendants to receive all keyboard input.

Fonts and Text

CloseFont	Disclaim interest in a particular font. If this is the last client to be using the specified font, then the font is unloaded.
GetFontPath	Get the path that the server uses to search for fonts.
ImageText8	Draw text string in 8-bit font. The bounding rectangle of the string is drawn in the background color from the GC before the text is drawn.
ImageText16	Draw text string in 16-bit font. The bounding rectangle of the string is drawn in the background color from the GC before the text is drawn.
ListFonts	List the fonts available on a server.
ListFontsWithInfo	List the fonts available on a server, with information about each font.
OpenFont	Load a font for drawing. If the font has already been loaded, this request simply returns the ID.
PolyText8	Draw text items using 8-bit fonts. Each item can specify a string, a font, and a horizontal offset.
PolyText16	Draw text items using 16-bit fonts. Each item can specify a string, a font, and a horizontal offset.
QueryFont	Get the table of information describing a font and each character in it.
QueryTextExtents	Calculate the width of a string in a certain font.
SetFontPath	Set the path that the server uses to search for fonts.

The Graphics Context

ChangeGC	Change any or all characteristics of an existing GC.
CopyGC	Copy any or all characteristics of one GC into another.
CreateGC	Create a graphics context, and optionally set any or all of its characteristics. If not set, each characteristic has a reasonable default.
FreeGC	Free the memory in the server associated with a GC.
SetClipRectangles	Set the clip region of a GC to the union of a set of rectangles.
SetDashes	Set the dash pattern for lines, in a more powerful way than is possible using **CreateGC** or **ChangeGC**.

Images

GetImage	Place an image from a drawable into a representation in memory.
PutImage	Dump an image into a drawable.

Interclient Communication

ChangeProperty	Set the value of a property.
ConvertSelection	Request that the owner of a particular selection convert it to a particular format, then send an event informing the requestor of the conversion's success and the name of the property containing the result.
DeleteProperty	Delete the data associated with a particular property on a particular window.
GetAtomName	Get the string name of a property given it ID.
GetProperty	Get the value of a property.
GetSelectionOwner	Get the current owner of a particular selection property.
InternAtom	Get the ID of a property given its string name, and optionally create the ID if no property with the specified name exists.
ListHosts	Obtain a list of hosts having access to a display.
ListProperties	List the IDs of the current list of properties.
RotateProperties	Rotate the values of a list of properties.

SetSelectionOwner	Set a window as the current owner of a particular selection property.

Keyboard and Pointer

AllowEvents	Release events queued in the server due to grabs with certain parameters.
Bell	Ring the keyboard bell.
ChangeActivePointerGrab	Change the events that are sent to a window that has grabbed the pointer or keyboard.
ChangeKeyboardControl	Change personal preference features of the keyboard such as click and auto-repeat.
ChangeKeyboardMapping	Change the keyboard mapping seen by all clients.
ChangePointerControl	Change personal preference features of the pointer, such as acceleration (the ratio of the amount the physical mouse is moved to the amount the cursor moves on the screen).
GetKeyboardControl	Get personal preference features of the keyboard such as click and auto-repeat.
GetKeyboardMapping	Return the keyboard mapping seen by all clients.
GetModifierMapping	Get the mapping of physical keys to logical modifiers.
GetPointerControl	Return personal preference features of the pointer.
GetPointerMapping	Get the mapping of physical buttons to logical buttons.
GrabButton	For all pointer events (button presses and motion) occurring while the specified combination of buttons and modifier keys are pressed, declare that these pointer events will be delivered to a particular window regardless of the pointer's location on the screen.
GrabKey	For all keyboard events occurring while the specified combination of buttons and modifier keys are pressed, declare that these keyboard events will be delivered to a particular window regardless of the pointer's location on the screen.
GrabKeyboard	Declare that all keyboard events will be delivered to a particular window regardless of the pointer's location on the screen.
GrabPointer	Declare that all pointer events (button presses and motion) will be delivered to a particular window regardless of the pointer's location on the screen.
QueryKeymap	Get the current state of the entire keyboard.

QueryPointer	Get the current pointer position.
SetModifierMapping	Set the mapping of physical keys to logical modifiers such as Shift and Control.
SetPointerMapping	Set the mapping of physical buttons to logical buttons.
UngrabButton	Release a grab on a button.
UngrabKey	Release a grab on a button.
UngrabKeyboard	Release a grab on the keyboard.
UngrabPointer	Release a grab on the pointer.
WarpPointer	Move the pointer.

Security

ChangeHosts	Modify the list of hosts that are allowed access to a server.
SetAccessControl	Turn on or off the mechanism that checks the host access list before allowing a connection.

Window Characteristics

ChangeWindowAttributes	Set any or all window attributes. For a brief description of the window attributes, see Section 1.3.2.
GetGeometry	Return the position, dimensions, border width, and depth of a window; return the ID of the root window at the top of the window's hierarchy.
GetWindowAttributes	Get the current values of some of the window attributes described for **ChangeWindowAttributes**; also find out the characteristics of the window that were set when it was created (**InputOnly** or **InputOutput**, and visual), whether its colormap is installed and whether it is mapped or viewable.

Window Manipulation by the Client

CreateWindow	Create a window.
DestroySubwindows	Destroy an entire hierarchy of windows.
DestroyWindow	Destroy a window.
MapSubwindows	Map all subwindows of a window.

MapWindow	Mark a window as eligible for display.
UnmapSubwindows	Remove all subwindows of a window, but not the window itself, from the screen.
UnmapWindow	Remove a window and all its subwindows from the screen.

Window Manipulation by the Window Manager

ChangeSaveSet	Add or remove windows from a save-set.
CirculateWindow	Lower the highest window on the screen or raise the lowest one, depending on the parameters of this request.
ConfigureWindow	Allow the window manager to move, resize, change the border width, or change the stacking order of a window.
QueryTree	Allow the window manager to get the window IDs of windows it did not create.
ReparentWindow	Allow the window manager to change the window hierarchy to insert a frame window between each top-level window on the screen and the root window. The window manager can then decorate this frame window with a title for the application, buttons for moving and resizing the window, etc.

Miscellaneous

CreatePixmap	Create an off-screen drawable.
ForceScreenSaver	Activate or reset the screen saver.
FreePixmap	Free the memory associated with an off-screen drawable.
GetScreenSaver	Get the characteristics of the mechanism that blanks the screen after an idle period.
GrabServer	Initiate a state where requests only from a single client will be acted upon. The server will queue events for other clients and requests made by other clients until the grab is released.
KillClient	After a client exits because of the **SetCloseDownMode** request, kill the resources that remain alive.
ListExtensions	List the extensions available on the server.
NoOperation	The minimum request, it contains only the opcode and request length.

QueryBestSize	Query the server for the fastest size for creating tiles or stipples or the largest support size for cursors.
QueryExtension	Determine whether a certain extension is available in the server.
SendEvent	Send any type of event to a particular window.
SetCloseDownMode	Determine whether resources created by a client are preserved after the client exits. Normally, they are not, but if the client can reclaim its resources in a later incarnation, the client can use this request.
SetScreenSaver	Set characteristics that blank the screen after an idle period.
TranslateCoordinates	Translate coordinates from a window frame of reference to a screen frame of reference.
UngrabServer	Release the grab on the server, process all outstanding requests, and send all queued events.

H
Alphabetical Listing of Requests

This appendix provides a table that lists all protocol requests in alphabetical order with brief descriptions.

Table H-1. Alphabetical Listing of Requests

Request	Description
AllocColor	Allocate a read-only colorcell specifying the color with RGB values.
AllocColorCells	Allocate read/write colorcells. This request does not set the colors of the allocated cells.
AllocColorPlanes	Allocate read/write colorcells for overlays. This request does not set the colors of the allocated cells.
AllocNamedColor	Allocate a read-only colorcell specifying the color with a color name.
AllowEvents	Release events queued in the server due to grabs with certain parameters.
Bell	Ring the keyboard bell.
ChangeActivePointerGrab	Change the events that are sent to a window that has grabbed the pointer or keyboard.
ChangeGC	Change any or all characteristics of an existing GC.
ChangeHosts	Modify the list of hosts that are allowed access to a server.
ChangeKeyboardControl	Change personal preference features of the keyboard such as click and auto-repeat.
ChangeKeyboardMapping	Change the keyboard mapping seen by all clients.
ChangePointerControl	Change personal preference features of the pointer, such as acceleration (the ratio of the amount the physical mouse is moved to the amount the cursor moves on the screen).
ChangeProperty	Set the value of a property.
ChangeSaveSet	Add or remove windows from a save-set.
ChangeWindowAttributes	Set any or all window attributes. For a brief description of the window attributes, see Section 1.3.2.
CirculateWindow	Lower the highest window on the screen or raise the lowest one, depending on the parameters of this request.
ClearArea	Clear an area of a window.
CloseFont	Disclaim interest in a particular font. If this is the last client to be using the specified font, then the font is unloaded.

Request	Description
ConfigureWindow	Allow the window manager to move, resize, change the border width, or change the stacking order of a window.
ConvertSelection	Request that the owner of a particular selection convert it to a particular format, then send an event informing the requestor of the conversion's success and the name of the property containing the result.
CopyArea	Copy an area of a window to another area in the same or a different window. If the source area is obscured, this request will generate a **GraphicsExpose** event to identify the area of the destination for which the source is not available.
CopyColormapAndFree	Copy into a new virtual colormap the colorcells that one client has allocated, and free these colorcells in the old colormap.
CopyGC	Copy any or all characteristics of one GC into another.
CopyPlane	Copy a single plane of one drawable into any number of planes of another, applying two pixel values to translate the depth of the single plane.
CreateColormap	Create a virtual colormap.
CreateCursor	Create a cursor resource from characters in a special cursor font.
CreateGC	Create a graphics context, and optionally set any or all of its characteristics. If not set, each characteristic has a reasonable default.
CreateGlyphCursor	Create a cursor resource from characters in any font.
CreatePixmap	Create an off-screen drawable.
CreateWindow	Create a window.
DeleteProperty	Delete the data associated with a particular property on a particular window.
DestroySubwindows	Destroy an entire hierarchy of windows.
DestroyWindow	Destroy a window.
FillPoly	Fill a polygon, without drawing the complete outline.
ForceScreenSaver	Activate or reset the screen saver.
FreeColormap	Free a virtual colormap.
FreeColors	Deallocate colorcells.
FreeCursor	Destroy a cursor resource.
FreeGC	Free the memory in the server associated with a GC.
FreePixmap	Free the memory associated with an off-screen drawable.
GetAtomName	Get the string name of a property given it ID.
GetFontPath	Get the path that the server uses to search for fonts.
GetGeometry	Return the position, dimensions, border width, and depth of a window; return the ID of the root window at the top of the window's hierarchy.
GetImage	Place an image from a drawable into a representation in memory.
GetInputFocus	Return the current keyboard focus window.
GetKeyboardControl	Get personal preference features of the keyboard such as click and auto-repeat.
GetKeyboardMapping	Return the keyboard mapping seen by all clients.
GetModifierMapping	Get the mapping of physical keys to logical modifiers.

Request	Description
GetMotionEvents	Some servers are equipped with a buffer that records the position history of the pointer. This request will return segments of this history for selected time periods.
GetPointerControl	Return personal preference features of the pointer.
GetPointerMapping	Get the mapping of physical buttons to logical buttons.
GetProperty	Get the value of a property.
GetScreenSaver	Get the characteristics of the mechanism that blanks the screen after an idle period.
GetSelectionOwner	Get the current owner of a particular selection property.
GetWindowAttributes	Get the current values of some of the window attributes described for **ChangeWindowAttributes**; also find out the characteristics of the window that were set when it was created (**InputOnly** or **InputOutput**, and visual), whether its colormap is installed and whether it is mapped or viewable.
GrabButton	For all pointer events (button presses and motion) occurring while the specified combination of buttons and modifier keys are pressed, declare that these pointer events will be delivered to a particular window regardless of the pointer's location on the screen.
GrabKey	For all keyboard events occurring while the specified combination of buttons and modifier keys are pressed, declare that these keyboard events will be delivered to a particular window regardless of the pointer's location on the screen.
GrabKeyboard	Declare that all keyboard events will be delivered to a particular window regardless of the pointer's location on the screen.
GrabPointer	Declare that all pointer events (button presses and motion) will be delivered to a particular window regardless of the pointer's location on the screen.
GrabServer	Initiate a state where requests only from a single client will be acted upon. The server will queue events for other clients and requests made by other clients until the grab is released.
ImageText8	Draw text string in 8-bit font. The bounding rectangle of the string is drawn in the background color from the GC before the text is drawn.
ImageText16	Draw text string in 16-bit font. The bounding rectangle of the string is drawn in the background color from the GC before the text is drawn.
InstallColormap	Copy a virtual colormap into the display hardware, so that it will actually be used to translate pixel values.
InternAtom	Get the ID of a property given its string name, and optionally create the ID if no property with the specified name exists.
KillClient	After a client exits because of the **SetCloseDownMode** request, kill the resources that remain alive.
ListExtensions	List the extensions available on the server.
ListFonts	List the fonts available on a server.
ListFontsWithInfo	List the fonts available on a server, with information about each font.
ListHosts	Obtain a list of hosts having access to a display.
ListInstalledColormaps	List the IDs of the colormaps installed in the hardware.
ListProperties	List the IDs of the current list of properties.

Request	Description
LookupColor	Return the RGB values associated with a color name, and return the closest RGB values available on the display hardware.
MapSubwindows	Map all subwindows of a window.
MapWindow	Mark a window as eligible for display.
NoOperation	The minimum request, it contains only the opcode and request length.
OpenFont	Load a font for drawing. If the font has already been loaded, this request simply returns the ID.
PolyArc	Draw one or more arcs, each of which is a partial ellipse aligned with the x and y axis.
PolyFillArc	Fill one or more arcs, without drawing the arc itself.
PolyFillRectangle	Fill one or more rectangles, without drawing the entire outline.
PolyLine	Draw one or more connected lines.
PolyPoint	Draw one or more points.
PolyRectangle	Draw one or more rectangles.
PolySegment	Draw one or more disconnected lines.
PolyText8	Draw text items using 8-bit fonts. Each item can specify a string, a font, and a horizontal offset.
PolyText16	Draw text items using 16-bit fonts. Each item can specify a string, a font, and a horizontal offset.
PutImage	Dump an image into a drawable.
QueryBestSize	Query the server for the fastest size for creating tiles or stipples or the largest support size for cursors.
QueryColors	Return the colors in the specified cells of a colormap.
QueryExtension	Determine whether a certain extension is available in the server.
QueryFont	Get the table of information describing a font and each character in it.
QueryKeymap	Get the current state of the entire keyboard.
QueryPointer	Get the current pointer position.
QueryTextExtents	Calculate the width of a string in a certain font.
QueryTree	Allow the window manager to get the window IDs of windows it did not create.
RecolorCursor	Change the foreground and background colors of a cursor.
ReparentWindow	Allow the window manager to change the window hierarchy to insert a frame window between each top-level window on the screen and the root window. The window manager can then decorate this frame window with a title for the application, buttons for moving and resizing the window, etc.
RotateProperties	Rotate the values of a list of properties.
SendEvent	Send any type of event to a particular window.
SetAccessControl	Turn on or off the mechanism that checks the host access list before allowing a connection.
SetClipRectangles	Set the clip region of a GC to the union of a set of rectangles.
SetCloseDownMode	Determine whether resources created by a client are preserved after the client exits. Normally, they are not, but if the client can reclaim its resources in a later incarnation, the client can use this request.

Request	Description
SetDashes	Set the dash pattern for lines, in a more powerful way than is possible using **CreateGC** or **ChangeGC**.
SetFontPath	Set the path that the server uses to search for fonts.
SetInputFocus	Set a window and its descendants to receive all keyboard input.
SetModifierMapping	Set the mapping of physical keys to logical modifiers such as Shift and Control.
SetPointerMapping	Set the mapping of physical buttons to logical buttons.
SetScreenSaver	Set characteristics that blank the screen after an idle period.
SetSelectionOwner	Set a window as the current owner of a particular selection property.
StoreColors	Store colors into cells allocated by **AllocColorCells** or **AllocColorPlanes**.
StoreNamedColor	Store colors into cells allocated by **AllocColorCells** or **AllocColorPlanes**.
TranslateCoordinates	Translate coordinates from a window frame of reference to a screen frame of reference.
UngrabButton	Release a grab on a button.
UngrabKey	Release a grab on a button.
UngrabKeyboard	Release a grab on the keyboard.
UngrabPointer	Release a grab on the pointer.
UngrabServer	Release the grab on the server, process all outstanding requests, and send all queued events.
UninstallColormap	Remove a virtual colormap from the display hardware, so it will not be used to translate pixel values.
UnmapSubwindows	Remove all subwindows of a window, but not the window itself, from the screen.
UnmapWindow	Remove a window and all its subwindows from the screen.
WarpPointer	Move the pointer.

Listing of
Requests

I

Xlib Functions to Protocol Requests

This appendix provides a table that lists each Xlib function (in alphabetical order) and the corresponding protocol request that it generates.

Xlib Function	Protocol Request
XActivateScreenSaver	ForceScreenSaver
XAddHost	ChangeHosts
XAddHosts	ChangeHosts
XAddToSaveSet	ChangeSaveSet
XAllocColor	AllocColor
XAllocColorCells	AllocColorCells
XAllocColorPlanes	AllocColorPlanes
XAllocNamedColor	AllocNamedColor
XAllowEvents	AllowEvents
XAutoRepeatOff	ChangeKeyboardControl
XAutoRepeatOn	ChangeKeyboardControl
XBell	Bell
XChangeActivePointerGrab	ChangeActivePointerGrab
XChangeGC	ChangeGC
XChangeKeyboardControl	ChangeKeyboardControl
XChangeKeyboardMapping	ChangeKeyboardMapping
XChangePointerControl	ChangePointerControl
XChangeProperty	ChangeProperty
XChangeSaveSet	ChangeSaveSet
XChangeWindowAttributes	ChangeWindowAttributes
XCirculateSubwindows	CirculateWindow
XCirculateSubwindowsDown	CirculateWindow
XCirculateSubwindowsUp	CirculateWindow
XClearArea	ClearArea
XClearWindow	ClearArea
XConfigureWindow	ConfigureWindow
XConvertSelection	ConvertSelection
XCopyArea	CopyArea
XCopyColormapAndFree	CopyColormapAndFree
XCopyGC	CopyGC
XCopyPlane	CopyPlane

Xlib Function	Protocol Request
XCreateBitmapFromData	CreateGC
	CreatePixmap
	FreeGC
	PutImage
XCreateColormap	CreateColormap
XCreateFontCursor	CreateGlyphCursor
XCreateGC	CreateGC
XCreateGlyphCursor	CreateGlyphCursor
XCreatePixmap	CreatePixmap
XCreatePixmapCursor	CreateCursor
XCreatePixmapFromData	CreateGC
	CreatePixmap
	FreeGC
	PutImage
XCreateSimpleWindow	CreateWindow
XCreateWindow	CreateWindow
XDefineCursor	ChangeWindowAttributes
XDeleteProperty	DeleteProperty
XDestroySubwindows	DestroySubwindows
XDestroyWindow	DestroyWindow
XDisableAccessControl	SetAccessControl
XDrawArc	PolyArc
XDrawArcs	PolyArc
XDrawImageString	ImageText8
XDrawImageString16	ImageText16
XDrawLine	PolySegment
XDrawLines	PolyLine
XDrawPoint	PolyPoint
XDrawPoints	PolyPoint
XDrawRectangle	PolyRectangle
XDrawRectangles	PolyRectangle
XDrawSegments	PolySegment
XDrawString	PolyText8
XDrawString16	PolyText16
XDrawText	PolyText8
XDrawText16	PolyText16
XEnableAccessControl	SetAccessControl
XFetchBytes	GetProperty
XFetchName	GetProperty
XFillArc	PolyFillArc
XFillArcs	PolyFillArc
XFillPolygon	FillPoly
XFillRectangle	PolyFillRectangle
XFillRectangles	PolyFillRectangle
XForceScreenSaver	ForceScreenSaver
XFreeColormap	FreeColormap

Xlib Function	Protocol Request
XFreeColors	FreeColors
XFreeCursor	FreeCursor
XFreeFont	CloseFont
XFreeGC	FreeGC
XFreePixmap	FreePixmap
XGetAtomName	GetAtomName
XGetFontPath	GetFontPath
XGetGeometry	GetGeometry
XGetIconSizes	GetProperty
XGetImage	GetImage
XGetInputFocus	GetInputFocus
XGetKeyboardControl	GetKeyboardControl
XGetKeyboardMapping	GetKeyboardMapping
XGetModifierMapping	GetModifierMapping
XGetMotionEvents	GetMotionEvents
XGetModifierMapping	GetModifierMapping
XGetNormalHints	GetProperty
XGetPointerControl	GetPointerControl
XGetPointerMapping	GetPointerMapping
XGetScreenSaver	GetScreenSaver
XGetSelectionOwner	GetSelectionOwner
XGetSizeHints	GetProperty
XGetWMHints	GetProperty
XGetWindowAttributes	GetWindowAttributes
	GetGeometry
XGetWindowProperty	GetProperty
XGetZoomHints	GetProperty
XGrabButton	GrabButton
XGrabKey	GrabKey
XGrabKeyboard	GrabKeyboard
XGrabPointer	GrabPointer
XGrabServer	GrabServer
XInitExtension	QueryExtension
XInstallColormap	InstallColormap
XInternAtom	InternAtom
XKillClient	KillClient
XListExtensions	ListExtensions
XListFonts	ListFonts
XListFontsWithInfo	ListFontsWithInfo
XListHosts	ListHosts
XListInstalledColormaps	ListInstalledColormaps
XListProperties	ListProperties
XLoadFont	OpenFont
XLoadQueryFont	OpenFont
	QueryFont
XLookupColor	LookupColor

Xlib Function	Protocol Request
XLowerWindow	ConfigureWindow
XMapRaised	ConfigureWindow
	MapWindow
XMapSubwindows	MapSubwindows
XMapWindow	MapWindow
XMoveResizeWindow	ConfigureWindow
XMoveWindow	ConfigureWindow
XNoOp	NoOperation
XOpenDisplay	CreateGC
XParseColor	LookupColor
XPutImage	PutImage
XQueryBestCursor	QueryBestSize
XQueryBestSize	QueryBestSize
XQueryBestStipple	QueryBestSize
XQueryBestTile	QueryBestSize
XQueryColor	QueryColors
XQueryColors	QueryColors
XQueryExtension	QueryExtension
XQueryFont	QueryFont
XQueryKeymap	QueryKeymap
XQueryPointer	QueryPointer
XQueryTextExtents	QueryTextExtents
XQueryTextExtents16	QueryTextExtents
XQueryTree	QueryTree
XRaiseWindow	ConfigureWindow
XReadBitmapFile	CreateGC
	CreatePixmap
	FreeGC
	PutImage
XRecolorCursor	RecolorCursor
XRemoveFromSaveSet	ChangeSaveSet
XRemoveHost	ChangeHosts
XRemoveHosts	ChangeHosts
XReparentWindow	ReparentWindow
XResetScreenSaver	ForceScreenSaver
XResizeWindow	ConfigureWindow
XRestackWindows	ConfigureWindow
XRotateBuffers	RotateProperties
XRotateWindowProperties	RotateProperties
XSelectInput	ChangeWindowAttributes
XSendEvent	SendEvent
XSetAccessControl	SetAccessControl
XSetArcMode	ChangeGC
XSetBackground	ChangeGC
XSetClipMask	ChangeGC
XSetClipOrigin	ChangeGC

Xlib Function	Protocol Request
XSetClipRectangles	SetClipRectangles
XSetCloseDownMode	SetCloseDownMode
XSetCommand	ChangeProperty
XSetDashes	SetDashes
XSetFillRule	ChangeGC
XSetFillStyle	ChangeGC
XSetFont	ChangeGC
XSetFontPath	SetFontPath
XSetForeground	ChangeGC
XSetFunction	ChangeGC
XSetGraphicsExposures	ChangeGC
XSetIconName	ChangeProperty
XSetIconSizes	ChangeProperty
XSetInputFocus	SetInputFocus
XSetLineAttributes	ChangeGC
XSetModifierMapping	SetModifierMapping
XSetNormalHints	ChangeProperty
XSetPlaneMask	ChangeGC
XSetPointerMapping	SetPointerMapping
XSetScreenSaver	SetScreenSaver
XSetSelectionOwner	SetSelectionOwner
XSetSizeHints	ChangeProperty
XSetStandardProperties	ChangeProperty
XSetState	ChangeGC
XSetStipple	ChangeGC
XSetSubwindowMode	ChangeGC
XSetTile	ChangeGC
XSetTSOrigin	ChangeGC
XSetWMHints	ChangeProperty
XSetWindowBackground	ChangeWindowAttributes
XSetWindowBackgroundPixmap	ChangeWindowAttributes
XSetWindowBorder	ChangeWindowAttributes
XSetWindowBorderPixmap	ChangeWindowAttributes
XSetWindowBorderWidth	ConfigureWindow
XSetWindowColormap	ChangeWindowAttributes
XSetZoomHints	ChangeProperty
XStoreBuffer	ChangeProperty
XStoreBytes	ChangeProperty
XStoreColor	StoreColors
XStoreColors	StoreColors
XStoreName	ChangeProperty
XStoreNamedColor	StoreNamedColor
XSync	GetInputFocus
XTranslateCoordinates	TranslateCoordinates
XUndefineCursor	ChangeWindowAttributes
XUngrabButton	UngrabButton

Xlib Function	Protocol Request
XUngrabKey	UngrabKey
XUngrabKeyboard	UngrabKeyboard
XUngrabPointer	UngrabPointer
XUngrabServer	UngrabServer
XUninstallColormap	UninstallColormap
XUnloadFont	CloseFont
XUnmapSubwindows	UnmapSubwindows
XUnmapWindow	UnmapWindow
XWarpPointer	WarpPointer

Protocol Requests to Xlib Functions

The following table lists each X protocol request (in alphabetical order) and the Xlib functions that reference it.

Protocol Request	Xlib Function
AllocColor	XAllocColor
AllocColorCells	XAllocColorCells
AllocColorPlanes	XAllocColorPlanes
AllocNamedColor	XAllocNamedColor
AllowEvents	XAllowEvents
Bell	XBell
SetAccessControl	XDisableAccessControl
	XEnableAccessControl
	XSetAccessControl
ChangeActivePointerGrab	XChangeActivePointerGrab
SetCloseDownMode	XSetCloseDownMode
ChangeGC	XChangeGC
	XSetArcMode
	XSetBackground
	XSetClipMask
	XSetClipOrigin
	XSetFillRule
	XSetFillStyle
	XSetFont
	XSetForeground
	XSetFunction
	XSetGraphicsExposures
	XSetLineAttributes
	XSetPlaneMask
	XSetState
	XSetStipple
	XSetSubwindowMode
	XSetTile
	XSetTSOrigin
ChangeHosts	XAddHost
	XAddHosts

Protocol Request	Xlib Function
	XRemoveHost
	XRemoveHosts
ChangeKeyboardControl	XAutoRepeatOff
	XAutoRepeatOn
	XChangeKeyboardControl
ChangeKeyboardMapping	XChangeKeyboardMapping
ChangePointerControl	XChangePointerControl
ChangeProperty	XChangeProperty
	XSetCommand
	XSetIconName
	XSetIconSizes
	XSetNormalHints
	XSetSizeHints
	XSetStandardProperties
	XSetWMHints
	XSetZoomHints
	XStoreBuffer
	XStoreBytes
	XStoreName
ChangeSaveSet	XAddToSaveSet
	XChangeSaveSet
	XRemoveFromSaveSet
ChangeWindowAttributes	XChangeWindowAttributes
	XDefineCursor
	XSelectInput
	XSetWindowBackground
	XSetWindowBackgroundPixmap
	XSetWindowBorder
	XSetWindowBorderPixmap
	XSetWindowColormap
	XUndefineCursor
CirculateWindow	XCirculateSubwindowsDown
	XCirculateSubwindowsUp
	XCirculateSubwindows
ClearArea	XClearArea
	XClearWindow
CloseFont	XFreeFont
	XUnloadFont
ConfigureWindow	XConfigureWindow
	XLowerWindow
	XMapRaised
	XMoveResizeWindow
	XMoveWindow
	XRaiseWindow
	XResizeWindow
	XRestackWindows

Protocol Request	Xlib Function
	XSetWindowBorderWidth
ConvertSelection	XConvertSelection
CopyArea	XCopyArea
CopyColormapAndFree	XCopyColormapAndFree
CopyGC	XCopyGC
CopyPlane	XCopyPlane
CreateColormap	XCreateColormap
CreateCursor	XCreatePixmapCursor
CreateGC	XCreateGC
	XCreateBitmapFromData
	XCreatePixmapFromData
	XOpenDisplay
	XReadBitmapFile
CreateGlyphCursor	XCreateFontCursor
	XCreateGlyphCursor
CreatePixmap	XCreatePixmap
	XCreateBitmapFromData
	XCreatePixmapFromData
	XReadBitmapFile
CreateWindow	XCreateSimpleWindow
	XCreateWindow
DeleteProperty	XDeleteProperty
DestroySubwindows	XDestroySubwindows
DestroyWindow	XDestroyWindow
FillPoly	XFillPolygon
ForceScreenSaver	XActivateScreenSaver
	XForceScreenSaver
	XResetScreenSaver
FreeColormap	XFreeColormap
FreeColors	XFreeColors
FreeCursor	XFreeCursor
FreeGC	XFreeGC
	XCreateBitmapFromData
	XCreatePixmapFromData
	XReadBitmapFile
FreePixmap	XFreePixmap
GetAtomName	XGetAtomName
GetFontPath	XGetFontPath
GetGeometry	XGetGeometry
	XGetWindowAttributes
GetImage	XGetImage
GetInputFocus	XGetInputFocus
	XSync
GetKeyboardControl	XGetKeyboardControl
GetKeyboardMapping	XGetKeyboardMapping
GetModifierMapping	XGetModifierMapping

Protocol Request	Xlib Function
GetMotionEvents	XGetMotionEvents
GetPointerControl	XGetPointerControl
GetPointerMapping	XGetPointerMapping
GetProperty	XFetchBytes
	XFetchName
	XGetIconSizes
	XGetNormalHints
	XGetSizeHints
	XGetWMHints
	XGetWindowProperty
	XGetZoomHints
GetSelectionOwner	XGetSelectionOwner
GetWindowAttributes	XGetWindowAttributes
GrabButton	XGrabButton
GrabKey	XGrabKey
GrabKeyboard	XGrabKeyboard
GrabPointer	XGrabPointer
GrabServer	XGrabServer
ImageText8	XDrawImageString
ImageText16	XDrawImageString16
InstallColormap	XInstallColormap
InternAtom	XInternAtom
KillClient	XKillClient
ListExtensions	XListExtensions
ListFonts	XListFonts
ListFontsWithInfo	XListFontsWithInfo
ListHosts	XListHosts
ListInstalledColormaps	XListInstalledColormaps
ListProperties	XListProperties
LookupColor	XLookupColor
	XParseColor
MapSubwindows	XMapSubwindows
MapWindow	XMapRaised
	XMapWindow
NoOperation	XNoOp
OpenFont	XLoadFont
	XLoadQueryFont
PolyArc	XDrawArc
	XDrawArcs
PolyFillArc	XFillArc
	XFillArcs
PolyFillRectangle	XFillRectangle
	XFillRectangles
PolyLine	XDrawLines
PolyPoint	XDrawPoint
	XDrawPoints

Protocol Request	Xlib Function
PolyRectangle	XDrawRectangle
	XDrawRectangles
PolySegment	XDrawLine
	XDrawSegments
PolyText8	XDrawString
	XDrawText
PolyText16	XDrawString16
	XDrawText16
PutImage	XPutImage
	XCreateBitmapFromData
	XCreatePixmapFromData
	XReadBitmapFile
QueryBestSize	XQueryBestCursor
	XQueryBestSize
	XQueryBestStipple
	XQueryBestTile
QueryColors	XQueryColor
	XQueryColors
QueryExtension	XInitExtension
	XQueryExtension
QueryFont	XLoadQueryFont
	XQueryFont
QueryKeymap	XQueryKeymap
QueryPointer	XQueryPointer
QueryTextExtents	XQueryTextExtents
	XQueryTextExtents16
QueryTree	XQueryTree
RecolorCursor	XRecolorCursor
ReparentWindow	XReparentWindow
RotateProperties	XRotateBuffers
	XRotateWindowProperties
SendEvent	XSendEvent
SetClipRectangles	XSetClipRectangles
SetCloseDownMode	XSetCloseDownMode
SetDashes	XSetDashes
SetFontPath	XSetFontPath
SetInputFocus	XSetInputFocus
SetModifierMapping	XSetModifierMapping
SetPointerMapping	XSetPointerMapping
SetScreenSaver	XGetScreenSaver
	XSetScreenSaver
SetSelectionOwner	XSetSelectionOwner
StoreColors	XStoreColor
	XStoreColors
StoreNamedColor	XStoreNamedColor
TranslateCoordinates	XTranslateCoordinates

Protocol Request	Xlib Function
UngrabButton	XUngrabButton
UngrabKey	XUngrabKey
UngrabKeyboard	XUngrabKeyboard
UngrabPointer	XUngrabPointer
UngrabServer	XUngrabServer
UninstallColormap	XUninstallColormap
UnmapSubwindows	XUnmapSubWindows
UnmapWindow	XUnmapWindow
WarpPointer	XWarpPointer

K
Events Briefly Described

The X server is capable of sending many types of events to the client, only some of which most clients need. Therefore, X provides a mechanism whereby the client can express an interest in certain events but not others. Not only does this prevent wasting of network time on unneeded events, but it also speeds and simplifies clients by avoiding the testing and throwing away of these unnecessary events. Events are selected on a per-window basis.

As mentioned in the sample session in Section 1.3, all events begin with an 8-bit type code. The following is a list of all the event types, what they signify, and any special notes about how they are selected.

ButtonPress, ButtonRelease
> A pointer button was pressed or released. These events include the pointer position and the state of the modifier keys on the keyboard (such as Shift).

CirculateNotify, ConfigureNotify, CreateNotify, DestroyNotify,
MapNotify, UnmapNotify
> This event is generated when one of these requests is actually made on a window. These are used to tell a client when some other client has manipulated a window. Usually this other client is the window manager. All these events and **GravityNotify** and **ReparentNotify** can only be selected together.

CirculateRequest, ConfigureRequest, MapRequest, ResizeRequest
> These events are selected by the window manager to enforce its window management policy. Once selected by the window manager, any request to resize, map, reconfigure, or circulate a window by any client other than the window manager will not be acted on by the server but instead will result in one of these events being sent to the window manager. The window manager then can decide whether to allow, modify, or deny the parameters of the request given in the event and then reissue the request to the server.

ClientMessage
> These events, or any other type, can be sent from one client to another using the **SendEvent** request. This event type is for client-specific information.

ColormapNotify
> This event tells a client when a colormap has been modified or when it is installed or uninstalled from the hardware colormap.

EnterNotify, LeaveNotify

The pointer entered or left a window. These events are generated even for each window not visible on the screen that is an ancestor of the origin or destination window.

Expose

As explained in Section 1.2.2, **Expose** events signify that a section of a window has become visible and should be redrawn by the client.

FocusIn, FocusOut

The keyboard focus window has been changed. Like **EnterNotify** and **Leave-Notify**, these events can be generated even for invisible windows.

GraphicsExpose, NoExpose

GraphicsExpose and **NoExpose** are generated only as the result of **CopyArea** and **CopyPlane** requests. If the source area specified in either request is unavailable, one or more **GraphicsExpose** events are generated, and they specify the areas of the destination that could not be drawn. If the source area was available, a single **NoExpose** event is generated. **GraphicsExpose** and **NoExpose** events are not selected normally but instead are turned on or off by a member of the graphics context.

GravityNotify

This event notifies a client when a window has been moved in relation to its parent because of its window gravity attribute. This window attribute is designed to allow automatic positioning of subwindows in certain simple cases when the parent is resized.

KeymapNotify

Always following **EnterNotify** or **FocusIn**, **KeymapNotify** gives the complete status of all the keys on the keyboard.

KeyPress, KeyRelease

A keyboard key was pressed or released. Even the Shift and Control keys generate these events. There is no way to select just the events on particular keys.

MappingNotify

This event tells the client that a client has changed the keyboard symbol table in the server. This event cannot be selected; it is always sent to the client when any client calls **ChangeKeyboardMapping**.

MotionNotify

The pointer moved. **MotionNotify** events can be selected such that they are delivered only when certain pointer buttons are pressed or regardless of the pointer buttons. Also, they can be selected such that only one **MotionNotify** event is sent between each query of the pointer position or button press. This reduces the number of **MotionNotify** events sent for clients that do not need complete pointer position history.

PropertyNotify

This event is issued whenever a client changes or deletes a property, even if the change is to replace data with identical data.

ReparentNotify

This event tells the client that a window has been given a new parent. Reparenting is used by the window manager to decorate and provide space around each window for a user interface for window management. One meaning of this event is that the coordinates of this window are no longer in relation to the old parent, which is normally the screen.

SelectionClear, SelectionNotify, SelectionRequest

These three events are used in the selection method of communicating between clients. See Section 1.3.2.1 for a description of selecting events. These events are not selected, but are always generated by the requests involved in the selection procedure.

VisibilityNotify

This event is generated when a window changes from fully obscured, partially obscured, or unobscured to any other of these states and also when this window becomes viewable (all it ancestors are mapped).

As mentioned in the list, a few of these event types cannot be selected because they are automatically delivered to all clients whenever they occur. This is either because virtually all clients need them or because they only get generated by clients that have an interest in them.

Unused bytes within an event are not guaranteed to be zero. Event codes 64 through 127 are reserved for extensions, although the core protocol does not define a mechanism for selecting interest in such events. Every core event (with the exception of **KeymapNotify**) also contains the least significant 16 bits of the sequence number of the last request issued by the client that was (or is currently being) processed by the server.

The server may retain the recent history of pointer motion and to a finer granularity than is reported by **MotionNotify** events. Such history is available by means of the **GetMotion-Events** request. The approximate size of the history buffer is given by motion-buffer-size.

Glossary

Access control list
X maintains a list of hosts from which client programs can be run. By default, only programs on the local host and hosts specified in an initial list read by the server can use the display. Clients on the local host can change this access control list. Some server implementations can also implement other authorization mechanisms in addition to or in place of this mechanism. The action of this mechanism can be conditional based on the authorization protocol name and data received by the server at connection setup.

Active grab
A grab is active when the pointer or keyboard is actually owned by the single grabbing client.

Ancestors
If W is an inferior of A, then A is an ancestor of W.

Atom
An atom is a unique ID corresponding to a string name. Atoms are used to identify properties, types, and selections.

Background
An **InputOutput** window can have a background, which is defined as a pixmap. When regions of the window have their contents lost or invalidated, the server will automatically tile those regions with the background.

Backing store
When a server maintains the contents of a window, the pixels saved off screen are known as a backing store.

Bit gravity
When a window is resized, the contents of the window are not necessarily discarded. It is possible to request that the server relocate the previous contents to some region of the window (though no guarantees are made). This attraction of window contents for some location of a window is known as bit gravity.

Bit plane
When a pixmap or window is thought of as a stack of bitmaps, each bitmap is called a bit plane or plane.

Bitmap
A bitmap is a pixmap of depth one.

Border
An **InputOutput** window can have a border of equal thickness on all four sides of the window. A pixmap defines the contents of the border, and the server automatically maintains the

contents of the border. Exposure events are never generated for border regions.

Button grabbing Buttons on the pointer may be passively grabbed by a client. When the button is pressed, the pointer is then actively grabbed by the client.

Byte order For image (pixmap/bitmap) data, the server defines the byte order, and clients with different native byte ordering must swap bytes as necessary. For all other parts of the protocol, the client defines the byte order, and the server swaps bytes as necessary.

Children The children of a window are its first-level subwindows.

Client An application program connects to the window system server by some interprocess communication (IPC) path, such as a TCP connection or a shared memory buffer. This program is referred to as a client of the window system server. More precisely, the client is the IPC path itself; a program with multiple paths open to the server is viewed as multiple clients by the protocol. Resource lifetimes are controlled by connection lifetimes, not by program lifetimes.

Clipping region In a graphics context, a bitmap or list of rectangles can be specified to restrict output to a particular region of the window. The image defined by the bitmap or rectangles is called a clipping region.

Colormap A colormap consists of a set of entries defining color values. The colormap associated with a window is used to display the contents of the window; each pixel value indexes the colormap to produce RGB values that drive the guns of a monitor. Depending on hardware limitations, one or more colormaps may be installed at one time, so that windows associated with those maps display with correct colors.

Connection The IPC path between the server and client program is known as a connection. A client program typically (but not necessarily) has one connection to the server over which requests and events are sent.

Containment A window "contains" the pointer if the window is viewable and the hotspot of the cursor is within a visible region of the window or a visible region of one of its inferiors. The border of the window is included as part of the window for containment. The pointer is "in" a window if the window contains the pointer but no inferior contains the pointer.

Coordinate system The coordinate system has X horizontal and Y vertical, with the origin [0,0] at the upper left. Coordinates are discrete and are in terms of pixels. Each window and pixmap has its own coordinate system. For a window, the origin is inside the border at the inside upper left.

Cursor

A cursor is the visible shape of the pointer on a screen. It consists of a hotspot, a source bitmap, a shape bitmap, and a pair of colors. The cursor defined for a window controls the visible appearance when the pointer is in that window.

Depth

The depth of a window or pixmap is the number of bits per pixel that it has. The depth of a graphics context is the depth of the drawables it can be used in conjunction with for graphics output.

Device

Keyboards, mice, tablets, track-balls, button boxes, and so on are all collectively known as input devices. The core protocol only deals with two devices, "the keyboard" and "the pointer."

DirectColor

DirectColor is a class of colormap in which a pixel value is decomposed into three separate subfields for indexing. The first subfield indexes an array to produce red intensity values. The second subfield indexes a second array to produce blue intensity values. The third subfield indexes a third array to produce green intensity values. The RGB values can be changed dynamically.

Display

A server, together with its screens and input devices, is called a display.

Drawable

Both windows and pixmaps can be used as sources and destinations in graphics operations. These windows and pixmaps are collectively known as drawables. However, an **InputOnly** window cannot be used as a source or destination in a graphics operation.

Event

Clients are informed of information asynchronously by means of events. These events can be generated either asynchronously from devices or as side effects of client requests. Events are grouped into types. The server never sends events to a client unless the client has specifically asked to be informed of that type of event. However, other clients can force events to be sent to other clients. Events are typically reported relative to a window.

Event mask

Events are requested relative to a window. The set of event types that a client requests relative to a window is described by using an event mask.

Event propagation

Device-related events propagate from the source window to ancestor windows until some client has expressed interest in handling that type of event or until the event is discarded explicitly.

Event source

The window the pointer is in is the source of a device-related event.

Event synchronization	There are certain race conditions possible when demultiplexing device events to clients (in particular, deciding where pointer and keyboard events should be sent when in the middle of window management operations). The event synchronization mechanism allows synchronous processing of device events.
Exposure event	Servers do not guarantee to preserve the contents of windows when windows are obscured or reconfigured. Exposure events are sent to clients to inform them when contents of regions of windows have been lost.
Extension	Named extensions to the core protocol can be defined to extend the system. Extension to output requests, resources, and event types are all possible and are expected.
Focus window	The focus window is another term for the input focus.
Font	A font is a matrix of glyphs (typically characters). The protocol does no translation or interpretation of character sets. The client simply indicates values used to index the glyph array. A font contains additional metric information to determine interglyph and interline spacing.
GC, GContext	GC and gcontext are abbreviations for graphics context.
Glyph	A glyph is an image, typically of a character, in a font.
Grab	Keyboard keys, the keyboard, pointer buttons, the pointer, and the server can be grabbed for exclusive use by a client. In general, these facilities are not intended to be used by normal applications but are intended for various input and window managers to implement various styles of user interfaces.
Graphics context	Various information for graphics output is stored in a graphics context such as foreground pixel, background pixel, line width, clipping region, and so on. A graphics context can only be used with drawables that have the same root and the same depth as the graphics context.
Gravity	See **bit gravity** and **window gravity**.
GrayScale	**GrayScale** can be viewed as a degenerate case of **Pseudo-Color**, in which the red, green, and blue values in any given colormap entry are equal, thus producing shades of gray. The gray values can be changed dynamically.
Hotspot	A cursor has an associated hotspot that defines the point in the cursor corresponding to the coordinates reported for the pointer.
Identifier	An identifier is a unique value associated with a resource that clients use to name that resource. The identifier can be used over any connection.

Inferiors	The inferiors of a window are all of the subwindows nested below it: the children, the children's children, and so on.
Input focus	The input focus is normally a window defining the scope for processing of keyboard input. If a generated keyboard event would normally be reported to this window or one of its inferiors, the event is reported normally. Otherwise, the event is reported with respect to the focus window. The input focus also can be set such that all keyboard events are discarded and such that the focus window is dynamically taken to be the root window of whatever screen the pointer is on at each keyboard event.
Input manager	Control over keyboard input is typically provided by an input manager client.
InputOnly window	An **InputOnly** window is a window that cannot be used for graphics requests. **InputOnly** windows are invisible and can be used to control such things as cursors, input event generation, and grabbing. **InputOnly** windows cannot have **InputOutput** windows as inferiors.
InputOutput window	An **InputOutput** window is the normal kind of opaque window, used for both input and output. **InputOutput** windows can have both **InputOutput** and **InputOnly** windows as inferiors.
Key grabbing	Keys on the keyboard can be passively grabbed by a client. When the key is pressed, the keyboard is then actively grabbed by the client.
Keyboard grabbing	A client can actively grab control of the keyboard, and key events will be sent to that client rather than the client the events would normally have been sent to.
Keysym	An encoding of a symbol on a keycap on a keyboard.
Mapped	A window is said to be mapped if a map call has been performed on it. Unmapped windows and their inferiors are never viewable or visible.
Modifier keys	Shift, Control, Meta, Super, Hyper, Alt, Compose, Apple, Caps-Lock, ShiftLock, and similar keys are called modifier keys.
Monochrome	Monochrome is a special case of **StaticGray** in which there are only two colormap entries.
Obscure	A window is obscured if some other window obscures it. Window A obscures window B if both are viewable **InputOutput** windows, A is higher in the global stacking order, and the rectangle defined by the outside edges of A intersects the rectangle defined by the outside edges of B. Note the distinction between obscures and occludes. Also note that window borders are included in the calculation and that a window can be obscured and yet still have visible regions.

Occlude	A window is occluded if some other window occludes it. Window A occludes window B if both are mapped, A is higher in the global stacking order, and the rectangle defined by the outside edges of A intersects the rectangle defined by the outside edges of B. Note the distinction between occludes and obscures. Also note that window borders are included in the calculation.
Padding	Some padding bytes are inserted in the data stream to maintain alignment of the protocol requests on natural boundaries. This increases ease of portability to some machine architectures.
Parent window	If C is a child of P, then P is the parent of C.
Passive grab	Grabbing a key or button is a passive grab. The grab activates when the key or button is actually pressed.
Pixel value	A pixel is an N-bit value, where N is the number of bit planes used in a particular window or pixmap; that is, N is the depth of the window or pixmap. For a window, a pixel value indexes a colormap to derive an actual color to be displayed.
Pixmap	A pixmap is a three-dimensional array of bits. A pixmap is normally thought of as a two-dimensional array of pixels, where each pixel can be a value from 0 to $(2^N-1$ and where N is the depth (z axis) of the pixmap. A pixmap can also be thought of as a stack of N bitmaps.
Plane	When a pixmap or window is thought of as a stack of bitmaps, each bitmap is called a plane or bit plane.
Plane mask	Graphics operations can be restricted to only affect a subset of bit planes of a destination. A plane mask is a bit mask describing which planes are to be modified. The plane mask is stored in a graphics context.
Pointer	The pointer is the pointing device attached to the cursor and tracked on the screens.
Pointer grabbing	A client can actively grab control of the pointer. Then button and motion events will be sent to that client rather than the client the events would normally have been sent to.
Pointing device	A pointing device is typically a mouse, tablet, or some other device with effective dimensional motion. There is only one visible cursor defined by the core protocol, and it tracks whatever pointing device is attached as the pointer.
Property	Windows may have associated properties, which consist of a name, a type, a data format, and some data. The protocol places no interpretation on properties. They are intended as a general-purpose naming mechanism for clients. For example, clients might use properties to share information such as resize hints, program names, and icon formats with a window manager.

Property list	The property list of a window is the list of properties that have been defined for the window.
PseudoColor	**PseudoColor** is a class of colormap in which a pixel value indexes the colormap to produce independent red, green, and blue values; that is, the colormap is viewed as an array of triples (RGB values). The RGB values can be changed dynamically.
Redirecting control	Window managers (or client programs) may want to enforce window layout policy in various ways. When a client attempts to change the size or position of a window, the operation may be redirected to a specified client rather than the operation actually being performed.
Reply	Information requested by a client program is sent back to the client with a reply. Both events and replies are multiplexed on the same connection. Most requests do not generate replies, although some requests generate multiple replies.
Request	A command to the server is called a request. It is a single block of data sent over a connection.
Resource	Windows, pixmaps, cursors, fonts, graphics contexts, and colormaps are known as resources. They all have unique identifiers associated with them for naming purposes. The lifetime of a resource usually is bounded by the lifetime of the connection over which the resource was created.
RGB values	Red, green, and blue (RGB) intensity values are used to define color. These values are always represented as 16-bit unsigned numbers, with 0 being the minimum intensity and 65535 being the maximum intensity. The server scales the values to match the display hardware.
Root	The root of a pixmap or graphics context is the same as the root of whatever drawable was used when the pixmap or graphics context was created. The root of a window is the root window under which the window was created.
Root window	Each screen has a root window covering it. It cannot be reconfigured or unmapped, but it otherwise acts as a full-fledged window. A root window has no parent.
Save set	The save set of a client is a list of other clients' windows that, if they are inferiors of one of the client's windows at connection close, should not be destroyed and that should be remapped if currently unmapped. Save sets are typically used by window managers to avoid lost windows if the manager terminates abnormally.
Scanline	A scanline is a list of pixel or bit values viewed as a horizontal row (all values having the same y coordinate) of an image, with the values ordered by increasing x coordinate.

Scanline order	An image represented in scanline order contains scanlines ordered by increasing y coordinate.
Screen	A server can provide several independent screens, which typically have physically independent monitors. This would be the expected configuration when there is only a single keyboard and pointer shared among the screens.
Selection	A selection can be thought of as an indirect property with dynamic type; that is, rather than having the property stored in the server, it is maintained by some client (the "owner"). A selection is global in nature and is thought of as belonging to the user (although maintained by clients), rather than as being private to a particular window subhierarchy or a particular set of clients. When a client asks for the contents of a selection, it specifies a selection "target type." This target type can be used to control the transmitted representation of the contents. For example, if the selection is "the last thing the user clicked on" and that is currently an image, then the target type might specify whether the contents of the image should be sent in XY format or Z format. The target type can also be used to control the class of contents transmitted; for example, asking for the "looks" (fonts, line spacing, indentation, and so on) of a paragraph selection rather than the text of the paragraph. The target type can also be used for other purposes. The protocol does not constrain the semantics.
Server	The server provides the basic windowing mechanism. It handles IPC connections from clients, demultiplexes graphics requests onto the screens, and multiplexes input back to the appropriate clients.
Server grabbing	The server can be grabbed by a single client for exclusive use. This prevents processing of any requests from other client connections until the grab is completed. This is typically only a transient state for such things as rubber-banding, pop-up menus, or to execute requests indivisibly.
Sibling	Children of the same parent window are known as sibling windows.
Stacking order	Sibling windows may stack on top of each other. Windows above other windows both obscure and occlude those lower windows. This is similar to paper on a desk. The relationship between sibling windows is known as the stacking order.
StaticColor	**StaticColor** can be viewed as a degenerate case of **PseudoColor** in which the RGB values are predefined and read-only.
StaticGray	**StaticGray** can be viewed as a degenerate case of **GrayScale** in which the gray values are predefined and read-only. The values are typically linear or near-linear increasing ramps.

Stipple	A stipple pattern is a bitmap that is used to tile a region that will serve as an additional clip mask for a fill operation with the foreground color.
Tile	A pixmap can be replicated in two dimensions to tile a region. The pixmap itself is also known as a tile.
Timestamp	A timestamp is a time value, expressed in milliseconds. It typically is the time since the last server reset. Timestamp values wrap around (after about 49.7 days). The server, given its current time is represented by timestamp T, always interprets timestamps from clients by treating half of the timestamp space as being earlier in time than T and half of the timestamp space as being later in time than T. One timestamp value (named **CurrentTime**) is never generated by the server. This value is reserved for use in requests to represent the current server time.
TrueColor	**TrueColor** can be viewed as a degenerate case of **DirectColor** in which the subfields in the pixel value directly encode the corresponding RGB values; that is, the colormap has predefined read-only RGB values. The values are typically linear or near-linear increasing ramps.
Type	A type is an arbitrary atom used to identify the interpretation of property data. Types are completely uninterpreted by the server and are solely for the benefit of clients.
Viewable	A window is viewable if it and all of its ancestors are mapped. This does not imply that any portion of the window is actually visible. Graphics requests can be performed on a window when it is not viewable, but output will not be retained unless the server is maintaining backing store.
Visible	A region of a window is visible if someone looking at the screen can actually see it; that is, the window is viewable and the region is not occluded by any other window.
Window gravity	When windows are resized, subwindows may be repositioned automatically relative to some position in the window. This attraction of a subwindow to some part of its parent is known as window gravity.
Window manager	Manipulation of windows on the screen and much of the user interface (policy) is typically provided by a window manager client.
XYFormat	The data for a pixmap is said to be in XY format if it is organized as a set of bitmaps representing individual bit planes, with the planes appearing from most-significant to least-significant in bit order.
ZFormat	The data for a pixmap is said to be in Z format if it is organized as a set of pixel values in scanline order.

Index

Index

Index

hosts
  adding and removing 67
  returning on access control list
    204
hotspot
  glossary definition 374

I

IDChoice error 325
identifier
  glossary definition 374
IDs
  abstract 20, 36
  colormap 25
  generating 20
  resource 81, 82, 83, 84
  window 28
illegal requests *see* errors
image data 16, 21
ImageText8 request 185
ImageText16 request 187 *see also*
    ImageText8 request
Implementation error 325
implementing X protocol 33
IncludeInferior GC value 107
indexing
  JIS/ISO method of 42
  linear 187, 229, 249
  matrix 187, 227, 229, 249
inferior windows 254, 268, 297
inferiors
  glossary definition 375
input focus 268
  glossary definition 375
input manager
  glossary definition 375
InputOnly window type 115, 116,
    136, 153, 291
  glossary definition 375
  in ClearArea request 82
InputOutput window type 116
  glossary definition 375
InstallColormap request 119, 188,
    205, 287
installing colormaps 146, 188,
    205, 287
INT8 type
  definition of 41
INT16 type
  definition of 41
INT32 type

definition of 41
interclient communication 37
InternAtom request 189, 333
Internet address family 67
interprocess communication chan-
    nels 9
Intrinsics
  description of 7
IPC *see* interprocess communica-
    tion channels
ISO encoding 57, 189, 199, 207,
    218, 238, 279

J

join-style GC component 106, 219

K

key clicks 69
key grabbing
  glossary definition 375
key masks *see* modifier key masks
keyboard grabbing
  glossary definition 375
keyboard-modes
  Asynchronous 177
  Synchronous 177
keyboards 335
  controlling 69
  encoding 336
  frozen 59, 179
  grabbing 59, 141, 175, 177, 297
  handling 11
  layout of 300
  mapping 72, 160, 210
  releasing 284
  returning control values for 158
  ringing bell on 62
KEYBUTMASK type
  definition of 42
KEYCODE type
  definition of 42
keycodes 162
  description of 335
  mapping 335
  returning symbols for 72, 160
  used as modifiers 270
  value of transmitted by server 45
KeymapNotify event 191

Index

in ClearArea request 82
in ConfigureWindow request 89
in CreateCursor request 101
in CreateGC request 103
in CreateWindow request 118
in GetImage request 155
in PutImage request 232
in RotateProperties request 256
in SetClipRectangles request
    263
matrix indexing 227, 229, 249
maximum-request-length *see*
    length field
max-keycode *see* keycodes
message types in X 10
min-keycode *see* keycodes
minor version *see* version num-
    bers
Mod2 modifier key mask 270
Mod3 modifier key mask 270
Mod4 modifier key mask 270
Mod5 modifier key mask 270
modes
    close-down 265, 286, 297
    Destroy 265, 297
    Grab 195
    Normal 195
    RetainPermanent 297
    RetainTemporary 297
    Ungrab 195
modifier key masks 270, 335
    glossary definition 375
    returning keycodes of 162
monochrome colormap 25
    glossary definition 375
motion
    events 214
    history buffer 163
    pointer 195
    pseudo- 195
MotionNotify event 64, 192, 193,
    195, 214, 214
multiplexing 9
multi-tasking systems 7

N

Name error 326
network protocol *see also* X proto-
    col
    asynchronous 5, 9, 13
    synchronous 5

networking on X 6 - 10
    and multi-tasking systems 7
    and single-tasking systems 7
    and the client/server relationship
        6
    and transferring data 10
networks
    efficiency of 33
    Ethernet 5, 7
    reducing traffic on 36
NoExpose event 94, 216
Nonconvex
    description of 138
None value
    in backgound-pixmap window
        attribute 118
    in colormap window attribute
        119, 146
    in cursor window attribute 119
noninferior windows 155
NoOperation request 217
normal events 195
Normal mode 195
NorthWest window gravity 90
NotUseful value
    in backing-store window attri-
        bute 119

O

obscured windows 291
    glossary definition 375
occlude
    glossary definition 376
OpenFont request 218
opening client/server connection
    15 - 21, 42
    and allocation of resource IDs
        44
    and DECnet connections 47, 48
    and TCP connections 47
    information received when 42
    process of 42
Opposite stack-mode value 91
OR type
    definition of 40
output buffer 34
override-redirect window attribute
    86, 89, 119, 209, 211
    False value in 213
owner window selection 276

Index

Index

☐ Please send me the information
I have asked for on the reverse
side of this card.

Name _____

Company _____

Address _____

City _____

State, ZIP _____

(Fill out or tape
business card here)

Nutshell Handbooks

 O'Reilly & Associates, Inc.
632 Petaluma Avenue
Sebastopol CA 95472

☐ Please send me the information
I have asked for on the reverse
side of this card.

Name _____

Company _____

Address _____

City _____

State, ZIP _____

(Fill out or tape
business card here)

Nutshell Handbooks

 O'Reilly & Associates, Inc.
632 Petaluma Avenue
Sebastopol CA 95472

O'Reilly & Associates, Inc.
Creators and Publishers of Nutshell Handbooks

Nutshell Handbooks

Learning the UNIX Operating System
DOS Meets UNIX
Learning the vi Editor
UNIX in a Nutshell, System V
UNIX in a Nutshell, Berkeley

Handbooks on Communications:

!%@:: A Directory of Electronic
   Mail Addressing and Networks
Using UUCP and Usenet
Managing UUCP and Usenet

Handbooks on Programming:

Using C on the UNIX System
Checking C Programs with lint
Understanding and Using COFF
Programming with curses
termcap and terminfo
Managing Projects with make

The X Window System series

Vol. 0 *X Protocol Reference Manual*
Vol. 1 *Xlib Programming Manual*
Vol. 2 *Xlib Reference Manual*
Vol. 3 *X Window System User's Guide*
Vol. 4 *X Toolkit Intrinsics*
   Programming Manual
Vol. 5 *X Toolkit Intrinsics Reference*
   Manual

For HyperCard on Macintosh:

UNIX in a Nutshell for HyperCard
(includes 1.8MB of HyperCard
stackware, *User's Guide,* and a copy of
Learning the UNIX Operating System)

Other UNIX books:

UNIX Text Processing

Send me more information on:

☐ Retail sales

☐ Licensing

☐ Review copies for instructors

☐ Magazine press kits for new books

☐ Education policy

☐ Bookstore locations

☐ Overseas distributors

☐ Additional copy of Nutshell News

☐ Upcoming books on the subject:

_____

_____

☐ Writing a Nutshell Handbook

O'Reilly & Associates, Inc.
Creators and Publishers of Nutshell Handbooks

Nutshell Handbooks

Learning the UNIX Operating System
DOS Meets UNIX
Learning the vi Editor
UNIX in a Nutshell, System V
UNIX in a Nutshell, Berkeley

Handbooks on Communications:

!%@:: A Directory of Electronic
   Mail Addressing and Networks
Using UUCP and Usenet
Managing UUCP and Usenet

Handbooks on Programming:

Using C on the UNIX System
Checking C Programs with lint
Understanding and Using COFF
Programming with curses
termcap and terminfo
Managing Projects with make

The X Window System series

Vol. 0 *X Protocol Reference Manual*
Vol. 1 *Xlib Programming Manual*
Vol. 2 *Xlib Reference Manual*
Vol. 3 *X Window System User's Guide*
Vol. 4 *X Toolkit Intrinsics*
   Programming Manual
Vol. 5 *X Toolkit Intrinsics Reference*
   Manual

For HyperCard on Macintosh:

UNIX in a Nutshell for HyperCard
(includes 1.8MB of HyperCard
stackware, *User's Guide,* and a copy of
Learning the UNIX Operating System)

Other UNIX books:

UNIX Text Processing

Send me more information on:

☐ Retail sales

☐ Licensing

☐ Review copies for instructors

☐ Magazine press kits for new books

☐ Education policy

☐ Bookstore locations

☐ Overseas distributors

☐ Additional copy of Nutshell News

☐ Upcoming books on the subject:

_____

_____

☐ Writing a Nutshell Handbook